A BOY
FROM
NOWHERE

VOL.1

by
David Mitchell

Published by

**MELROSE
BOOKS**

An Imprint of Melrose Press Limited
St Thomas Place, Ely
Cambridgeshire
CB7 4GG, UK
www.melrosebooks.com

FIRST EDITION

Cover designed by Tanya Fukes

ISBN 978 1 906050 31 3

Printed and bound in Great Britain by:
CPI Antony Rowe, Bumpers Farm,
Chippenham, Wiltshire, SN14 6LH, UK

CONTENTS

INTRODUCTION v

1: My Early Life in the East End Docklands 1

2: Life in the East End During the Early 1930s 9

3: Poplar Town Hall, Sadness and Charity Organisations 24

4: Evacuation – The War Begins – My Spell at Windsor –
   I Discover There is a Better Life and I Almost Become
   a 'Toff' 34

5: I Return to the East End from Windsor 44

6: I Start to Work, 1942–1946 and The War Continues 56

7: Hitler's V2 Weapon Strikes, My Childhood Pal,
   Alfie, Dies Near Arnhem, and Finally The War Comes
   to an End. 69

8: 1946–1950, National Service and Marriage. 84

9: Back in Civvy Street Again 95

10: The Early 1950s – My New Job In Business. 102

11: My Introduction to Communism and the Late 1950s. 118

12: Going up in the World – the Late 1950s and
    the Early 1960s. 141

13: Continuing to Develop Sugosa and Our First Trip To
    Czechoslovakia by Car. 172

AFTERWORD 214

INTRODUCTION

THE MITCHELL & GEARY FAMILIES

Family legend, plus an old Family Tree formulated by a relative long since dead, suggested that the paternal side of our family, the Mitchells, descended from a WILLIAM b 1785 and a DAVID, his son, b 1805, both supposedly born at Speymouth, Morayshire, Scotland.

After many fruitless searches, during which I was helped by a number of extremely kind Scottish people and organisations, I finally had to accept that, as far as could be traced, these ancestors were not born in Speymouth in those years. It remains a mystery where our deceased relative obtained his information, but it may have been passed down through time from other ancestors also long since dead.

However, one fact that we did know from this Family Tree was that DAVID, my great-grandfather, had married an Anne Jackson in WIGTON, Cumberland, in 1828. Therefore it seemed to me that it would be a more accurate search to begin with this known fact. In this we were helped very much by a family search organisation up in the North West called Relative Research.

They unearthed the apparent truth, which showed that in the 1851 Census at Wigton, our DAVID declares that he was born in Ireland. No indication of whether he came from the North or South, and no indication of which county. We are trying to trace him via The Tithe Applotment Books in Ulster but it really is like looking for a needle in a haystack and I have a feeling that we may not succeed.[1]

---

[1] *Since the above was written we have discovered that a WILLIAM MITCHELL and a DAVID were in fact mentioned in the Tithe Applotment Books in the village or town of DRUMLEA, Co. Tyrone – we are investigating further via the local church there.*

As far as DAVID is concerned, some years after his marriage in 1828, by which time two children had arrived, he moved down into the Birkenhead/Liverpool area – probably for reasons of work or better pay. In Birkenhead/Liverpool three more children followed, one of which was my grandfather, and from such beginnings a widespread family developed who now live in Northern England, Southern England, Spain, Canada and the USA.

My own grandfather broke away from the Birkenhead area following his marriage to my grandmother, MARY HUGHES, at Higher Bebington, Cheshire, in 1882. They came down to London, again probably for work or for higher pay; for at that time, with the development of the great London docklands which eventually became the largest and busiest port in the world, the demand for dock labour must have been considerable.

After living at various addresses in Poplar, all very near to the docks, my paternal grandparents settled in 2 Prestage Street. That became the family home where I grew up, as I shall explain. Prestage Street was a typical East End street and was sandwiched between the East India Docks and the ship repair yard owned by Green, Silley & Weir. It was a turning off Blackwall Way and only 200-300 yards or so from Blackwall Stairs and the River Thames. On the right side, it consisted of a pub, The Ivy House, which was virtually on the corner, and then about forty terraced houses which led right down to the high wall beyond which was the East India Docks warehousing section. On the left side it began with a block of tenement flats, then a few terraced houses, then the entrance to Harrap Street, and then a further twenty houses or so. It was a typical East End street with a variety of people and it is true to say that those who resided towards the bottom end of the street were not as familiar with those of us who lived in our half – there was a kind of mysterious divide between the two halves. We were all on nodding terms, of course, and we would wish each other a "Good Morning" greeting, but in our half of the street we had the big attraction of having the local pub, The Ivy House, where neighbours met to enjoy a glass of ale and more often or not, after a few glasses, they would break into song. Those who lived in the lower half of the street would no doubt prefer to visit an alternative pub, The Steamship, just around the corner in Naval Row. I was the pianist in both these pubs in my younger days.

In conclusion on the subject of family origins, I understand that in the years before the 20th century there was a considerable number of people exchanged between Scotland and Ireland (especially Ulster due to it's close proximity), most probably for reasons of labour, agriculture, fishing etc., and so it is not beyond the realm of possibility that our family line originated in Speymouth, Morayshire or somewhere in that region. If only we knew where our long dead relative obtained his information, when putting his family tree together. Unfortunately, there is now no way of knowing. This shows the importance of making notes and leaving behind documentary evidence that others can pick up when recording family history.

On my maternal side, my grandfather's family originated in Kent and my grandmother, whose maiden name was GEARY, was born in Youghal, Co. Cork. They married in Wales, which possibly may have resulted from my grandfather having been transferred to a training ship there; my grandmother may have crossed over from Cork to Wales, perhaps to enter service. Therefore, one supposes, they met and eventually married. They evidently decided to return to the general London area and lived at various addresses before settling in Prestage Buildings. There in three rooms they raised a family of two girls and two boys. My grandfather was a ship's cook. He died in the early part of the Second World War, but my dear old Irish Granny survived until 1950 and then she too passed away. I am still trying to research my grandmother's family but there is nobody now in existence who knows anything at all about her and so it is a matter of referring to records. This is not easy in either the Irish Republic or in Northern Ireland for a variety of reasons. Very often it is a matter of referring to old parish records and in many instances the poor priests, as if they had not enough to do, are bombarded by requests from all over the world – the USA, Australia, Canada and the British Isles of course being the main sources, where people want to know about their family backgrounds. Thus, one can understand to some extent the priests' reluctance to spend time poring over old records. So this makes for a difficult task.

1

MY EARLY LIFE IN THE
EAST END DOCKLANDS

It is said that there is a story and a book in every man. In my life there are many stories and perhaps even more than one book. I have always been a prolific letter writer and in the course of writing I have related a number of my stories to both friends and relatives. Quite a number of them urged me to write a book because they felt my life had been unusual, exciting, and very interesting. After a lot of consideration I decided to do so, and share my life's story with others. But it has been a long life filled with so much that I was not confident I could confine it to one book. Therefore, in agreement with my publishers, I have decided to write two volumes of which this is the first, taking us to a very exciting point in my life. I sincerely hope that Volume 2 will follow shortly.

So, this is my story – a story of a boy born in very humble circumstances, without proper education, who, like the majority of working class lads back then, had to start work at fourteen without a single educational or any other qualification, working as a builder's labourer running around the roofs of East London repairing bomb damaged houses to earn some money before National Service, but who managed nevertheless to pull himself up by his bootlaces by his own efforts, and make something of himself.

I am an old man now but, as a confirmed nostalgic, I always take great pleasure, as well as a tinge of sadness sometimes, in looking back to all those memories of yesteryear, all those wonderful people I have had the good fortune to meet in my long, varied, and adventurous life and thanking all, especially my dear wife, Lynne, to whom I have been married these past 57 years, and of course my dear family, who have all contributed to what has been a very happy life; I am very contented.

When sitting quietly by myself at the end of the day, I often recount some of those memories and I go back, back, over the years, recalling names, faces, and places. I have tried to write about those memories of occasions, experiences, and adventures as they happened to me.

I am writing this for the following reasons: Firstly, I think it is nice for my family that my descendants will know something of where they came from, how we lived, and the kind of lives we led in those days in the past. They ought to know that the fine lives of comparative luxury and plenty which they have always enjoyed did not always exist and that there were times when it was not nearly so good and were indeed very tough. I am disappointed that neither my grandparents nor my parents left so much as a scrap of paper to tell of their lives, and yet I for one would have loved to know how they lived, what they did, what problems they had etc.

Secondly, I write this in the hope that maybe one, two, or even more of those young people I knew all those years ago, when we sat in the park dreaming of what we would like to be when we got older and wondering what life held in store for us, will maybe read this.

And thirdly, I would like to leave something behind so that I might be remembered in days to come by my great grandchildren and their children too. I urge them to follow the example I have endeavoured to set and never think their ambitions are too high; to work hard and conscientiously, and to remember that provided you have the will and the determination to see things through to the very end, there is very little on this earth that you cannot achieve if you want to badly enough.

I have no idea if my story will interest everybody but I hope and believe that it will interest many, because I describe a diverse life filled with stories of humble beginnings in the East End of London, how we lived before the war, experiences during and after the war, battling against the odds to make a success of life. How business brought me into close contact with Czechoslovakia and Communism, and apart from explaining some of the problems generally encountered in business and the means by which we overcame them, it includes a political element too, when the reader can go behind the Iron Curtain with me and find out what it was really like to live under Communism. I describe why and how I severed my connections with the Czechs and how I built my own successful business leading to early retirement and our subsequent emigration to Spain. I paint a picture of our lives there and explain why we eventually decided to return to England after nine glorious and happy years.

It is not exactly a rags to riches story, although it so easily could have been had my wife and I not decided upon early retirement. Financially, we were on the way up into the millionaire class; that was more or less guaranteed by our property possessions alone. But we reached a point when we decided that to live a good and enjoyable life was far more important than money and, therefore, it was the joint decision of my wife and myself to take early retirement. It is true that the properties we owned are today valued at around £1.75 million and had we stayed in business we would still have owned them. But we do not have one single regret for our actions as, for us, everything has worked out more perfect than we could ever dream. We could not have planned it better.

As I have already said when giving my reasons for writing this book, I am especially keen that some of those old pals with whom I sat in the park dreaming when we were kids and talking about our futures, and about our ambitions, will read this. I would very much like them to know that from the backstreets of the East End Docklands, where we all grew up, I was indeed fortunate enough to realise almost all of my dreams and lived a life that was full of adventures and experiences which, back in those days, I never would have imagined possible; I hope that some of my old pals had an interesting life too and that they were successful in what ever line they chose to follow. Fortunately, I am a writer – I suppose it is my main hobby. I hope, therefore, that my book will be accepted as a true account, according to my memory, of a good and honest life of which I am very proud and sometimes, often quite amazed.

So, I invite the reader to come with me whilst I relate my thoughts, actions, and experiences and my journey through the past 79 years. Let me, therefore, start at the beginning:

I was born in 1928 in Poplar, East London, in the very heart of the docklands. I cannot be sure precisely where but it would have been probably either at home, or at Poplar Hospital. Unfortunately there is no information of exactly where I or any of my brothers and sisters were born; only the areas. Sadly, there is nobody now alive whom I can ask, for I am the only survivor of my immediate family. However, I do possess one Application for Unemployment Benefit completed by my father in one of the many periods in which he was unemployed, and this has given me some clues. This form is dated August 1935 and records that following their marriage in 1917 my eldest brother, BILL, was born in Silvertown in 1918, my sister ELSIE was born at Mile End, Old Town in 1921, my brother LENNY was born at Bow & Bromley (almost certainly at St. Andrews Hospital, Bow) in 1927, but I was born in Poplar in 1928.

Another boy was born to the family, tragic little Derek, and I shall write about him later. There then followed in 1933 a little sister, DOREEN, who sadly was born with Downs Syndrome. She too was born in Bow & Bromley in 1935 – very probably also at St Andrews Hospital.

So it can be seen that following their marriage in August 1917 my parents moved around quite a lot to different addresses in different areas; however, always in the East End region. At some point after the birth of my sister in 1921 my parents returned to the family home in Prestage Street which was occupied then by my father's younger brother, Frank, his wife, Nell, and their son Frankie. This puzzles me for I have no idea why my parents decided to return to No 2 Prestage Street; I rather suspect that they must have been destitute with nowhere else to live, or had hit some crisis or other, because I cannot otherwise understand why they should have been willing to live in such poor conditions, i.e. a family of six, later seven, existing in just two upper rooms, unless it had been very necessary or unavoidable.

Now No 2 Prestage Street consisted of two basement rooms which were below the street level; one of these served as a sort of kitchen and coal store where the cooking was carried out. The other room was where the family congregated and ate. A door led from this room into the backyard where the wash house was situated, and beyond that was the outside toilet. Then there were two rooms on the street level, used as sleeping rooms, and finally two rooms on the upper level – and it was these two rooms which my parents and my immediate family occupied. My own belief is that these houses were possibly constructed so as to house two families, in quite primitive conditions, which is why there were three sets of stairs, one set inside bringing one from the upstairs rooms to the ground floor level, a further set of inside stairs leading to the basement rooms, but also an external stone staircase at ground floor level accessed by a door from the passage to the backyard. So these houses were not, in my view, constructed solely for one family and this may have been a quite normal kind of arrangement in Victorian times.

In the backyard was the wash house which consisted of a stone wash boiler with a wooden lid under which it was necessary to light a fire to warm the water. Then a contraption we called 'the mangle' or 'the wringer' which extracted most of the water from the washing before it was hung out to dry fully. There was also a cold water tap and a three-inch deep stone sink. At the end of the small yard was the toilet. I would suppose that my mother was given permission by my aunt to use the wash house from time to time to carry out her laundering.

There was of course no bathroom – these houses were built in Victorian times and probably, for that period, they (as well as the tenement flats opposite, i.e. Prestage Buildings) may have been regarded as quite suitable for the working classes – although why they thought the working classes were not deserving of a bathroom I can only wonder! But despite all, the fact was that the housewives did their best to keep their homes clean and tidy, and would often be seen scrubbing their front doorsteps until they were almost white whilst calling out to each other with little titbits of gossip. However, it was inevitable that these habitations would become almost slum-like in time. My abiding memory of my early life is the cold and dampness of the house in which we lived.

Anyhow, my father and his brother, Frank, must have come to some agreement to the effect that our family, consisting at that time of six people (my parents and four children), would occupy the upper two rooms. Knowing my mother in particular, I can only think that my parents must have been quite desperate, and in dire straits, to agree to live like that. I know that my mother would have wanted us to live in greater comfort if it had been possible.

My mother managed to have a small gas cooker fitted and this was situated in the only place possible – out on the landing. So there she cooked, and there in those two rooms she brought up her children. But every cup of water and bucket of coal had to be carried up from downstairs and of course if you wanted the toilet it was necessary to go down one flight of stairs inside, exit by the backyard door, and then down another flight of external stone steps – all in darkness and very unpleasant in winter in the bitter cold. How on earth my parents managed in such conditions is beyond understanding – but they did, for they very probably had no other choice. It is hard to believe but there were people even worse off than us. As far as we kids were concerned we knew no better and so became quite accustomed to these conditions into which we were born; therefore, we regarded them as quite normal. When children are born into a tough lifestyle it is quite amazing how resilient they are.

My parents were basically good people. My mother had a typical Irish temper and at times didn't we know it! I recall the occasions when she would chase my brother Lenny and I around the house with a broomstick when we were being naughty; she never, ever, caught us, we were too swift for her, but if she had, I believe she would have hesitated, looked at the broomstick, and then given us a good telling off! I believe she was as good a mother as those hard times permitted but she had a tendency to hold back her emotions somewhat.

For example, like all boys there were times when we thought our mother was wicked and cruel and nasty, and the very devil herself, if sometimes she became angry with us or wouldn't allow us to go out to play; but we didn't mean it of course. We really loved our mother very much. On the other hand, although she no doubt fussed over us when we were babies, I have to say that she rarely, if ever, gave either Lenny or I any kisses or cuddles that I can remember, and it is in that sense that I mean she held back her emotions somewhat. I am sorry to say that I think my brother and I lost out a little bit on mother love. But I am sure, in her own way, she did love us.

In her later years her Irish temper died away and she mellowed quite a lot; she became a very nice and gentle, kind of lady. I was very upset when she died and wished I had been able to spend more time with her in her later years. She wanted so much to see The Black & White Minstrels show which was playing at The Victoria Palace then. My wife and I planned to take her out in style with dinner either before or after the show and give her a really good time. But somehow, to my everlasting and deep regret, I couldn't find time to do so and therefore that occasion never took place. And then she became more and more unwell until it was impossible for her to go out. I do not doubt that many people experience feelings like that after the death of their loved ones. We have, all of us, experienced regrets, having perhaps spent too much time thinking of ourselves and our own problems. And the very sad thing is that so often we only realise it when it is too late to do anything about it. We should, all of us, learn from such experiences – but we don't.

My father started out in life being a steward on board a liner. During one voyage he had an ear infection which the ship's doctor endeavoured to deal with but succeeded only in making worse. Thus my father suffered from deafness from a fairly young age. No doubt this affected the development of his personality because he became a quiet, inoffensive man and he found it hard to participate in debate or discussion.

I think it would be true to say we received more obvious affection from him than from my mother and in true Mitchell style he was a joker and made us laugh when we were small. Unfortunately he never studied or trained for any profession or skill and so, after his marriage to my mother, he earned his living as a labourer in the docks. He was old fashioned in his outlook and never encouraged us boys to be anything but working class lads from the East End. He simply believed that we all had our places in the world, as it existed, that we should recognise that we were working class people, and that we should not have delusions of grandeur. He thought any kind of responsibility should be avoided by the working class – we should leave such things to those above us and be content with the position in life that had been ordained for us.

He did not have an ounce of ambition in his whole body, except maybe to win a prize at pigeon racing which was his hobby – and he didn't think we should have any either! I am sorry to have to put it this way but anything we, his children, may have achieved in life was down to us – not our parents. But in no way do I blame them. They were not educated people and could not see that even in the 1920s and 1930s the world was beginning to awake from the times of old and a new world was on its way! Sadly, it took another war for this progress to start developing in earnest.

My very first living memory is of sitting on a bed in one of the two rooms in which we then lived and being looked after by my sister, Elsie. I was very small – probably not more than two or three years old, but it was my first conscious memory.

Those times were very tough – not only for us but for the majority of people living in the East End Docklands. Without doubt there were people worse off than our family, and some I knew! It was the time of the Great Depression, unemployment was rife, and money was therefore short. For some the situation was sometimes so bad that they did not know where the cash might come from to put the next meal on the table. In that case it was off to 'Uncle's' (Mr Blackmore) in Poplar High Street to see what could be pawned. In bad periods one would often see a small queue outside the pawn shop – especially on Monday mornings.

In Prestage Street we had a variety of people, a few of whom, but only a very few, seemed to be a little better off than others; perhaps some had lower managerial positions or, if they were lucky, worked in the docks offices or maybe even in the City. Their family situations were not so bad but for the clear majority there is no question but that they were very hard times.

However, my further memory of that period was that despite the poor conditions, the unemployment, and the recurring financial crises etc., people were not for the most part unhappy, and seemed to go about their daily lives in a cheerful and good natured manner. In later years I often reflected upon this anomaly and tried to analyse why it was that, although the general situations of people, i.e. in terms of living conditions and of deprivation, should have generated misery and unhappiness, with people walking around in a downcast manner, it was not like that at all and they remained perky, relatively cheerful, and in quite good spirits.

I came to the conclusion that life then, if you were at the bottom of the pile, did not contain a great deal of hope of a better future and so people tended to accept their situation in a resigned manner and got on with living. In other words they taught themselves mentally to accept what life had meted out to them.

Of course, that is not to say that we did not have our dreams; perhaps of more disposable cash, maybe better food, a small car, and even a cottage in the country one day and a somewhat better life – even a proper holiday perhaps? But those days never arrived for they were only dreams and not at all within the realms of possibility. We didn't know then that the whole situation would indeed change for the better. However, we also did not envisage what a terrible price would have to be paid for those improvements in our lifestyle and standard of living. Matters became much worse before they became better and as the 1930s advanced, so war became that much nearer.

2

LIFE IN THE EAST END
DURING THE EARLY 1930s

In September 1931, when I had just reached the age of three, I began to attend Woolmore Street Infants School, Poplar, just around the corner from the main school. I have confirmed this by documents about Woolmore Street School held at the London Metropolitan Archives which my deceased cousin's widow, Colleen Mitchell, very kindly obtained for me. Although I was surprised to discover that I began school so early I have quite good memories of this period and even recall the name of the teacher who looked after us – a Miss Towner. She had short, cropped, hair and I liked her because, even though she looked a bit odd, she brought us cherries to school, which we loved. Cherries have always been an expensive fruit and they certainly were then; I cannot remember ever having cherries at home. But Miss Towner made sure we little ones had them at school. I remember how she taught us to put them over our ears in pairs as decorations.

The school must have been more of a nursery school to have taken children so young and I recall that every afternoon camp beds were laid out in the classroom and all of us, little boys and girls, had to lie on these beds and were urged to try to sleep. Of course, very few, if any, of us did – but we did try!

I also recall that we did little tasks of embroidery. We were given a blank piece of material and then Miss Towner would demonstrate how to make a nice pattern with needle and coloured threads. We boys took a dim view of this kind of work of course, for we didn't want to be cissies, but how very proud we were when taking our handiwork home to show our parents. Although I do not remember learning much there, I am sure we obtained good basic training.

In October 1934, when I was six, I was transferred to the main school just around the corner. Here boys went in one section and girls in a separate section. I remember some of the teachers then; firstly I recall Mr Grimm who was quite young and taught us how to sing; through him we learned some lovely songs and music to which I was attracted from the beginning. He had a nice voice but when he sang his head would shake up and down – with the effort of singing, I suppose, or maybe it helped him to produce a vibrato sound! Then I recall Mr Gibson, a strong disciplinarian with a grey, gingerish, moustache. He had a cork finger which he would not hesitate to dig into you quite sharply if you were misbehaving; I wonder if that hurt him more than it hurt us? And then in charge of the more senior boys we had a Mr Carter and after him perhaps the finest teacher of them all – a Mr Williams, a quiet, inoffensive, but very likeable man, who was Welsh but whom we nicknamed 'Jock' for some unremembered reason. Mr Williams we shall meet again a little later. But the Headmaster was a German whose name was Mr Wenzel and I often wondered what happened to him following the outbreak of war. Records show that he did come to Windsor with part of our school for a short spell, but returned a little later to London. What happened to him after that I do not know. He was a rather short man and had to stand on a chair sometimes in order to administer the cane when our class teacher sent us to him for punishment.

The class of boys I was in numbered about thirty-five I would estimate. The rather well dressed boys in blue serge suits, evidently the sons of the managers and somewhat better off parents, sat in the front rows. We rather more scruffy urchins were placed towards the back of the classroom, perhaps to be less noticeable. Thus those in the front obtained a greater amount of attention and therefore, I suppose, a somewhat better education compared to the rest of us. Anyway, it was those boys who tended to 'pass the scholarship', as we used to say, and then go on to George Green's Secondary school which would now be described as a grammar school. I cannot remember one single child who sat at the back of the class, as I did, who made it to George Green's.

On the whole we were reasonably well behaved and our teachers saw that we were. There was a disciplinary code and most of the time we observed it and maintained a respect for authority – a little different from these days in many schools I understand. The teachers were, however, people we really did look up to. They were always very smartly dressed and they set us a very good example; furthermore, we also liked and respected them.

Our class was something of a mixture; we had one Jewish boy, Benny Bornstein, whose parents ran the Army Surplus shop in East India Dock Road. Benny was a 'blue serge suit' boy but he was my pal; I knew his family and on a number of occasions sat in their back room behind the shop eating unleavened bread – Motzas I think they called it. Also I recall we had an Indian boy named Ayoub Khan. I mention him because lads of ethnic background were actually few and far between before the war. Furthermore, we also had one boy who was destined to be charged and convicted of murder when he reached his teens! I do not doubt for one moment that there were thieves and rascals in the remainder of the class. But I was not one of them – providing we conveniently forget about the apples I used to pinch from the stalls in Chrisp Street market!

I tried to absorb as much learning as I possibly could, but I never thought of myself as clever or brainy – too busy dreaming of what I was going to be when I grew up and how to make my fortune. Just before my eleventh birthday I sat for what is now called the 11-plus I believe, but we used to say 'the scholarship'. Nobody could have been more surprised than I, therefore, when somewhat later I was informed that I had 'passed the scholarship' to the Central School level.

In those days there were Elementary Schools, with a level of education much as the name suggests. The next stage up was Central, a higher standard of education but a kind of halfway house, and then, for the very brainy girls and boys, they qualified for what we called in those days the Secondary School level. All the names have been changed now to Comprehensive and Grammar Schools, and I believe that the Central school level for those scholars who were not quite brainy enough to go to a grammar school but a little more clever than for the elementary level, has been abolished. Now, it seems to me that these days all types of children have been thrown into the same educational pot and I am not sure this is a good idea.

Apart from schooling we kids had a life to lead as well. In Prestage Street we had a collection of small boys and girls all of about the same age and so we formed a group. First of all we had to find a way to earn ourselves some money. The first method I can recall involved going down to Blackwall Stairs, River Thames, collecting wood which was washed up on the small shore there from time to time. This we would chop, tie, and then sell at 1d (one penny) per bundle.

But the wood supply at Blackwall Stairs was not very consistent and so we had to find other ways to earn some money. Our salvation came by courtesy of the London County Council who decided, for the sake of hygiene and cleanliness, to issue free disinfectant to the poor people of East London. The only problem was that the depot issuing the free disinfectant was sited in Pennyfields, just by Chinatown, at the far end of Poplar High Street, nearer to the West India Docks, quite a distance from the Prestage Street area which was almost adjacent to the East India Docks. And so our idea of setting up a disinfectant service was born. Our gang had managed to construct a small cart which consisted of an old wooden fish box with two wheels attached to the back and a plank nailed along the bottom. To the front end of this plank we attached another piece of wood, fitted with a swivel bolt, to which was attached another two wheels and with the aid of a piece of string this enabled us to guide it to the left or right.

Of course we all fought to be given the chance of guiding this contraption but as I was rather small I was forced to be a 'pusher' rather than a 'guider' for most of the time and I took a dim view of that sometimes – never mind, we were earning money! But the point was that we had the means of carrying things and so we went around the houses and flats in our street and in the streets nearby collecting empty bottles. These we transported to the LCC depot, right at the very top of the High Street, in our little cart and there we took our place in the queue. The bottles were filled with free disinfectant which we then carried back to our area and distributed. For this service we charged 1d per bottle and shared out the proceeds among those taking part. Some Saturday mornings I made as much as 6d (2.5p)! And believe me, 6d was a fortune to us kids in those days.

It was usually spent in the following manner: tuppence for the 'tuppenny rush' at The Grand Cinema, (there was very little 'grand' about it by the time we had finished), tuppence for peanuts and maybe a bit of fruit. And tuppence for sweets. Sometimes it was possible to save a penny or even more and I kept these coins in the top pocket of an old blazer I used to wear sometimes if I went anywhere 'posh'. One Saturday evening Lenny and I were going to the slide show and silent movies held at our school, Woolmore Street, when my father happened to tap my breast pocket. Of course it tinkled with all the pennies I had saved. My father immediately came to the conclusion that I had stolen this money somehow and just wouldn't believe that it was money I had saved. He took the lot away from me, about 10d I think it was – not much of an encouragement to save, I thought!

I would like at this point to write a little more about Blackwall Stairs which is a spot we kids frequented very often. It consisted of just a few steps and after mounting these there was a causeway leading right down to the river where we used to paddle and throw stones into the water. We did this sometimes with our shoes on as boys do – our mothers were not best pleased with us because new shoes meant more money which had to be found from somewhere. To the right was a rough kind of small beach, where as I have earlier related we used to collect wood, but to the left was a gully. Now in those days I can only assume there was no strict discipline imposed on the liners and large boats that sailed up the Thames to the great docks and so, sometimes, they used to discharge their oil sumps on their way up river which washed up on the various small shores and especially in that gully at our Blackwall Stairs.

This resulted in a carpet of thick grey-black mud forming there and the young bravos of the day would get down in to this gully, smear themselves from head to foot with this filthy, oily, mud, and then climb up on the railway parapet above. As that was well forward they could dive into the water from there and come up spotlessly clean – or as clean as the dirty River Thames would allow. We young ones would watch in awe and all of us resolved that when we grew up we would do the same. However, I do not think any of us did.

But the amazing thing is that we had no idea at all how historical the Stairs actually were. It is only recently that I have learned from Jim Fitzpatrick M.P. (currently Minister for Post Offices) that in the year 1606 the very first English speaking group of settlers set forth from Blackwall Stairs in three ships to settle in the Americas – they in fact preceded all others – even The Pilgrim Fathers. I researched this further via the Internet and found that the expedition was granted permission in the form of a Charter by our King at that time, King James, and paid for commercially. The expedition consisted of 104 settlers plus their crews. Their voyage was not a good one as at first they were becalmed off the Irish coast and then, afterwards, ran into very bad weather conditions. However they eventually arrived off the American coast, landed, but were immediately attacked by Indians from the Powhatan tribe. They beat the Indians off but skirmishes continued to take place.

In one of these the leader of the expedition, Captain John Smith, was captured and sentenced to be put to death by the Chief. I believe the traditional method employed by the Indians was to club the poor victim until he died. But the daughter of the Chief pleaded for Smith's life to be spared and the Chief relented. This Indian Princess was none other than the famous Pocohontas! In Walt Disney's lovely film about Pocohontas he depicted her falling in love and marrying Captain Smith but this was not correct. There was no romance between these two – not that we know of anyway!

Mistrust between the settlers and the Indians continued and so Smith decided to build a fort which he named Jamestowne, after our King. Today, Jamestown is of course a large city. Smith also founded the State of Virginia – named after our Queen of course.

Pocohontas did eventually find romance with an English captain, however, after three or so years. His name was Captain John Rolfe and he became famous for instigating the very first tobacco plantations in Virginia. Pocohontas married Captain Rolfe and they had a child, a boy whom they named Thomas. All the family returned to England and landed at Blackwall Stairs; in fact they actually made their residence nearby.

Pocohontas conducted herself with dignity, was presented at Court, and pleaded for peace on behalf of her people. She wanted to return to her country but before doing so took a trip to Gravesend and there she contracted a fatal disease and died. She was given a full Christian burial and her remains lie there in Gravesend to this very day. Her grave is visited often by American tourists.

We kids never knew all of this, and nobody taught us about it in our history lessons. Had we known, I believe we would have been even more proud of where we had come from. As I have related, I was alerted to this by a response from Jim Fitzpatrick M.P. to some of my writings that were published in *The Island History Trust Magazine* during 2006 in which I specifically mentioned Blackwall Stairs and it was Jim Fitzpatrick's response that caused me to investigate the full story further.

But to return to my narrative, for entertainment we didn't have a lot. When the planners designed the East End Docklands they forgot about us kids and so we had no grass to play on although we did have a small play park with a hard surface area just by Blackwall Tunnel where we played sometimes. However, we were very adventurous kids and in any case we wanted to play on grass. And so our gang, all boys and girls together, wandered far and wide and for miles and miles to do just that. Our nearest and most often visited venue was Millwall Park – only about a mile or so from us but it seemed like 10 miles to us small kids. We also went further; through the foot tunnel from Millwall to Greenwich Park and on to Blackheath for example.

I always remember that tunnel when first of all we went down in a cranky old lift. When we had arrived down below, the lift attendant would open the gates and out we all would burst, whooping and shouting at the tops of our voices as we ran through the tunnel, just to hear the lovely echo of the sounds we were making, which seemed to spread from one end of the tunnel to the other. They were pleasant sounds to us, we were just letting off steam, but I doubt they were pleasant to others.

Our adventures and the next target journey of our gang was always planned by our leader. I recall two leaders, a boy called Teddy Brown who lived in Prestage Buildings ran it for a couple of years; he grew older and then Johnny Ives, my cousin who lived opposite us in Prestage Buildings was our leader right up to just before the war I think. To see us kids setting off for one of our great adventures must have been a sight. In those days we did not seem to have those nasty people around who preyed on young children, or if there were we never encountered them. And so our mothers never minded us going off for the day, God knew where or in which direction. They probably appreciated the fact that we did. They would pack us up two slices of bread and margarine, wrapped in newspaper of course, and a bottle of water flavoured with cheap lemonade crystals and off we would go, chattering and laughing excitedly, into the 'unknown', returning in the late afternoon, tired, hungry and thirsty. Then we were scrubbed up in the outside wash-house, a quick supper before our father came home from work, if he was at work that is, probably another two slices of bread and margarine – but maybe with a little jam too as a treat, and off to bed we were sent to dream about our next big adventure the following day.

I remember one occasion when we decided to go just to Millwall Park to play. Now at the top of Prestage Street was Blackwall Way and opposite to the top of our street, i.e. in Blackwall Way, was Green's Dining Rooms which were frequented by our teachers from Woolmore Street School and the managerial people from the ship repair yard and other places. Sandwiched between Green's and a small pub called Star of India, was a large, grim looking, three-storey house in which lived a German family by the name of Muller.

They must have been a very poor family for this house was always cold and bleak without any carpet (or even lino) on the floors or stairs – just the bare floorboards. When you entered the house you always experienced the unforgettable atmosphere and smell of poverty. We were all poor, but they appeared to be poorer than most. I have no idea what the father did for a living but the family consisted of the parents, two girls, and a small boy whose name was Little Henry. Now Little Henry, who was a little younger than I, used to like me for some reason and he would follow me everywhere like a lamb; everywhere I went Little Henry would follow. On this particular occasion I had wolfed down my two slices of bread and margarine quite early in the day and by early afternoon I was ravenous. So I announced to the rest that I was heading for home sooner than was normal in the hope I could get a bite to eat there, and off I went – followed by Little Henry of course.

Being so hungry, thirsty, and somewhat tired, the journey home seemed much longer than usual; but we continued to trudge our way along Manchester Road when suddenly we arrived at Christ Church. Outside this church was a monument of Jesus Christ on the cross which stood on a plinth of steps. It is still there to this day. But by now the pangs of hunger were getting worse and worse and as we approached the statue I had what I thought was a brilliant idea! As a matter of fact something similar had happened to me some little while before when I stood with my nose pressed up against the window of the brightly lit sweets-and-small-toys shop that used to be in the lower part of Poplar High Street. There I stood looking at all the wonderful things; but I had no money. If only I had 6d, I thought to myself, I would go in and buy up the shop almost! So, with my nose still pressed up against the window I prayed silently for 6d – in those days you could buy a lot for such a small amount. For some reason that I cannot for the life of me explain, I turned my head and lying there in the gutter, I swear to you dear reader that this is absolutely true, was a shiny sixpenny piece!

I looked around – nobody was in sight, and so I quickly picked the sixpence up and entered the shop. I left the shop with my arms filled with goodies and hurried around the corner, along Blackwall Way and into Prestage Street. But here I came unstuck as my mother was standing in the street gossiping with one of the neighbours. Seeing me with all those goodies in my arms she immediately demanded to know where I had obtained the money to buy so many things. I told her the absolute truth – that I had found 6d in the gutter – but she didn't believe my story and smacked me so hard she nearly knocked me to the other side of the street – it was her Irish temper you see! And she thought I was lying to her. So I found myself in deep trouble for she was certain I had stolen money from somewhere; however I was truly totally innocent. It is bad enough to be accused of something when you are guilty – but what an awful feeling it is to be accused of something when you are entirely innocent and nobody believes you!

But that experience didn't deter me and so on this occasion I said to Little Henry, 'Come on Henry, let's pray to Jesus for something to eat!' Henry was all for it. So, picture if you will these two little boys, very hungry and very thirsty, and probably very grubby, kneeling at the foot of the statue of Jesus praying so earnestly and in such an innocent manner; it must have been a touching scene. Suddenly, a deep but kind voice addressed us, 'Hallo boys, I see you are praying to dear Jesus. Would you like to come into the Vicarage for something to eat and a cup of tea?' Well, we did not need to be asked twice and so we accompanied the Vicar, trooping behind him to the Vicarage which was just a few steps away and there a plump, rosy cheeked, and smiling lady, like someone from a Charles Dickens book long ago, greeted us and invited us to sit down. She evidently was the Housekeeper and she reacted as though she had done this sort of thing many times before. So we sat down and the Vicar chatted to us. We explained about our trip to Millwall Park and how hunger had overcome us. He nodded in a kindly manner. Very soon the Housekeeper appeared with a plate filled with cakes and pastries and a steaming hot pot of tea on a tray. We looked at the cakes hungrily, and observing this, the Vicar invited us to tuck in. I cannot recall exactly now but I do believe Little Henry and I emptied that plate. I wonder if the Vicar wanted one! When we had finished we thanked the Vicar, and his Housekeeper, over and over for their kindness. We may have been poor children but we were polite and knew our manners.

So we continued on our way towards the two bridges which separate the Isle of Dogs from Poplar and eventually reached Prestage Street. That event must have taken place around 1934-5 or so. Some 70 years later Eve Hostettler, the Archivist at The Island History Trust, very kindly sent me a copy of a celebratory book on churches on the Isle of Dogs. On the front cover were two priests; one was Edward Hartley, Vicar of Christ Church from 1902-1920, and the other was John Harold Hardy, Vicar of the same church from 1920-1940. I cannot truthfully say I immediately recognised the Rev. Hartley but this must have been the kind vicar who took pity on two small, hungry boys all those years ago and it gave me an eerie feeling when I gazed at his photo.

But I should like to return to Saturdays and especially Saturday nights in Poplar High Street. The description 'High Street' conjures up in the imagination a wide, busy, road with lots of big shops on both sides. Well, our High Street was not like that at all. It was a narrow thoroughfare and began up near West India Docks, Pennyfields, and Chinatown.

Before the East India Dock Road was constructed, the High Street was indeed the main thoroughfare between the West India Docks and the East India Docks, Blackwall etc. and a well populated and very busy street. But after the East India Dock Road came into existence – a wider and much better road – the old High Street became less used; although it was frequented by those of us who lived in the locality. There at the Western end, on the corner of Garfield Street and West India Dock Road, opposite to the beginning of the High Street, you would find Charlie Brown's pub – made widely famous (I believe even world famous) because of the novel curiosities and perhaps even antiques that use to adorn the Saloon Bar. It is said that Charlie Brown would give beer to sailors arriving at the docks from all over the world in exchange for interesting mementos; and the sailors, if they had no money, were glad to trade such items for beer. Further down was another pub called The Blue Post – an establishment of ill repute I once heard – and then the old cinema, called The Ideal. It was a real 'flea-pit' but very popular with us kids because they gave lots of bags of sweets away to those children whose tickets bore the right lucky number – I never won one of those!

And then we go on to the Recreation Ground on the left. I understand that this quite substantial area, with an old church, St. Mathias (which had a graveyard where officers and crews were buried many years ago), was presented to the people of Poplar by The East India Company in the early 1800s. As the name suggests, it served as a place of recreation for the general public. It had a very nice bowling green, tennis courts, and swings etc., as well as a memorial to the eighteen children who were killed and the thirty-seven injured during World War 1 when a German aircraft dropped a bomb on a school in North Street. I would like to point out that North Street was a considerable distance from any of the docks; there was no excuse for this act of inhumanity. But in their general plans for the Recreation Ground they provided not a blade of grass for us kids to play on.

Opposite the Recreation Ground is a building which used to be The London School of Engineering. During World War II it was used as a temporary Elementary School, which, as I will tell later, I was obliged to attend during 1941-2, there being no Central School available. So many schools had either been bombed or evacuated. It was also used as a British Restaurant where members of the public could get a quite decent meal for one shilling and for which I do not believe they had to surrender rationing points.

Going further down on the right side was the Poplar Public Library and then Solly Spector's confectionery shop where, as a schoolboy, I used to buy most of my black market chocolate and confectionery; then came Constance House, a Council block of flats which I remember well as it was there we were fitted for our gasmasks in the early part of 1939. There was a pub on the corner there which I think was called The Resolute. On the opposite corner was the old Dockland Settlement and still further down there was Wickes – my sister Elsie, when young, was for a short while in service there. Wickes was an old, established, rather upmarket family business where they sold meat, poultry and most foods. Thereafter, there were various shops, including the most important of them all – the pawn shop!

This took us down to the Cotton Street Junction and that part of the High Street I considered to be the most interesting. On the left we would find Enevers, the butchers, then The Bargain Stores which we kids used to go to, poke our heads in, and ask 'Have you any broken biscuits?' and when the answer was 'Yes' we would cry out 'Well bloomin' well mend 'em!' and run off; that sounds a bit tame now but at the time we considered it a laugh.

And then of course we come to The Queen's Theatre & Music Hall. On the opposite side to the theatre was a great favourite for all – the local fish and chip shop where you could buy a handsome piece of fish for tuppence and a good portion of chips for a penny; total cost of a substantial meal was therefore less than 2p in today's money. Mostly we kids had to be satisfied with just the chips – fish was only for the grown ups, but sometimes they would give us a taster!

Just past the fish 'n' chip shop was a public house, The Ship, which was always full at the weekends – but not exactly empty during the week either! As the story goes, The Ship was bought for his parents by Teddy Baldock, a Poplar boy who rose to become the Flyweight or Bantamweight Champion of the World in the 1930s. I am told that the Baldock family had very little before Teddy became famous and so were very happy then to be grandly regarded as landlords of The Ship. I knew Teddy personally and would often have a chat with him whilst supping a pint in his pub. Sadly, Teddy himself became a victim of drink, as sometimes happens, and from time to time he made a nuisance of himself to the extent that his family threw him out. He deteriorated to a level of which he would have been thoroughly ashamed when in his prime. I heard that his family did not want anything to do with him and he became almost a vagrant. He died penniless. I believe he was found lying dead in the gutter somewhere near to Aldgate. What a tragic end to a fine athlete and a top sportsman.

Now the means of entertainment were very sparse in those days – it was only the cinema or the theatre, if your locality had one. We did, and The Queen's Theatre and Music Hall was of course a big attraction. To be sure of getting a good seat it was always better to arrive at the theatre early and join the queues. These queues naturally attracted the street entertainers and, if our mothers were in a good mood, they would allow us to go to the High Street on Saturday nights; not every week mind, just now and then because there was another attraction, which I have mentioned earlier, for on Saturday evenings silent movies or slide shows were held at our school, Woolmore Street. Anyway, on the occasions we were given permission to go to the High Street we would beg or borrow a penny for a packet of chips, all wrapped in newspaper in those days and plenty of salt and vinegar (we used to have a big debate as to which newspaper had the best flavour – my favourite was the Daily Herald because it was my Dad's newspaper!). And so our little gang of boys and girls would sit on the kerb opposite the theatre, munching away, and enjoying the entertainment supplied gratis for us by the street entertainers. There we would be in a row cheering the good artists and booing those we did not care much about.

As each act finished they would go along the queues with their hat or a small bowl and then make way for the next act. Our two favourites were, first of all, old Mutton-eye. We called him that because he had a funny eye. But he was there every Saturday with his bowler hat on and with his collapsible organ tucked under his arm. After he had assembled his equipment, which he did remarkably quickly, he played his organ, pumping away with his foot, and sang old, funny music hall songs which made us laugh. My cousin, Joyce, tells me that sometimes his wife accompanied him and sang too but I truly can't remember her.

The second favourite act was either two men, or sometimes three, dressed in Egyptian clothing. They would sprinkle some sand on the roadway and then perform a very funny sand dance. They were very good. The other acts were mainly singers and some of those sang so well they should have been singing inside the theatre, not outside, for they were excellent.

Of course this wonderful atmosphere of Poplar High Street on Saturday nights was not only magical for us kids, it was magical for everybody. There was an atmosphere of excitement in the air and this was also sometimes added to when The Ship had to eject a drinker from the pub who had obviously had one over the eight and such people were either fighting mad and wanted to fight the whole world, or in a soppy sentimental state of inebriation in which case they wanted to sing 'Danny Boy' or 'Nellie Dean' at the top of their voice. But in either case they too, in their way, contributed to Saturday nights in the High Street.

Eventually, the queues began to slowly disappear as they entered the theatre and the street entertainers would melt away as well as did the apple and orange lady, the roasted peanut man, and the chap who sold hot, roasted chestnuts which were very popular on cold evenings. Sometimes the entertainers, where suitable, would continue by performing their acts in the local pubs – if the landlords would allow it. But it was quite remarkable how quickly the High Street turned from the hustle and bustle and excitement of an hour earlier into just an ordinary street and so people, including us kids, would gradually disappear into the gloom of the night and the High Street returned to normality.

Those were times which have now vanished into the past, and we shall never see the like of them again, I fear. As far as The Queen's (originally called The Oriental when it opened in the 1800s) is concerned, that too has gone. I will write a little more detail about the history of The Queen's below. The advent of television in many homes affected all theatres and The Queen's was closed in the 1950s and demolished and sold for development later on. Many famous stars of the past appeared there; indeed it was the very first theatre in London in which our dear Gracie Fields appeared. It is true to say that before the advent of TV every town and city had one or more theatres or music halls like The Queen's and so throughout the country there were hundreds and hundreds of them. They were served by the revues or variety shows that travelled the country, appearing usually for just one week and then moving on to the next venue. These shows were put together by entrepreneurs and agents who were responsible for booking the show tours and paying the artistes which, if it was a revue, consisted of the principal artist, usually a comedian, a couple of singers, or maybe a magician, a group of dancing girls; perhaps seventeen to twenty people in total. If it was a variety show then that would consist of six to eight individual acts with a compere introducing each one to the audience.

It was a wonderful nursery for talent and for budding artistes to hone their skills and learn the business of entertainment and, providing you had some evident talent, it was not too difficult to find a touring show that would accept you. In the days of the provincial theatre this 'theatrical nursery' produced a lot of famous actors and actresses who in later years appeared on TV to entertain the nation. Today we have no such nursery and so there are fewer places for up and coming stars of the future to develop and improve and I for one, but joined by many, believe this is a tragedy. But it was what they call 'progress' and in my opinion is one of the main reasons why the quality levels or standards in entertainment have deteriorated so much these days and why there are fewer real stars than there were years ago. With the end of the music halls and provincial theatres there seems to be almost nobody around today who can hold an audience in the palm of their hands like the old stars. They had a kind of magical attraction. But then, they had the opportunity in those days to learn how to do that!

As far as the history of The Queen's Theatre is concerned, the first music hall on this site was licensed in 1865 and the performances took place at the rear of The Queen's Arms public house. An inn, The Angel, had occupied the site previously as early as 1765. The Abrahams family took over The Queen's Arms in 1863 and they were connected with the development and ownership of what eventually became The Queen's Theatre (originally called The New Albion and then The Oriental) for almost a century.

Apparently it was a 'pub' theatre right up to the 1920s. It went through a bad patch in the late 1880s and early 1890s which was perhaps due to the poor economic conditions which existed then and the dock strike of 1889 could not have helped. But it survived and went on into the 20th century. It closed in 1956 but was purchased by a theatrical group which intended to re-open it within 18 months or so as a West End theatre in the East End. But sadly these plans came to nought and the site became derelict. It was eventually purchased by the London County Council in 1964 for development and for a very low price. Thus The Queen's was demolished and with it went a lot of treasured memories on the part of so many people, and also, certainly, the author. But in my heart of hearts I believe that the ghosts of the many stars who performed at The Queen's are wandering abroad – maybe seeking a heavenly opportunity to display their artistry as they once did on that stage many years ago!

I would like to mention that there was a little 'cubby hole' at the side of the stage where the Stage Manager sat or stood and watched that everything was proceeding according to plan. On the wall of this cubby hole was a glass case containing signed photographs of many of the great stars of the past who had performed there – from Charlie Chaplin to Gracie Fields and many wonderful performers even before them. I often wonder what happened to that when The Queen's was demolished. It must have been worth a tidy penny to any collector!

After the excitement of Saturday nights, followed the quietness of Sunday mornings. Our mother always packed us off to church, either St Nicholas or All Saints. When we returned home she would send me or Lenny (mostly me I seem to recall, despite my protests) off to Cobb's Wet Fish shop in lower High Street. Cobb's had their own fishing smack and in those days they used to sail up to the Thames Estuary, or perhaps even farther, returning either late on Saturday night or very early Sunday morning. They moored their vessel off Blackwall Stairs, dealt with their catch, and I would pop along rather later with a precious shilling in my hand which I guarded with my life. My job was to buy a pint of fresh winkles and a pint of shrimps; for that was Sunday tea for the family and how we fought in the family for the best pins and needles with which to tackle the winkles. Sometimes, if things were good, I would be given a little extra to buy some large prawns which my father, especially, liked very much. And if things were very, very good we sometimes had a slice of ham, too! But that was only a treat which occurred now and then before the war – after the war it became a regular habit. I cannot explain why but every time I hear the song 'In My Sweet Little Alice Blue Gown' my thoughts go back to those wonderful, quiet Sunday mornings in Poplar. There must be an unconscious connection there somehow.

3

POPLAR TOWN HALL, SADNESS AND CHARITY ORGANISATIONS

I should also like to write a few words about the old Poplar Town Hall in Newby Place and what a magnificent building it was. On those very steps at the entrance, George Lansbury made many a fiery speech in defence of the poor and the working classes. But what I remember most are the Mothers' Meetings which were held there. Sometimes my mother would take me with her when I was small and quite often they would arrange a small stage show. For some mothers that was about the only entertainment they ever got! These shows were very entertaining and I recall two main entertainers there. One was an older man we called 'Uncle Ernie' who sang funny songs from the music hall which amused the mothers who were, incidentally, ladies of all ages – they were just glad to have the opportunity of getting out of the house for a little pleasure. The other chap was named Jimmy Emms, a younger man who loved to entertain. He just lived for any chance to perform. I shall always recall his imitation of Shirley Temple when she was just a tot. Jimmy would come on to the stage wearing a blonde curly wig and a short girly dress; with his hairy legs he had the mothers in fits of laughter, and me too! Jimmy was at one time quite sweet on my sister, Elsie, but nothing came of it. Pity, he was a very nice young man and very likeable. I do not think these, or any other willing participants in these shows for the mothers, were paid for their services; if they were it would only have been a pittance. Years later I saw 'Uncle Ernie' performing in The White Hart pub on the corner of the High Street and Robin Hood Lane; he was still singing the same old songs. And I know Jimmy Emms used to delight in performing at people's private parties if he was asked; he certainly came to parties at our house. If I remember correctly, I believe his theme tune was 'Music, Maestro, Please'; back in the 1930s – it was a very popular tune. Sadly, the Town Hall was badly damaged by a bomb during The Blitz; it remained as a shell for a time and was finally demolished either just before the end of the war or immediately after. I am not sure what stands in its place today.

Another who performed occasionally at The Old Town Hall was our own little angel from Prestage Street. Her name was Little Joanie Cruise. She was pretty and sang and danced in a very cute and perfect way. She appeared not only at the Town Hall shows but also occasionally at The Queen's, in talent contests and other places, too. We all loved Little Joanie for she was the darling of the neighbourhood. She was invited to all the parties that were held in our district, lifted on to a table in the centre of the room, and there, with many watchful eyes upon her to see that she didn't fall, she would perform her act to rapturous applause from the whole room. We often spoke of and wondered if Little Joanie would have become a big star. Alas, it was not to be and I shall relate the tragic end to Little Joanie's short life later on in this narrative.

I used to love Good Friday mornings in Prestage Street and looked forward to them. For that was the day that out came the thick skipping rope that stretched easily from one side of the street to the other. All the neighbours came out and others stood at their doorsteps to watch the fun. The young girls began the skipping; at first they had to get used to the rhythm of the rope holders and so the beginning was always a bit ragged. But after a few minutes the girls got used to it and then skipped in earnest with great smiles across their faces as they bobbed up and down. Then came the turn of the Mums and older women to shouts of 'Come on gels, lift yer knees up!' There were many humorous scenes and funny quips from both the women who were skipping and their husbands mocking them. And then, eventually, it was the turn of the men. They all joined in and this time the tables were turned and it was the women that mocked the men. Finally, it became a free for all with everybody – young and old, fat and thin, men, women and girls – all gaily skipping away and laughing all the while. My cousin, Joycie Ives, says that during the skipping it was customary to sing the old song: 'Hot Cross Buns, Hot Cross Buns, one a penny, two a penny, Hot Cross Buns' and I myself have a vague memory of this.

I only ever witnessed one not very nice accident during this annual skipping occasion and that was an older neighbour who lost the rhythm and the thick rope caught her ankle. She fell down and injured herself but not seriously; I saw her going to Chrisp Street market the following day so she couldn't have hurt herself all that badly. I have tried very hard to find the origin of street skipping on Good Fridays which took place in many streets other than ours but without success so far. One source suggests that the rope has some significance or connection with the rope that Judas used to hang himself on another Friday, long, long ago after Jesus was crucified. But I am not sure that I can swallow that one!

Of course, after the skipping all the adults retired to The Ivy House – to replenish their lost energy, they said! Well, to hear them burst into song after a few pints showed that they didn't lose their singing energy, that's for sure and it was lovely to listen to – even we kids were enthralled!

In the 1930s the main scourges of the working classes were (1) Unemployment, (2) Diphtheria and (3) Tuberculosis. My father was an unskilled dock labourer and whether he had work or not was dependent upon a number of factors but mainly on whether a ship was in and further men were required. So my father was out of work many times and for varying periods.

As a particular point of interest it should be remembered that back in those days there were not the generous allowances available to the unemployed that exist today and that made family situations very difficult in times of unemployment. When my father was out of work he would line up with all the other unemployed along the wall which separates Robin Hood Lane from Blackwall Tunnel, hoping to be picked for a day's work – even a half day sometimes was better than nothing! Then along would come the foreman in his black bowler hat, hands clasped behind his back, and often without even looking up he would just mutter 'You, and you, and you...' etc. But my father was a rather short man and so was one of the last to be picked – the big strong chaps were preferred.

On our way to school we had to walk up Robin Hood Lane and spying our Dad we would call out 'Hi Dad'. But he never answered or returned our greeting or acknowledged us in any way. I think he felt degraded and rather ashamed that his children should see him standing there almost like a beggar with a look on his face that was quite desperate and evidently pleading for work. But he needn't have – we were never ashamed of our Dad because we knew he was trying his very best to find work to keep food on the table for us all. And I have to say that I can never recall being really hungry. Yes, there were times when we could have eaten a little more and we always wished we could afford food of a better quality. I never ate a steak in my whole younger life until I reached the age of 20-21 or so, for example. We never went hungry – my dear old Mum always saw to that – even if we had only a pennyworth of chips for lunch. My God! What would the poor people of The East End have done without the fish n' chip shop?

As I have mentioned, Prestage Street contained a mixture of various kinds of people, but it would be true to say that the majority were those we must describe as poor, as indeed my family was, i.e. my father earned £2.10.0d per week – when he was working – and that had to keep a family of six, and later on seven! Some were even below the poverty line. I think most people earned that or perhaps a little more if they had a good job. I wonder how many readers will remember the old song 'He's The Little Boy That Santa Claus Forgot', which used to tug at my heart strings when I was small? Well, whenever I play that song on the piano or maybe hear it on the radio, which today means almost never, I am reminded of one extremely poor family named Tighe, an old Irish name I believe, who lived in the lower part of the street; they had one son in particular called Patsy. The Tighes were so poor they didn't even have mice!! There was never a Mr Tighe! This could mean a number of things; either he had left the family to fend for itself or he was in prison.

Anyway, I knew Patsy although he was a couple of years younger than I, and I always felt sorry for him and his brothers and sisters. When going into their house I was always pleased to get out and back in the street again. My cousin Joyce swears that if little Patsy saw her mother at the front of Prestage Buildings he would ask her, 'Can yer give us a slice of bread and marge Mrs Ives – can yer, please, Mrs Ives?' Knowing my Aunt Bec I am sure she obliged every time. And that's why that song reminds me of Patsy because at Christmas time it fitted him to a T and I felt truly sorry for him because if we had very little then Patsy had even less and, just like the words of the song, I am sure he must have envied all those lucky boys who played in the streets showing off their new toys. I expect Patsy, too, wandered home to play with last year's broken toys – if he had any that is!!

Meanwhile, around 1932-4 The London County Council announced the semi or maybe full completion of their house building schemes in Becontree and Dagenham districts. My Uncle Frank and Aunt Nell, together with their son Frankie, were successful in obtaining one of those charming semi-detached houses with a garden and so they moved to 283 Ivy House Road, Becontree. My own immediate family either did not apply or did not want to move away or could not afford to move, and so we stayed where we were, in Prestage Street. But this meant that my parents could now take over the whole family house and so, instead of existing in just two rooms upstairs, we now added the two rooms at street level and the two basement rooms. For my mother especially, it must have been a happy moment because although 2 Prestage Street was by no means a palace, the transformation from two rooms to six meant that she must have been, by comparison, in Seventh Heaven.

There was another event in our family which I should like to mention and this concerns that other scourge of the working classes then – Diphtheria. When I think of how we kids played marbles in the filthy gutters of the East End it is a wonder that with all that dirt we didn't all catch illnesses as bad or worse; on the other hand, having survived the early period maybe our little bodies were groomed and strengthened to accustom ourselves to the myriad of bacteria, viruses and diseases that were out there. Anyhow, our family was blessed in 1930, when my parents were still living in two rooms mark you, with a little baby brother who was named Derek – so there were now seven of us. Everyone fell in love with Derek for he was one of those perfect children. He never cried, was good looking, with fair hair; he danced and sang and kept all our family very amused. He was loved not only in our house by us but by the whole neighbourhood and especially by my maternal grandparents who lived just across the road from us in Prestage Buildings. My grandfather took much delight in taking little Derek to the local park almost every day and he loved him very much. Tragically, when he was about five or so, little Derek contracted diphtheria. He fought very hard to combat it and the hospital did their very best; but all to no avail. Our beloved little Derek passed away and I cannot find the words to describe the terrible grief we all felt.

My grandfather, who had such a close relationship with him, was a broken man and as best as I can remember I do not think he ever fully recovered from this very sad loss of a lovely little boy. I can recall being lifted up to see poor little Derek in his white coffin lying in the front room (my parents must have asked the permission of my Uncle and Aunt to use this room); he looked so very peaceful, just as if he was having a short nap, and he wore his favourite sailor suit. Even I, as a child, was broken-hearted and could hardly believe that we would never see our lovely little brother again. I remember asking my mother, 'Mum, why is it that God takes the best ones?' Sadly, I cannot remember the actual funeral but I am sure the whole neighbourhood would almost certainly have been there.

Everybody cried that day for little Derek!

Before terminating my description of those pre-war years, no account would be complete without mentioning the various charity organisations that did so much for the poor children of the East End. To give just one example, my brother Lenny and I were walking along the street quite near to home when we were stopped by a well-dressed lady and gentleman. They spoke extremely well and plied us with a whole variety of questions. They wanted to know how we lived, what my father did for work, and when and where did we spend our last holiday. Well, we answered all the questions and as for holidays we just didn't have any. Holidays were out of the question for most working people in the East End. Many of them went hop-picking in Kent and regarded that as their holiday. And I would suppose that in many respects, it was.

Every September you would see them all going off and most families or even two or three families, would club together and hire a lorry to take them. Loaded on to the lorry was everything they might possibly need to live and to cook. Pots and pans, favourite chairs – all went on to the lorry – plus the people of course. As they drove away we would cheer them and they went singing their hearts out.

At the other end the hop farmers provided wooden sheds in rows for the hop pickers. Usually it was one shed to a family with all the cooking being carried out over a wood fire outside. The confirmed hop pickers knew the ropes and settled in immediately, but I expect those who were trying it for the first time were possibly shocked by the primitive conditions. It was like a great big camping holiday, gypsy style.

The families formed working groups with everybody piling in to pick as many hops as they could. There were various calls that were made; like 'Hops ready', which I believe meant that they wanted their bin to be emptied. And then 'Vine cutter', which was the call when the tops of the vines could not be pulled down easily and they needed the assistance of the cutter who was armed with a long pole with a sort of knife on the end with which he could cut the vines. As a matter of fact, those hops which grew on the top of the vines were considered the best quality of all and so it was important to gather them in.

At the end of a long day in the hop fields the pickers would return to their huts and a meal was prepared. I do not know if each family group was paid daily or weekly but one way or another they shared the money out between them. Anyway, they always had money for beer and they would descend en masse to the local pubs, firstly to quench their thirst and then to sing their favourite songs of the time at the very tops of their voices. I think they mostly had a good time. It was in any case a break from the normal monotony back home and a chance to breathe God's good air.

For some reason, of which I am unaware, my parents never went hop-picking. We kids would have loved every minute of such an adventure but my parents preferred not to go. Today there are no hop-pickers. That was a Cockney tradition which is long dead and buried. Today the operation of cutting and gathering hops is carried out automatically by machines. People are no longer required to do this job and in any case the descendants of those old hop-pickers now have money and seek their holiday destinations in far away and sunny places. Today it is a different world where money is not in such short supply as it was back in those days and so people can afford holidays to exotic places; so even if hop-picking still existed, I think it would be doubtful if they could persuade sufficient people to take part.

Anyway, let me return to our well-dressed couple. At the end of this brief questionnaire they asked for our address and said they would speak with our parents about the possibility of our going on a fortnight's camping holiday down by Chichester. They in fact represented the Toc H Charity Organisation; they did indeed visit our parents who agreed to their proposals and so we enjoyed the first and only holiday of our lives up to that point. My brother Lenny and I were absolutely delirious with joy. I believe my parents were asked to make a small contribution towards our keep for two weeks of five shillings (25p today) each. I imagine it was a bit of a struggle for our parents to find ten shillings but they did; they were probably glad to get rid of us for a fortnight. And so, we had a great holiday during which a very brave Lord and Lady Something or other, who owned a very large house not far from our camp with huge gardens and which led right down to the beach and the sea itself, invited a group of us poor boys from the East End to spend some hours with them. We did so and were entertained royally; to us little Cockney urchins it was another world of which we knew nothing. I remember that from their garden we saw the S.S. *Normandie* going in one direction either to or from Portsmouth, and the Queen Mary sailing in the other direction. Anyway, as I have said, we had a wonderful time – and all because of the Toc H and that Lord and Lady of course!

But that was not all. Various charity organisations operated in the East End and they made the lives of us children much more enjoyable as a result of their efforts. As another example, they always gave us poor kids a terrific Christmas party every year at The King George Hall (as I wrote earlier, this lovely building was sadly bombed in the Blitz and subsequently demolished), where we ate ourselves silly on sandwiches and jelly and all kinds of nice things to eat, watched a good show with jugglers and magicians etc., and then returned home with a bag of goodies plus a marzipan fish wrapped in cellophane – I cannot say why but I shall always remember that marzipan fish and its little chocolate eyes – and yes, in case you are wondering, I *did* pick the eyes out and eat them!

Also the bus drivers and taxi drivers did their bit and organised days out for us. So all in all, these very generous and unselfish people made the lives of us little ones much better and gave us something to look forward to. They brightened our lives, which were sometimes grim, and I for one will not forget them. I hope that applies to the many children whom they helped. I do believe that where it was called for they also gave assistance in various forms to the parents if they thought it was needed. But I am not well informed in that respect.

It was in this period that a hardware shop in East India Dock Road called Eaton's began to sell cheap imports of small toys. They came from Japan, and the first one I recall was a little tin boat with a tiny little receptacle for water in the back and underneath it a tiny candle. When you lit the candle this produced heat which, in turn, produced power that propelled the boat forward. We clubbed together and bought one of these; they were only 6d each and after a good disinfectant run on a Saturday that was within our reach.

But the only place where we could play with our little boat was in a horse trough situated in Blackwall Way. In those days horses continued to be used by many tradesmen and so there many water troughs all over for them to drink from. So we kids gathered around and watched our little boat putt-putt away round and round the trough, stopping only when a horse and cart drove up and the horse wanted to drink. We then stood to one side and moved back into position when it had finished and gone on its way.

Another small toy I remember (indeed how can I forget?) and which also cost 6d, was a small burner. We had to buy a small quantity of methylated spirit to make it work but our idea was that if we took one of these burners with us together with some water, a little milk and sugar cadged from our Mums, we could then make our own lovely cups of tea when we went on our adventures far and wide. Great idea – we thought!

Well, one day we decided to set off for Blackheath, complete with burner and accessories. I recall that Blackheath then was in part covered with gorse bushes; so we found a nice little spot, set up the burner, lit it and waited for the water to boil – just as Mum and Dad did at home. But someone (I think it was my cousin Joycie Ives, but she denies it to this very day) knocked the whole thing over, the methylated spirit spilt on the ground and the flames shot up! Very quickly the dry gorse bushes caught fire and this rapidly spread from bush to bush! We kids stood there for a moment transfixed and terrified out of our wits! We were scared and that's a fact – not of getting burnt but of being caught and accused of arson or something like that. We decided at that point that a swift exit from the scene of the crime was the best plan and so with a cry of 'Come on, let's scarper!' our whole gang legged it across the heath, anxiously looking behind us to see if anyone was trying to follow and catch us 'vicious criminals'. But all we could see and hear was the pall of smoke rising and the clang-clang of the fire engines. Of course we were never caught but if ever anyone wants to know why there is so little gorse on Blackheath these days – it was us! Sorry!

And so the lazy, hazy, days of the 30s went by. I remember the Jubilee of King George V, his death, and the subsequent Coronation of King George VI. In both instances we had terrific street parties. There was much celebration in the street and a wonderful atmosphere – especially in our local pub, The Ivy House, where the singing went on for hours and hours; for us children, and indeed everyone, those were memorable occasions for there existed in the East End a very strong love and admiration of the Monarchy.

We actually lived just two doors away from the pub and many were the nights when my brother Lenny and I fell asleep with the sound of singing coming from the Saloon Bar. What good singers they seemed to be in those days; and what lovely, sentimental songs they had to sing then! Also, from time to time, an accordionist or other musician would open the Saloon Bar door, render their piece of music, and go round with their hat hoping for a small reward. I remember the haunting sound of a trumpeter who regularly used to play such songs as 'O Play to Me Gypsy' and 'Little Man You're Crying, I Know Why You're Blue' at the Saloon Bar door. Many years later I would have cause to recall the song 'Gypsy' in the heart of Eastern Europe, but I will relate that story later on.

We kids, of course, never had a care and went about our lives exploring new places to play, and trying to think up new ways to earn some money. We both saw and heard Oswald Mosley and his blackshirt mobs who held at least one march in the East India Dock Road – it was so obvious that he was just aping Adolf Hitler. We also heard much about the bad man, Adolf Hitler, and some of us became rather apprehensive at the mention of his name.

But much of this went over our little heads; we had much more important things to think about, or so we thought, like 'what are we going to do tomorrow and where are we going?' However, it was on the day in early 1939 when we had to go to Constance House (a Council block of flats in the High Street) to be fitted for our gasmasks that we began to feel that our pleasant little world was coming to an end. Also our parents, and people in general, began to display worried looks on their brows. We knew something was up – but what? The one good thing to come out of whatever had changed was the fact that the unemployment levels had now greatly improved. Many ships were coming into the docks and my father had plenty of work and we could see this in the rise in our standard of living. We were eating better food. For example, we had roast meat every Sunday, not the best cuts perhaps but we had roast meat. And so we began to feel more comfortable and perhaps even more confident that life was going to get even better.

Well, it did get better in a number of respects as we neared the end of the 1930s, but as I have intimated before, what we kids (and many of the adults) did not realise was that there would be a terrible cost to us all for these improvements in our standards. This would be brought home to us quite soon now!

4

EVACUATION – THE WAR BEGINS –
MY SPELL AT WINDSOR – I DISCOVER THERE
IS A BETTER LIFE AND I ALMOST BECOME
A 'TOFF'

As the rumours and stories of an impending war were growing by the day, one of the great worries was the clear fact that if London were to be bombed then the East End Docklands would be a target of great importance to the Luftwaffe. Hitler was posturing and making threatening speeches at one moment and then pleading that he only wanted peace the next but I believe most people knew what he really wanted. Meanwhile Britain and France had signed a Pact with Poland guaranteeing both her freedom and that we would come to her aid if she were attacked.

We had already let down Czechoslovakia and agreed that Hitler should take over part of that country – this despite the fact that they had a first class army and excellent mountain border defences. To this day the Czechs and Slovaks believe that with the combined help of Britain and France they could have effectively resisted the German Army who most certainly would not have wished to fight on two fronts – and so our Czech and Slovak friends have never completely forgiven us for deserting them in their hour of need.

What might have happened had we supported Czechoslovakia and forced Germany to fight on two fronts can now only be conjecture. But there are a number of military historians who believe that, as Hitler had not yet fully built up his war machine at that time, it is quite possible that he would have been forced to the negotiating table, at the very least, and the freedom of the Czechoslovak nation may well have been preserved.

But the authorities were obliged to take the situation as it in fact was and consider how matters might develop, and so it was decided that the evacuation of children and young mothers with babies, to places of greater safety outside London, was of paramount importance. Therefore urgent plans were made to achieve this objective. My parents did not hesitate and placed the names of my brother, Lenny, and myself on the list of children to be evacuated.

On Friday, September 1st 1939 we were ordered to report to our school at Woolmore Street at 9.00am. My mother took Lenny and I there; lined up in the whole length of the street was a long queue of double-decker buses. First of all we were divided into classes and as Lenny was older than me, and in a different class, he went one way and I went the other. Somehow they sorted us out and I went with my class on to one of the buses. I rather think that this collection of children and parents were not just from one school – there were too many, so it must have been appointed as a central meeting place for a group of schools. Exactly how they managed to sort us out Heaven only knows.

Gradually the buses began to move off and then the harrowing scenes began with some mothers running after the buses calling out the names of their children, perhaps to say a last Goodbye. It was a heart-breaking scene made somewhat worse by the fact that nobody seemed to know where in England we were going! We were going into the unknown and I think that worried our parents more; most of us kids thought it was a great lark and an adventure – but only to begin with!

I do not know if all the buses ended up at Waterloo Station but that is where ours went. Inside the station were thousands upon thousands of children milling about all over the place. How on earth were they going to control this situation efficiently? It would take a miracle. But that miracle was in fact achieved – somehow. Mainly, I think, due to the excellent and very efficient teachers we were lucky enough to have.

At this point, we return to my favourite teacher at Woolmore Street School, Mr 'Jock' Williams, for he was in charge of our group. Upon our arrival at Waterloo Station he asked us to remain quiet, to stay where we were, and explained that he had to go off to find out what was going to happen to us and where our destination was to be. After a while he returned and led us to a platform where a train was waiting. He then announced we were going to Windsor. At last we knew where we were going; but where on earth was Windsor? I am afraid that our knowledge of places outside the East End area of London was very minimal. So we boarded the train and it seemed as though we were sitting there for ages whilst other groups who should be on the train were located. Eventually the train began to move and soon we had left London behind and were travelling in the direction of Berkshire. During all these activities I cannot remember anybody giving us a drink or something to eat and if I have a criticism at all it would be that factor. Fortunately, we were so excited at this big adventure we hardly noticed.

It seemed like a long journey but it could not have taken us much more than an hour and a half or so; finally we arrived at what was then called The Great Western Station at Windsor. Once again, a great crowd of children were congregated there and one has to say that the teachers, who were at their wits' end, did a wonderful job. To view the scenes at both Waterloo and Windsor Stations one could be forgiven for thinking the whole thing was just a complicated, disorganised mess. How they rescued order from that chaos, only God knows, but somehow the teachers sorted us out, received or obtained their instructions, and took us in the right direction – although I am sure that some mistakes were made and that some groups ended up where they should not have been! That didn't happen to us and so we formed ourselves into a line of twos and followed Mr Williams as we trooped out of the station.

Mr Williams had been handed a list of Windsor residents who had previously been asked, or had volunteered, to accept one, two, or more evacuees, so off we went. But it proved to be not so easy since one or two of the volunteers had changed their minds – or maybe their own circumstances had changed. Others had volunteered to take two but now could only take one and so on. The exhausted teachers had to cope with all that – they must have had the patience of angels. I recall one lady who only wanted an attractive little girl with long blonde hair and blue eyes – no other would do! But we didn't have one! And so it went on. For poor Mr Williams it must have been an absolute headache – even a nightmare. But full credit to him – he managed admirably. We owe a great deal to such dedicated people.

However, slowly but surely our line of children became smaller and smaller until there were only eight of us left. But I had not yet been chosen! I wondered if something was the matter with me and began to be a little concerned! Did I have a dirty face or something? And just then we entered a street called Alexandra Road and there, at No 10, was a small grocery shop. A lady came out, looked us all over, looked back at me – and at last I was selected! She took me through the shop into the parlour at the back, invited me to put my gas mask and small cardboard attaché case down and take a seat; she then explained that it was a busy time in the shop but that she would return within a short while.

So I sat there, looking around and waiting for my new foster parents, Mr and Mrs Maxwell, for that was their name, to close the shop. In that time I reflected upon the whirlwind day I had experienced. Strangely, despite the fact that I had not had anything to eat or to drink the whole day long, I cannot recall being either very hungry or thirsty; no doubt the excitement of the day had something to do with this. I looked around once more; it was all very strange to me and at once I began to feel the first pangs of homesickness. Homesick? I had only been away from home 10 hours or so! Was this a sign of what my feelings would be in the coming months or God knows how long? Perhaps years?

After 20 minutes or so Mr and Mrs Maxwell came into the parlour, having closed the shop for business, and I had a proper introduction to them both. They asked me a number of different questions and after 15 minutes or so, Mrs Maxwell went into the kitchen to prepare something to eat. Meanwhile I chatted with Mr Maxwell, who was not a very talkative type of person. You could not say that of me – I was a little Cockney chatterbox and so I kept the conversation running. In times to come, when he saw what a healthy appetite I had, he gave me the nickname of 'Bunter' after Billy Bunter from *The Beano*. After dinner Mrs Maxwell said I had experienced a very long day and she suggested I have an early night. Now normally, at home, when it was suggested I go to bed early I would object very strongly, as most kids do. But on that evening it seemed even to me that to go to bed early was a good idea.

Mrs Maxwell took me upstairs to where I was going to sleep – it was a bathroom! A very long and large bathroom to be sure but still a bathroom. As a matter of fact I believe it was the very first bathroom I had ever seen – No! I tell a lie; it was the second I had seen for how could I forget the beautiful bathrooms at the magnificent residence of the Lord and Lady down by Bognor during our Toc H camping holiday! But it was in no way uncomfortable, and my bed was in the middle of this long room, with the bath at one end and the toilet at the other; I was in the middle of the two. I undressed and Mrs Maxwell helped me unpack my small case, which took about two minutes because I didn't have very much, and immediately asked me where my pyjamas were. A little embarrassed, I explained that I didn't have any! We didn't wear pyjamas back in Prestage Street! I am not sure how, but Mrs Maxwell rectified that little problem quite soon. Probably she obtained a pair of her nephew's cast offs for me.

I do not remember much about the next day, which was a Saturday and so a busy day in the shop. But I know we had to report to Mr Willams at a church hall in a side street off Alexandra Road during the morning. He was a very caring teacher and therefore wanted to know if we had settled in alright and if any boy had any problems. Nobody seemed to and so we wandered back to our billets. When I arrived there, a lady and a boy were waiting and Mrs Maxwell introduced me for they were her sister and nephew, a Mrs Hunt and the lad was named Kenneth. Mrs Maxwell explained to me that because she and her husband were often very busy in the shop I would be spending quite a lot of time at the Hunts' house which was No 235 St Leonard's Road, which ran parallel to Windsor Great Park and very near to the Windsor and Eton Football ground. So I went with them, had lunch at their place, and went with Kenneth that afternoon to see Windsor & Eton F.C. play. So began my first interest in watching football which has stayed with me all my life.

The next day was Sunday, 3rd September and it was a day I shall never forget. Mr and Mrs Maxwell and I sat in the parlour waiting for 11.00am, when Mr Chamberlain, our Prime Minister, was due to speak to the nation. We knew that the situation was very grave – you could feel it in the atmosphere at that time and I can recall his speech even now when he said 'This morning the British Ambassador in Berlin handed a Note to the German government requesting an undertaking, etc. etc.' and then finishing with the chilling words 'I have to tell you now that no such undertaking has been received and that, consequently, this country is at war with Germany.' We sat there for a minute or two digesting those dramatic words and then Mr Maxwell said 'Well, that's it then ... we are at war.' I didn't say a word, and, as far as I can remember, neither did Mrs Maxwell. But despite my young age I realised that this was a moment in history as indeed it was.

I got on rather well with Kenneth. He was a couple of years older than I but that didn't seem to make much difference. I learned from him that not only was he an Eton College Choirboy – he was the Captain! It was as well that I got on, not only with Kenneth, but with Mr and Mrs Hunt too, because I was destined to spend a lot of time with them. Kenneth was, after Mr Grimm at Woolmore Street School, the second person who had kindled an interest in music within me. Kenneth played the piano and although I was not too interested at that time, I tried to show that I was. I wish now that I had paid more attention as playing the piano became a big part of my later life.

The next development was in the form of two Jewish children whom Mrs Hunt agreed to take in. Their names were Renee and Harold Herskovitch. However their stay did not last long for, after they informed their parents where they were, the parents came to Windsor as quickly as possible, maybe two weeks or so later. Now the parents must have been fairly strict orthodox Jews because when they saw what their children were eating and maybe also the fact that they were living in a Christian home, they went back to London, returning within days to collect Renee and Harold and presumably take them back to London with them. What happened to them after that I have no idea. I have tried to locate them via the Internet and, with a name like Herskovitch, I thought it would be easy but I have had no luck. Maybe they changed it as so many Jewish people with foreign sounding names have done.

Meanwhile, the arrival of so many evacuees at Windsor was causing a number of problems. The main problem was that there were of course no schools for them to go to for they were already full with local children. Our group, led by Mr Williams, first of all met each morning at a church hall in which we had our first gathering the day after our arrival. But it was almost impossible to either learn or teach in those circum-stances and so Mr Williams had the bright and, in our opinion, excellent idea that we should learn as best we could in the mornings and then spend each afternoon in Windsor Great Park. So that is what we did and our days were pleasantly passed playing football and cricket on the verges of the Long Walk, Windsor Great Park. In those days a herd of deer roamed around in the main part of the park but for some reason they were removed and are no longer there. I remember, too, that there were fine batches of primroses to be found in the main park area. Millions of them. I had never seen anything like that in my life.

I shall always recall that the autumn of 1939 which was very fine, thank goodness; it was an Indian summer and the sun seemed to shine every day. But of course, lovely as it was for us kids, this situation could not be allowed to go on for ever and so those responsible for the evacuees negotiated with the Windsor educational authorities. They reached an agreement whereby the Windsor children would occupy the schools in the morning periods and the evacuees would attend in the afternoons. In this way the school space was shared and even though it was not a satisfactory solution to the problem, nothing better was apparently possible. Eventually, of course, they sorted the problem out in a more satisfactory way.

I shall always remember Christmas 1939. It was my very first Christmas away from home and we, i.e. Mr and Mrs Maxwell and myself, spent it with Mr and Mrs Hunt. I really thought I might be rather sad, homesick and perhaps a little bit weepy (being a sentimental little soul) but I wasn't. Of course I missed my family very much but the Hunts and the Maxwells were such nice, kind people they made me feel as if I was at home. We had a nice Christmas lunch and I volunteered to do the washing up, which I did satisfactorily and which was much appreciated by Mrs Hunt. Funny – I wouldn't dream of offering to do the washing up at home but here I wanted to do everything I could to help! Afterwards we sat around the fire and listened to King George VI speaking to the nation over the radio. In those days we paid great respect to the royal family and so we sat silently listening to those words of comfort and encouragement from him.

But I should remark that very shortly before Christmas, Mrs Hunt had asked me if I would like to accompany her to the Eton College Christmas Carol Service. I was keen on virtually anything and everything and so I happily accepted because the College choir would be leading the singing and I would hear my new pal Kenneth sing. On the day, we caught a bus to Eton and entered that famous building under the archway, noticing the statue of Henry VIII, the founder of the college, in what I suppose you would call the quadrangle. And what a hallowed quadrangle it was and what very famous people had trodden those ancient stones with which it was paved. Then, at a half-right direction, were the steps leading to the Eton College Chapel. I thought to myself once again what a wonderful variety of famous names must have walked under that arch and up those steps. This was the school of royalty, both British and foreign, future prime ministers and leading members of government, of dukes, earls, barons and lords, as well as a great number of very wealthy people. As a little Cockney urchin I felt very proud to be there but, strangely, not out of place at all.

After taking our places the carol service began. I have learned through my long life that I am quite easily inspired and get very enthusiastic and so it was on that occasion. Back in the East End I had attended church at All Saints and also at St Nicholas by Blackwall Stairs – but never had I experienced anything as majestic as this. It was quite fantastic; the music and especially the beautiful singing in that wonderful chapel was truly something very special indeed and I was greatly impressed.

As we were given word sheets of the carols that were going to be sung, I very soon joined in with gusto and with much effort I tried to produce, if I could, something similar to what I was hearing. Well, I think I must have succeeded to a degree because the people around us heard me, as well as Mrs Hunt, and afterwards they gathered for a short while in the quadrangle and chatted to each other – obviously the parents of the choirboys knew each other – and in the conversation, one lady remarked to Mrs Hunt that they had heard me singing and that I would make a good choirboy. Afterwards, Mrs Hunt must have spoken with Kenneth about it and he told her that very shortly there would be an audition session for new boys held before Dr Lee (or perhaps Leigh), the Music Master at Eton and in overall charge of the choir at that time.

So later on, perhaps 10 days or so, Mrs Hunt spoke to me about it and asked if I would be prepared to sing before Dr Lee. I said that I would and the prospect of becoming an Eton College choirboy really appealed to me. My God – what would they say back in The East End? If I succeeded I am sure that such an event would have made news at least in *The East London Advertiser*. I began to imagine the headlines:

'LOCAL BOY SUCCEEDS AT ETON'!

And how very proud my parents and family would have been. One must bear in mind that although the choirboys were taught separately, they received the same quality of education by the same masters as the Eton College boys themselves. I wasn't very keen on the idea of wearing the thick, rigid, collar and the small coat which all choirboys had to wear. But that would be but a small sacrifice on my part. And so my name was registered for this audition and I eagerly awaited the day when it was to be held and got quite excited about it all.

But then disaster struck! It was discovered that I was an evacuee and I was informed that the rules of the college did not permit evacuees to be choirboys at Eton. Of course, I was bitterly disappointed. But it was probably all too good to be true anyway. What on earth was I doing thinking I might be raised to such a level? The whole thing was preposterous! Never mind, I consoled myself, something else will turn up – and it did! Not so grand, it was true; I *would* be educated at Eton – but not at the College! However, despite my disappointment I still wanted to attend any services at Eton College Chapel I could, because I did enjoy them so much – but more especially the Carol Services – and I did for as long and often as possible.

The Elementary School I attended at Windsor for a short period was Clarence Road School, a quite modern school and fortuitously near to Mrs Hunt. But not for long, as news had filtered through from London that I had been partially successful in my examination back in Woolmore Street and that I had qualified for Central School level. Well, it so happened that housed just across the river in Eton, in a temporary but quite large and adequate accommodation called The Baldwin's Institute, was a Central School called The Hamlet of Ratcliffe and they had a place for me. So I would be educated at Eton after all! The name of this school sounded very grand. But I then discovered that it was in fact from the backstreets of Stepney! However, it was a good school, and quite historical, there is no question about that.

I duly presented myself there; it wasn't all that far – just a walk to the bridge separating Windsor from Eton and through a small gap in the High Street – and there was The Institute. I now began a whole new curriculum of studies which took me into the world of languages, higher mathematics and other subjects of which I knew little or nothing – and I enjoyed it very much and tried as hard as I could to study properly. I also made a number of new friends. In later years whenever the subject of education arose and if asked where I had been educated I would always answer 'Eton'. This would be received with looks of surprise and a touch of admiration. I then always explained the situation correctly – but only afterwards, and was then met with a series of groans.

But all was not well within my mind. My mother and father came to visit me whenever they could but they also had to visit my brother Lenny, who, as he was in a different class to me, ended up at a small place called Tatling End, near to Gerrards Cross in Buckinghamshire and train journeys during the war were not so easy and there were many hold-ups and delays. Unfortunately, poor Lenny was billeted with an old couple who were extremely religious and forced him to go to church every single day and twice on Sundays!

My parents did allow me to come home on two occasions for a short holiday with the full permission of Mr and Mrs Maxwell but each time I returned to Windsor I was clearly very upset and very, very homesick. As I say, they came to visit me as often as they could, but not as often as I would have liked, and on each occasion I walked back with them to the railway station to say our last Goodbyes. After they had gone, I felt so miserable and homesick and often tears would roll silently down my cheeks as I walked slowly, and very sadly, back home. I was in a very comfortable home, I was being well looked after, I was happy at school – so why should I feel like this? Why would I want to return to the East End after experiencing the better food and living conditions at Windsor? Well, who can fathom or understand what makes us homesick? The simple fact was that I felt this very keenly and so I began to write pitiful letters home pleading to be allowed to come back. I must say that I was capable of writing quite good pleading letters which I knew would touch the hearts of my parents and I dropped little spots of water on the paper so that they could see that I had been crying. Deceitful – yes. But sometimes one has to resort to such method to achieve one's aims!

Yes – there had been The Blitz but things had gone rather quiet on that front and a number of people felt that maybe the very worst was over. Hitler and Goering and their Luftwaffe had done their worst and now perhaps they would leave not only London, but other British cities, alone. The real truth we would learn only later on.

5

I RETURN TO THE EAST END
FROM WINDSOR

Eventually, in the autumn of 1941, my pleading letters had their desired effect, my parents relented and gave their permission for me to return home. Hitler had now invaded the Soviet Union, Operation Barbarossa had begun, and so he evidently needed all his aircraft to support his invasion of that vast country. Therefore London was quiet for a while and little seemed to be going on. It was their belief, and many others were of the same opinion, that the terrible bombing had possibly ended, and so they permitted me to return home. How very wrong we all were!

I sadly said my last Goodbyes to Mr and Mrs Hunt, Kenneth, and Mr and Mrs Maxwell, who, in my boyish way I had come to love as they had all been so kind to me. I cannot truthfully say that I recall the journey home. I seem to have a vague recollection that I was put on a train at Windsor and met at Waterloo by my father or mother but I cannot be sure. No matter, I was going home and that gave me a deep sense of satisfaction. But I do recall seeing the severe damage to dear old London as I travelled through on my way to East London. And when we arrived at Prestage Street I could hardly believe my eyes.

On our side of the street about 60% of the houses were smashed to smithereens and what remained of them were derelict empty shells; the house next to ours, No 3, was completely burned out – by incendiary bombs it transpired! The local pub, The Ivy House, was okay and on the opposite side the tenement flats, Prestage Buildings, were intact but all the houses further down on that side were destroyed and uninhabitable. I was in total shock when I saw the state of our street; how dare they ruin our wonderful Prestage Street, I thought!

Of course we knew in Windsor that the bombing was severe, not only in London but many other cities, but I never expected to see anything like this. It really was a terrible sight! Looking at London as it is now, one can hardly believe that The Blitz had created so much widespread damage and it was truly shocking to see. I am sure that other cities were in a similar state. One cannot easily speak of The Blitz being in any way good because many people lost their lives (some 46,000 in 1940 alone) and many lost their homes; but if anything good came out of it the widespread bombing did at least enable the authorities to demolish many slum buildings that existed before the war. Of course, the high rise blocks of flats they put up in their place were, in many cases, not a success and gave birth to a lot of new social problems – so that was not the answer to the housing shortage that existed then and has continued ever since. Today, the East End is nothing like it used to be. My East End has gone and only silly old nostalgics like me yearn to see it as it once was. If only it could be possible to re-create it just for a day – just for a visit – that would be something to treasure.

At this point I must tell the tragic story of little Joanie Cruise, whom I described earlier in Chapter 2. As I wrote, she really was the darling of the neighbourhood and, apart from performing at all the local parties, at The Queen's Theatre at talent contests, at The Town Hall concerts, and other places, she also entertained in the deep air raid shelters where people sought protection from the bombing and very often slept overnight. They, and everybody, found little Joanie's cute performances fascinating; quite often the entertainment that went on in those shelters was truly excellent and was a great lift to the morale of those taking refuge. I rate such entertainers heroes, too!

It was quite a sight most evenings, in 1940 certainly and the early part of 1941 as well as later years, to see people carrying their bed-clothes, blankets etc. to the shelter. When I came home for a short holiday I did this myself when I helped my grandmother. We too stayed all night until the 'All clear' sounded, for this told us that, for the moment at least, it was safe to go home again. But it often happened that no sooner had you arrived home than the air raid warnings went off again – and so back we all trooped to the shelter.

I last saw Joanie on my last visit home and played in the street with her. It appears, so my mother told me, (who was an ARP Warden by the way) that very shortly after I had returned to Windsor, Joanie's mother took her to see her grandmother who lived somewhere at the bottom of Chrisp Street. There was an air raid, a bomb fell where they were, and little Joanie, her mother and grandmother all perished. Her poor, broken, little body was dug out of the rubble and taken to the Mortuary. What a terrible and tragic waste of life; what a terrible waste, in the case of Joanie, to lose such a wonderful talent which was just beginning to blossom.

There was great sadness in the neighbourhood, my mother told me; people cried uncontrollably and almost everybody in the street and the surrounding area, where she was well known and loved, attended her funeral.

I often think of little Joanie and wonder, if things had turned out differently, what might have happened to her. Would she have further developed as an entertainer? Would she, perhaps, have become a big star in the West End theatres with her name in lights? Sadly, we shall never know. But in my heart of hearts I am certain that had she lived, she would have been famous and well known everywhere. She was that good. I was very proud of the fact that she liked me, too; we were not exactly childhood sweethearts – but nearly! Maybe just a small kiss away!

War is recognised as man's inhumanity towards man but that war was much more than inhuman and I cannot think of a word in the English language which adequately describes it. The words evil and horrific do not even come close. It is awful enough when we think of war in general, but when we are affected by individual cases involving children and people we ourselves knew, then I can only describe it as man's madness towards man. It should never have happened – but we must remember that it was we who allowed it to happen.

Now back at home again, the first thing to do would be to get me back to school. We searched and searched for a Central school so that I could continue my better grade of education. But not only were we unsuccessful in finding a Central school, we found great difficulty in finding any kind of school! Those that had not been bombed were closed as the majority of pupils had been evacuated. My parents were quite busy and occupied and, although admittedly it was wrong of them, they allowed me to run the streets going in and out of bombed-out houses to find wood, chopping it up and once again selling it to people in the neighbourhood.

This went on for a while and then one day whilst walking along, I was stopped by a well-dressed and authoritative man. He introduced himself to me as a Schools Inspector, at which I froze! I knew I had been doing wrong and that we should have made greater efforts to find a school for me to attend. I had to give my address and quite soon my parents received a letter instructing me to attend an appointment at the London School of Engineering in Poplar High Street, opposite the Recreation Ground. My mother and I were both a bit mystified by this at first and she came with me.

There before us was the Schools Inspector and the Headmaster of the elementary school that was temporarily created in the upper part of the building – the lower part as I explained earlier was the British Restaurant. I remember feeling very nervous about this meeting because there is no doubt that I had misbehaved by running the streets and not attending school, and my parents were also wrong for not making me, or by failing to find out from the proper authorities where I could actually attend. It is hard now to recall the exact exchange of words between these gentlemen and my mother but I seem to remember that both she and I received a telling off. And so the very next day I began attending at the only school open in that part of Poplar.

However, after the superior education I had been receiving at the Hamlet of Ratcliffe School at Eton, I really was learning nothing here at all that I didn't know already. So when a volunteer was requested from the school by the British Restaurant below to peel potatoes, I quickly held my hand up and got the job! I didn't have to peel the spuds with a knife; there was a machine into which I poured the potatoes and then turned a handle for about 10 minutes and Hey Presto! the potatoes were ready for cooking. Of course, I had to keep filling and emptying the machine as a lot of potatoes were required. I was not paid to do this, my reward was a free lunch in the restaurant. I think my stay at this elementary school was a complete waste of everybody's time.

I was 13 years of age now and I wanted to earn some money. The first job I took was selling newspapers outside the Green & Silley Weir ship repair yard just around the corner from where we lived. I would collect my papers from Poplar Railway Station from my 'boss', who was named Alby, and carry them to my pitch. Outside the entrance to the yard was a very large stone which must have been there a very long time; and on this stone I would place my papers and also sit waiting for my customers to pour out at 5.00pm, at which point I was exceedingly busy and sold about eighty papers within minutes. For this I received 3d per day, less than 1½p in today's money. In later years there was a time when I wanted to buy that stone and have it transported to my home in Surrey where it would have been placed in the centre of my lawn – as a memento and to remind me of where I had come from. But for some reason I didn't progress with the idea.

Not long afterwards, my brother Lenny, who had an evening job shining the spotlights at the Queen's Theatre, told me that they needed another boy to shine the lights on the opposite side to him and that he had put in a good word for me. So I went to see Morrie Abrahams, the owner of the Queen's. He asked how old I was and I fibbed and said I was fourteen. Even though I was only thirteen, but looked about twelve years of age, he agreed to give me the job and I began the next week. I started at about 5.30pm when I had to charge my spot lamps with new carbons and make sure I had my list of instructions as to what to do, which colour to show and when etc., for each separate act. There were two shows every night and I usually arrived home sometime after 10.00pm. I worked six nights per week and my pay for this was 15/- per week (75p in new money). But for a boy of thirteen that was a fortune in those days.

Of course it was a bit of a struggle to hold two jobs down but I found that as soon as I had finished selling my papers, if I rushed home for a quick something to eat and a cup of tea, I could get to the Queen's in time to prepare my spot lamps. I enjoyed my job at the Queen's, which enabled me to see all the acts free of charge!

I witnessed the house being 'brought down' three times; twice during the period in which I was spotlight boy. The first occasion was an act by a so called 'Dutchman' who called himself Van Luin but was about as Dutch as I was! He sang and yodelled a couple of songs and then did some impressions. The best he saved until the last when he did an impression of Winston Churchill making that famous speech in 1940 when things were looking so black for poor old Britain, 'We shall fight on the beaches, we shall fight on the landing grounds,' etc. etc. and then finished with a thunderous 'We shall never surrender!'

The imitation was excellent – he sounded exactly like Winnie and maybe, because he was an actor, he may have added a little more drama in his voice than Winston himself. Well, the whole theatre rose to their feet as one and they clapped and cheered and stamped their feet. It was absolutely deafening and it shook the old theatre to the rafters; even the stage hands and us spotlight boys sitting aloft in our little cubby holes were caught up in this extraordinary atmosphere and joined in – it was a quite fantastic moment the like of which I had never seen or experienced in my life!

The next time something similar happened, it was a dark-skinned chap who sang extremely well. I think perhaps he may have been Indian or from somewhere around that part of the world. His last and his best song by far was 'Begin The Beguine' and it was sung so perfectly and in a way I had never heard this popular piece sung before. When he finished, I once again witnessed the crowd leaping to their feet applauding and cheering, for this was an act which was something very special. It is a pity that I do not remember his name or whether he went on to greater heights in his singing career.

The third occasion when I witnessed the audience at the Queen's going crackers occurred when I was in the Army and had come home on leave. I had only been serving a short while and was glad to be home again. It was now 1946 and my parents had developed a habit of going to the Queen's every Tuesday evening now that money was not so tight. In those days it cost just 1/- (5p) for a good seat in the stalls. As I was at home they asked me if I would like to go with them. I asked who was on and they said it was Kate Carney.

Well, I had heard the name but I really didn't know much about her except that she was one of the old time music hall stars back in the good old days of music hall. I didn't have anything to do so I agreed to accompany my mother and father. We sat in the stalls and at the Queen's the Saloon Bar stretched almost from one end of the stalls to the other; so if you were sitting there in the auditorium you could see the people drinking through the glass window. There we sat waiting for the show to begin, when my mother nudged me and pointed towards the bar which was now full of Cockneys in their special suits covered with what I can only call shirt buttons – even the gents' hats. These were the famous Cockney Kings and Queens. I recall that the ladies wore big hats with plumes. It was like a scene from yesteryear! In the middle of this crowd was a little old lady with bright orange hair. 'That's Kate Carney,' my mother told me.

I sat there wondering what was to come and eventually Kate appeared, for she was the final act. When she entered the stage there was rapturous applause – she had been a great favourite in the East End many years ago and they still remembered her. She then began to sing but her voice sounded only like a frog! She was croaking! But the audience didn't mind that at all it seemed. She went through a number of the songs which had made her famous when she was younger and saved the best one until the last. This was a song called 'Are We To Part Like This, Bill?' I think it was, and the audience sang it along with her; I can only say it was very nice, and very touching, that people remembered her in this way – even if she could not sing. But no matter, she held that audience in the palm of her hand like the exquisite artiste she must have been in her younger days; she had not forgotten how to do that and she had a magical effect when on the stage – the kind of artistic magic that one does not often see these days. When the closing bars of the song came, we had a repetition of what I have described before. The audience went mad and would not let her leave the stage unless she sang another song and she was happy to oblige again and again.

So those are the three occasions I remember most but I saw a lot of excellent acts. I would just like to say that it is really a great pity that theatres like the Queen's were forced to close down with the development of television. The Queen's was the scene of some great moments and many is the star who worked to improve their skills and performances in similar theatres around the country. Today, as I have already remarked in the previous chapter, talent has far fewer such places where they can do that and this, I think, is reflected in the quality of performers we have these days. It is not that talent is any the less now – it is mainly the fact that budding talent has far fewer places and opportunities where they can hone their skills and get better at their chosen profession.

Just a few more words about the Queen's; I realise I have written something about its history in the preceding chapter and I will try not to repeat myself. I wrote earlier that the Queen's was taken over by Frederick Abrahams, a theatrical impresario, around the 1860s and that his family retained a connection with the theatre for almost a century. In fact it was Morrie Abrahams who gave me my job. After further alterations it opened as the New Albion. Subsequent to that it was demolished and a new theatre emerged which was named the Orient and which could seat some 3,100 people. There were even further alterations and it again re-opened in 1905 as the Queen's Theatre Of Varieties, and then became simply the Queen's Theatre and Music Hall. It was bombed twice during the Second World War, but as far as I know it didn't close, or if it did, it was only for a very short time.

With the availability of television throughout the country from the early 1950s, many theatres, except in the West End of London and perhaps the larger theatres in other cities, began to close, and the Queen's closed its doors for the last time in 1956. It was a great pity that although in 1958 it was bought by a theatrical group with the intention of re-opening it as a West End theatre in the East End, these plans came to nothing. And so the poor old place was becoming derelict. The site was bought by the London County Council in 1964 at a price below £10,000 and the theatre was totally demolished shortly thereafter. As far as I know they didn't leave a plaque to show where the old music hall had once stood, which I think is a pity. But with it went a lot of memories shared by a great number of people, and certainly by me. And I am still mystified as to what happened to that glass case in the Stage Manager's cubby hole.

My mother, who was not averse to making some extra money, let our spare room to theatricals from the Queen's from time to time. You will learn later that this fact helped me to meet my dear wife. We had quite a few well known people stay with us, but although our house was looking much better than it used to before the war, I cannot for the life of me, understand why these theatricals would want to come and stay in a house like ours. However, the people at the theatre accepted my mother's name – and they came! In fact, in Prestage Street there were two people who took in theatricals; my mother and Mrs Boater who lived a little way down the street, at No 5, I think.

At our house I remember we had little Robbie something or other, who was very famous on the radio during the war; his stage name was Enoch and he made up this comic trio with his colleagues Harry Lovejoy and another chap. Robbie's well-known saying or catch phrase was 'Let me tell you' in a Northern accent and the three of them had a signature tune called 'We Three We're Not Alone, Working for the BBC, Ramsbottom and Enoch and Me' which everybody knew and whistled on their way to work. 'Let me tell you' doesn't sound funny when you read it but the way Robbie said it was humorous and appealing and so it caught on.

And then we had Tony Mercer who became very well-known as the bass singer (the fat one!) in *The Black & White Minstrels Show* – one of the very finest shows ever to grace our television screens and the winner of golden awards in Europe. Tony took a shine to me and as the theatricals received free tickets to the cinema, he took me with him on one or two occasions.

Many years later my football team, Crystal Palace, where I was a season ticket holder, was playing at home to Sheffield United and Tony was one of their staunch supporters. It was customary to have a drink in the bar before the match – we always did. Well, on this day I observed Tony also enjoying a drink with his pals. So, just for fun, I went to him and said, 'I'll buy you a double brandy if you can remember who I am.' He looked at me quizzically, trying very hard, but try as he may he could not recall ever having seen or known me before. And so he said 'There is something about your face that is familiar but, sorry, I just can't place it.' I then asked him if he remembered appearing at the Queen's many years ago in a show called 'Soldiers in Skirts' and staying at Prestage Street with our family. . He did, and he said he now remembered me. But I think he was just being nice – he didn't recall me at all, really. Well, I was only a boy then and it was a very long time ago.

Another artiste I knew was Hylda Baker, the comedienne; I used to run to buy cigarettes for her at the bar. She became very famous and well-known on TV in the 1970s. I was sad to read of her death, in the 1990s I believe, in a nursing home for theatrical people.

Also in this period I joined the Poplar Boys' Club which was held down below the church at the bottom of St. Leonard's Road. There have been so many changes that I am not even sure that St. Leonard's Road exists anymore. But it did in the 1940s and full marks to Mr Boorman who took care of us, encouraged us, and generally kept us in order – a tough job. What a wonderful man he was and what a terrific job he did in controlling us boisterous, and sometimes naughty, lads. He did this in a humorous but firm manner and we all respected him. Mr Boorman was also a hero in his sphere and thank God for such people.

With the club I played table tennis and got quite proficient at that; I also played football, at which I was, at that time, only passable; we played at Hackney Marshes where many a brilliant player learned to play and became famous. I also swam for the club – once at a well publicised tournament held at Seymour Hall. I was entered for the 100 yards backstroke and apparently I was doing quite well and keeping up with the leaders when I unfortunately crooked my arm over the dividing ropes between the lanes and that was me finished; that was a great pity for I might have finished up with a medal which would have made me mighty proud.

I used to attend the club with my pal at that time, Willie McIlveney, who also lived in Prestage Street and with whom, incidentally, I once cycled all the way to Deal, near Dover – an unforgettable journey; we followed almost the exact tracks of David Copperfield! We started out on the first day rather later than we had planned and by the end of the day we had only reached Sittingbourne.

We didn't quite know what to do but we spied a canvas hut on a grass verge – obviously there for workmen. It was quite empty apart from two benches so we had one each and tried to sleep that way. It had started to rain a little earlier and it looked as though the rain might return. So the canvas hut seemed like a jolly good idea to us.

Later that evening a lady passed by who was evidently walking her dog. She saw us and asked us if we would be alright sleeping there; we assured her that we would be okay but she was quite concerned about our welfare and after about 10 minutes she returned and told us to follow her. She took us to her lovely home and introduced us to her husband, made us a nice hot cup of tea, and then showed us to a bedroom – a room that boys such as us had never seen the like in our whole lives. It was simply beautiful for they were obviously well-to-do people. The next morning she prepared new laid boiled eggs (they had their own chickens) and toast for us and then saw us on our way.

Such kindness is rare and when I arrived back home after our stay in Deal, I told my mother of our experience. I must have kept the address because she wrote a nice letter of thanks to this very kind couple for which I was very pleased. It is rare to encounter such care and generosity these days and I shall always be grateful to that elderly couple who rescued two hungry, tired and lonely boys from a not very pleasant night in that workmen's hut.

And so the months passed by. The war carried on and the bombing had resumed towards the latter part of 1941 onwards. Evidently Hitler and/or Goering had found some extra planes from somewhere or had borrowed them from the Russian front maybe, and so had decided to show the British public that they had not finished with us yet.

Many were the times that Willie Mac, as I called him, and I were caught in air raids on our way home from the Boys' Club. By this time our anti-aircraft guns had been improved and strengthened and they gave the German planes a fright or two with ferocious barrages that, when they were firing together, was quite deafening; they also frightened us by the way! Not only that but the shrapnel from our own shells fell like rain – and shrapnel was a killer! One of our neighbours, Billie Thatcher, was killed by a piece of shrapnel which struck him in the chest.

My mother, in her capacity as ARP Warden, told me of other instances she came to know about which resulted in death or injury as a result of shrapnel from our own guns. I do not know if it is true but I read somewhere that with all the firing of the guns against the marauding German aircraft, not one was ever shot down by them throughout the whole war. Apparently our guns were not capable of reaching the heights at which the bombers were flying. But it was felt that it should be carried out as the noise of the guns firing gave the general public some comfort in the supposed knowledge that we were also giving it as well as taking it!

I recall one particular night when there was a heavy raid and the anti-aircraft guns were firing virtually non-stop. For some reason, Willie and I took the Abbots Road route home, off which was a street called Moness Street. The terraced houses in this street had recessed alcoves before the front door and so we decided to take shelter because the shrapnel really was as severe as we had ever known it to be. So Willie sheltered in one alcove and I in another. I had not been there long when a large jagged piece of shrapnel whizzed down and hit the door behind me just about 3-4" above my shoulder. That was the first of two narrow escapes I had in the war. The other one concerned a V2 rocket which dropped in Poplar and I shall tell about that later on.

But now I was rapidly approaching school leaving age, for in those days most working class lads traditionally left at the age of 14 in order to make a contribution towards the upkeep of the family. There was very little possibility for lads like us to even think of further education then – unless you were the type who could study every evening at night-school; I did try this but found I was not that type at all. Even then you had to be able to pay the fees. I forget what they were but it was money that had to be found from my rather meagre resources. I was helped by a retired Colonel to whom Mrs Maxwell's other sister, Hilda, was a private nurse. I kept up correspondence with Mrs Maxwell and told her of my ambition to be an architect. So the Colonel, hearing of my ambitions, bought and sent me a drawing board and a T square. This was of course extremely kind of him. He also sent me an introduction to a well-known architect of those days, a certain A.S.G. Butler, whom he knew and who tried to advise me. He recommended that I attend the London School of Art in Kennington which I did for a while. I enjoyed my art studies there to some extent but I was the only one there for architectural studies and was mostly placed in a large room by myself with various stone effigies and ornate pieces of masonry which I had to draw. Well evidently I didn't have what it takes to stick at it, or maybe I felt I was chasing a lost cause or perhaps it was because I lacked any form of encouragement from my family. And so I didn't pursue it for very long. I did raise the subject with my father some years later, after I had finished my National Service, but I'll tell about that in the correct sequence later on.

Well, eventually Christmas came and it was time for me to leave school. But with what? Nothing! I had not a single qualification to my name and I sat and wondered what on earth would become of me. Boys from my background were accustomed to becoming van or lorry drivers, navvies, dock workers, store men or factory workers and I had enough common sense to realise that with no qualifications, the cards would be stacked very heavily against me. But I resolved to worry about that tomorrow or maybe the day after – but not to forget it! I knew I had a mountain to climb but, strangely, I never felt that I couldn't achieve something in this life. I was ambitious and I was confident – despite the dire circumstances I was in.

My brother Lenny had a job in the office of an import company which dealt in hemp and jute for rope-making. Of course, with a war on, shipments coming in were few and far between but it seemed as though it was enough to keep the business going. Lenny was an office boy and he didn't want to be an office boy! So when my time came to leave school he asked if I would like to take over his job, as he would be leaving to engage himself in more lucrative employment. Well, I had nothing else in mind and no other possibility had occurred and so I agreed. I duly presented myself to a certain Mr Thorn, and the only Director (others were serving in the forces), a Mr Sibley; and they approved of me, so I began my first ever real full time employment for which I received £1.10.0d per week!

6

I START TO WORK, 1942–1946 AND
THE WAR CONTINUES

Well, now I was a working lad and earning £1.10.0d per week, which at first sounded like a lot of money to me, until my mother informed me that I would have to give her £1 per week for my keep! I think I protested that such an arrangement would only leave me with 10/- with which to pay my fares and my lunches. But my mother insisted and when my mother had made up her mind nobody, but nobody, could change it.

I remember my very first day at work. I was the first person to arrive and so I waited outside for either Mr Thorn or Mr Sibley to arrive. Mr Thorn arrived first and so I was shown to my desk and given a description of my duties and what was expected of me. I had no job of any importance – just licking stamps, posting letters, wrapping parcels and running messages; I never learned anything there and no attempt was made to teach me anything. Lunch time came and my instructions were that I was to have one hour for lunch between 1-2 pm. I left the building and tried to find some place where I could buy a sandwich. I think the cheapest sandwich I could find was 1/- each (5p) and if I paid that every day that would be half of my total pocket money! In the days and weeks that followed I searched far and wide for somewhere where I could get a cheaper sandwich but as far as I can recall, I did not have a great deal of success.

During my daily lunch hour, I made searches for food at a reasonable price that I could afford. I wandered out of the City and down to Aldgate on occasions. There, at the City end, used to be a Chop House where they cooked all kinds of delicious foods in the window. Of course, the window was quite steamed up more often than not but still you could see the sausages, pork chops and other items all sizzling hot and if you peered through you could see people inside munching away; the smells coming from that place were quite fantastic and only increased my pangs of hunger. I was very envious and gazed longingly at those lucky people; what wouldn't I give, I thought to myself, to be one of those. I think the cheapest meal there was 1/6d (7½p) and that was far too much for me.

I resolved that one day, when I am rich, I will return to that shop and treat myself to a slap up meal. In fact, years later I found myself in a new office in Mark Lane. I was now a Director and obviously in a very much improved financial state and so one day I wandered down to Aldgate, to the Chop House, in great expectations of a truly wonderful feast – but I was devastated to find that the shop had just closed down! I remember to this very day how deeply disappointed I was that I was unable to carry out my promise to myself. What a meal I would have had!

But to return to my boyhood plight, with just a limited amount of money at my disposal and a budget of about 9d per day (about 4p) I quite often went without lunch and just strolled around the City and nearby districts in my lunch break. I investigated this street and that one, I went to all of the sites of the Jack the Ripper murders which still existed then, I visited Leadenhall Market where I liked the atmosphere very much – especially at Christmas time. I went to the Tower of London and often stood there listening to some of the political speeches on Tower Hill and I even went as far as St. Paul's Cathedral. I did anything just to while away the time, i.e. to take my mind off food, and so, after a few months of this, I came to know the City and its surroundings extremely well.

One small point I would like to mention is that I had to go to the Bishopsgate branch of the Royal Bank of Scotland to deposit cheques from time to time and so I became known there. At Christmas I went there as usual but when they handed the company passbook to me they also presented me with a brand new half crown! I was very deeply touched by this unexpected gesture and I always had a soft spot for the RBoS after that.

I also recall that one day in the office Mr Thorn asked me to clear out some cupboards. As I did so I noticed that they were filled with old contracts dating back years and years. Now such contracts were only legally binding if they were duly stamped with the appropriate stamp value which seemed to vary – perhaps in accordance with the values of the different contracts. Anyway, I saw there were old stamps of King George V, and King George VI, but none, I think, of Queen Victoria.

So I asked Mr Thorn if he wanted these stamps and he said he didn't and that I could have them if I wanted them. So I tore them all off before destroying the contracts themselves and saw that they varied in value from £1 to £5, and maybe some at £10 – I am not sure. These I placed in a large envelope. I felt that they must be worth something and so I took them to a stamp shop in a turning just off Fenchurch Street. Well this man rooked me good and proper. He pretended to hesitate and began to shake his head when going through the collection I had brought to him, as if to indicate that they were not really of interest. But then he said he would give me a £1 note for the lot. In my ignorance and foolishness I eagerly agreed and so I passed him all these stamps which I know now were worth quite a lot, even then, took the £1 note and ran back to the office smiling all the way. What a nitwit I was; if that stamp man had given me £10 or even £20 he would still have bought them very cheaply!! Of course I never told Mr Thorn what I had done; he had given them to me and so, as far as I was concerned, that was that! OK, I was a fool but to me in those days, a £1 note was a very considerable sum.

Despite the shortage of money, I did try very hard indeed to save enough to visit the cinema once a week either locally at the Pavilion or Grand, but sometimes on my way home from work at the Troxy in Stepney. On one occasion at the Troxy they showed a trailer advertising the programme to be shown the following week, which was the famous wartime film *Dangerous Moonlight*, the theme music of which was the Warsaw Concerto.[2] When I heard those dramatic opening chords of what I considered to be a beautiful and inspiring piece of music, I was determined to save enough money to see this film the following week. Of course, the inspiration of the music can be appreciated so much more if one has seen the film. I did so and was absolutely enthralled – in fact, I was mesmerised! I stayed to watch the film twice and when I walked out of the cinema I was in something of a daze. I thought about it very seriously and I resolved that I would teach myself to play the piano, and

---

[2] *The Warsaw Concerto – this was written for the film by the composer Richard Addinsell, an English composer, and I read that due to certain circumstances and delays, he was only given one week in which to write it! He did a wonderful job, and it made him famous not only in the UK but in many other countries. Abroad it is not widely known that this is a British composition. When I have asked European people who they think composed the Warsaw Concerto, quite a lot of them reply, 'It was an American wasn't it?' Naturally I proudly correct their assumptions.*

if possible, even the Warsaw Concerto. After all, mountains are there to be climbed!

At home we had the proverbial 'front room', which in our case contained a piano (bought by my mother over at Stratford just before the war, when things had started to improve, for 2/6d per week, which must still have been something of a struggle for her), a rather worn three-piece suite, and of course an aspidistra plant. No front room was ever complete without an aspidistra plant in those days. A bit later it also included a radiogram. However, the 'front room' was like a holy place; it was never used, and we weren't allowed in it, unless my parents had a party and I must say that many a nice party was held in that room, too. So I asked my mother for permission to go to the front room and when she asked why I told her that I wanted to teach myself to play the piano. At this my mother laughed. She thought it was a hilarious idea, but she gave me the necessary permission. In time to come she was very proud of me when I became more and more proficient.

And so, at every possible spare moment, I practised. First of all, I reasoned, it was necessary to understand the instrument. I wondered why there were many white notes and then quite a number of black notes. I played both but decided that it was less confusing and easier just to use the white notes if this was possible. So I attempted a tune and, being a very proud Englishman and a monarchist, the very first tune I learned was 'God Save the King' – Good! No black notes needed for that!

I made a number of mistakes to begin with, but after repeating the same tune over and over and with a combination of hearing and memory, I could play it all the way through without a mistake. I then tried other tunes that I knew and gradually I learned and memorised those too. I learned as I progressed that I could not ignore the black notes completely for these were half notes and there were times when they too had to be used, but I kept away from them as much as I could. Being a musical coward, I still do my best to avoid them today! I was making very good progress with my right hand but what about the left hand? That was either doing nothing or just making a dull thumping noise that didn't sound nice at all.

Looking back, if I could have my time over again, I think I would have done better to have sought lessons in harmony and bass co-ordination and had I done so then, I think I would have been a better player somewhat sooner, because when you play by ear and memory as I do, you tend to develop habits, some of which stay with you always, and some are not conducive to good sound. But I didn't have the money or any possibility to take lessons, and my parents could not afford to pay for them, and so I plodded on. Soon I began to make sense out of the bass and although it remains the weakest part of my piano playing, I believe I mastered it to a reasonable degree. I should really team up with a piano player who is good on the bass to leave me what I am best at which is playing the main theme of a melody – like Rawicz & Landauer, the famous piano duo.

But what about the Warsaw Concerto? Well, when my sister's husband bought a new radiogram and offered his old one to my mother, she accepted immediately and that went straight into our front room of course. So now I had the means to play back a recording.

I therefore bought the recording of the Warsaw Concerto and sat there listening over and over again. Then I played very small parts and immediately went to the piano to copy what I had heard and after much practice and to-ing and fro-ing from piano to radiogram, I found I could eventually play this lovely piece of music. Not perfectly by any means, but what I may have lacked in perfection I think perhaps I made up for in the intense feeling and passion I tried to put into my playing; I made some mistakes, of course, and occasionally I still do, especially now that I am old and my faculties are not as efficient as they once were; but bearing in mind that I had never had a lesson in my life, I thought I didn't do too badly.

When I later became a pub piano player people asked me to play on occasions the Warsaw Concerto, which was very popular indeed, and it was said that I played it quite well. I thought that I could do better and so even today, when I am 78 years of age, I am my own biggest critic and am still trying to improve. But my powers of concentration are no longer the same as when I was young and when the mind wanders so one tends to make errors, but the best thing about playing by ear is that quite often you can make a mistake but rectify it as you continue to play, i.e. as if you hadn't made a mistake at all! Sometimes you can get away with it, and sometimes not. It's funny how people who play by ear often envy those who can read music whilst those who play by music envy the ability of those who play by ear and so can play more or less anything without music having to be in front of them.

The trouble is that today a lot of the music I play, such as the Warsaw Concerto as well as popular melodies of our younger years, are now somewhat dated, although once upon a time the *Family Favourites* programme on the radio had many requests and played such music, especially the Warsaw Concerto, every Sunday. Maybe people do not want to sit quietly and listen to good music any more – or at least not many people. Certainly not the young ones. The film, *Dangerous Moonlight*, of which I keep a permanent copy now, brings a thrill and an awful lot of nostalgia but, it seems, only to me in my family – nobody else. It is an old film and long out of date and the script and acting are both corny; however, it brings back some very special memories to me.

As I have mentioned already, I think the appreciation of the music is helped a lot if one sees the film and knows the story behind it. At least that is what I have found but maybe I am just prone to easy inspiration. The fact is that, as I have said, I have never been taught and some very nice people have remarked, after hearing me play, that they find this hard to believe and that I have done very well considering I achieved this on my own. I take that as a compliment but learning to play taught me a lesson which was that there are few things in life you cannot achieve, provided you have the will and determination to succeed and see it through to the end. I am so glad that I taught myself to play the piano; it has given me a lot of pleasure, and still does, and some nice experiences too. I wish I could play better than I do but on the whole I am satisfied. To play also became the means to earn some extra money when I was young and when it was badly needed, by playing in pubs in the days when the majority of pubs had piano players. Later on I bought a piano accordion and taught myself to play that as well; being mobile meant that I could play at parties where they had no piano and also I played on coach outings which my mother organised after the war.

She always insisted that we left the street singing at the tops of our voices and that we return at the end of the day also singing loudly to show those neighbours who had not joined us on these coach outings what a wonderful time we had enjoyed and what they had missed. As I recall, it was 'Oh I Do Like To Be Beside The Seaside' when going and 'Show Me The Way To Go Home' when coming back.

I still enjoy playing the piano today and have equipped myself with a brand new Yamaha piano which does just about everything except the washing up! I have conquered the basic principles of this remarkable instrument but the complexity of it means that I am constantly finding new sounds and combinations and I then promptly forget how I managed to find them! I get a lot of enjoyment and relaxation from playing in my twilight years and despite my age I do believe I am improving a little! But I realise, and accept, that I shall never be a brilliant pianist – different, yes maybe, but brilliant, no. What might have happened if my mother could have afforded music lessons when I was young I shall never know. But these days, as the piano is situated in the lounge where the TV is also positioned, I am a little restricted as to when I can play and practise and so I usually do so at night, after Lynne has retired to her room to read, using the earphones, which means she cannot hear the music but she can hear the thumping because as an old pub piano player, I am still a thumper!

Also, I look forward to Sunday mornings which are mine alone and I have the sole freedom of the lounge until some time after 11.00am when Lynne returns after carrying out her chores; it is then I try to make recording tapes which I sometimes send to friends. But now that I am writing this autobiography, piano playing is taking a bit of a back seat. I tried to interest all of our children in playing the piano – but without success, I regret to say. But my son, Philip, did become quite proficient with the guitar.

Meanwhile the war continued. Our food rations were reduced, I remember, and when Hitler's armies smashed their way through to the gates of Moscow, things began to look even blacker. Could nothing or no-one stop Hitler's mighty war machine? Was he as invincible as he claimed? Earlier in the war, we all had a very severe shock when Rudolf Hess, Hitler's Deputy, had flown to Scotland and demanded to speak and discuss peace terms with higher authorities. He was considered to be barking mad and was imprisoned. But perhaps one of the worst features of the war was the fact that shipping, bringing us precious food supplies as well as badly needed war equipment, was being sunk by German U-Boats at a colossal rate. Many thousands of tons of precious cargo, as well as many lives, were being lost and going to the bottom of the sea.

So many things were in very short supply and that is why the Government was forced to reduce our rations. Simple things like bananas, oranges and even sometimes eggs, and many other items, were simply unavailable. Of course, any shortage of anything will give rise to a 'black market' and so, if you had plenty of money, you could usually get what you wanted if you also had the right connections. Sometimes you could not even buy a packet of cigarettes unless you were a known and regular customer; if you were, then the shopkeeper, who stood before his empty shelves, would reach under the counter and give you what you wanted – but not all you wanted and maybe not the brand you wanted; for example if you wanted a pack of twenty cigarettes of a particular brand, he might give you a packet of ten, and maybe then it would be another brand, and feel he was doing you a big favour.

From the end of 1941 until 1944, the bombing of London and other cities resumed. Not with the same ferocity as during the Blitz in 1940, but still bad enough to send people back to the shelters again and a number of tragedies occurred. One I recall was in an air raid shelter built under a factory in Poplar which made or stored ground pepper and spices. It received a direct hit and many people died, suffocated by the pepper and spices.

Many people chose to use the underground railway stations to take refuge from the raids. Strictly speaking, it was not allowed but people did it anyway and nobody tried to stop them. On one occasion in March 1943 at Bethnal Green Tube Station, the air raid warning had sounded and people began to enter the station. Unfortunately, a woman with a baby slipped and fell on the staircase; people then began to trip over her, those that were behind began to trip too and further back people foolishly began to surge forward not knowing what was causing the hold-up; then panic set in, and a terrible situation quickly developed with people being crushed by the pure weight of bodies and suffocated by people on top of them. Some 173 men, women, and children died in that tragedy.

What caused this panic? Well I have read different theories but it seems a likely explanation was that a secret and new anti-aircraft weapon was being tried out in a nearby park. This weapon sent sixty rockets into the sky with a terrible roar and it may have been this very unusual and unknown sound that set off the panic. Perhaps some of them thought it was a bomb that was falling upon them or very close by.

I also remember vividly an air raid during which they dropped not only high explosive bombs but also thousands of incendiary bombs. These incendiaries were about fourteen inches long and if you could get to them quickly enough you could deal with them by placing sand over them. If I remember correctly it was highly dangerous to put water on them. On this occasion a block of slum flats in Poplar High Street had been set alight by incendiaries and it was raging, for these rather ancient flats were like a tinder box. Quite poor people lived in them. I, and by now a small crowd, stood there watching these flats go up in flames and smoke, when a man tried to break through in order to reach them. The police, aided by Air Raid Wardens, held him back but he fought them furiously, screaming for them to let him go as his wife and two children were inside. Apparently, he had popped out to get a bottle of beer or something and returned maybe half an hour later to find that the place where he lived was up in flames. He shouted and screamed and struggled until he could struggle no more but the police could not let him go and tried to tell him that it was hopeless and that he would only die in that furnace himself. It was a tragedy and one of those experiences that remain in one's mind for always. I was only a few feet from this poor, tormented man who had to watch whilst his wife and family burned to death.

In this period of bombing, we younger ones had the idea to go camping at weekends. At least we could get a little fresh air and maybe a decent night's sleep. My brother Lenny had been evacuated to Tatling End near Gerrards Cross, so he knew that area very well. He particularly knew a stretch of woodlands there with a number of open spaces where there were good camping sites. And so on Friday evenings, if possible, otherwise first thing Saturdays, off we would go in a group of about six chaps, having begged some food from our mothers to take with us.

We cycled from Poplar, towards the West in the direction of Uxbridge, and from there it was only about a forty minute ride to Tatling End. There, in the woodlands, we would set up camp, light a fire, and begin to cook what food we had. I will always recall that camping site of ours for two reasons. The first is that at the bottom of the woods was a field leading down to a very attractive stream where sometimes we would get our water. From that point you could see a small factory and an odd kind of construction outside which looked as though it had come from a fairground. On occasions we could see this in operation when a man sat in a seat at the very bottom and he would then be catapulted to the top. This was the factory that developed and made the automatic ejection seats for air pilots and which saved many lives!

The second reason I remember Tatling End calls to mind one Sunday morning. I was always very keen on reading the newspapers and keeping myself well informed and so I decided to walk up to the confectionery and newsagents shop up on the main road. When I got there I saw a car parked on the frontage of the shop. I looked at the people sitting inside and it was Vivien Leigh and Laurence Olivier, the world famous actors.

I have to say that Vivien Leigh on the screen looks a very attractive lady indeed but to see her in the flesh on that never to be forgotten Sunday morning – well, I can only say she was like a dream. Absolutely beautiful. In fact, the second most beautiful woman I ever saw in my life. (I have to put that in – just in case the wife reads this!!). She actually looked at me – but she didn't smile. I learned afterwards that their house was in Iver and in the general vicinity of Tatling End and with stars like John Mills and others also living there, it was a kind of film star's haven. It is a wonder we didn't see more stars!

Of course, being in the country, we took advantage of the scrumping opportunities, as boys do, and most times returned home with a bagful of apples or plums or, very infrequently, pears. Had we been discovered by the owners we most certainly would have seen stars of a different kind then!! Once, on our way back to Poplar, I was stopped by a policeman who demanded to see what was in my bag which I had hanging from my crossbar. I was quite scared because I thought I was going to be arrested but he looked in, saw the apples which I had stolen, took a nice large one, winked at me, and sent me on my way!

For other forms of recreation we went over to Victoria Park by bus. There you could take a rowing boat out on the lake; we used to like that a lot and it was always disappointing to be called in when our time was up. Also they had a large, open-air swimming pool which was very nice when the weather was good, which I seem to remember happened quite frequently in those days.

In 1941 the Japanese bombed Pearl Harbor and simultaneously Hitler made one of the biggest mistakes of his life by declaring war on the USA. Winston Churchill had tried for a long time to persuade President Roosevelt to join in the war but Roosevelt steadfastly refused. He did not think the American people would be in favour of such a move. He permitted much aid in the way of food and war materials to be sent to the UK – but he would not join in the war.

It is very interesting, I think, to study the situation at that time, for we have the benefit of hindsight, but had Hitler not declared war on the USA I wonder if Roosevelt might not have directed all their attention to defeating Japan and left us to stew in our own juices? It is a fact that since 1940 the USA had supported us in food and war materials without which it is doubtful that we could have survived for very long. I, for one, will always remember, will greatly appreciate, and be very grateful for, the help they gave us in those dark days. We could not have survived without them.

After the attack on Pearl Harbor it would have been quite understandable if, after this treacherous act on the part of the Japanese, the Americans had decided to devote all their strength and power to defeating the Japanese. However, after Hitler's ghastly error in declaring war on the USA, and following a meeting between Churchill and Roosevelt, the USA agreed to make the defeat of Germany the first priority. This pleased not only Churchill but the whole British nation and Commonwealth because despite the encouraging and inspiring speeches of Churchill, there were many people who could not see how we were going to defeat Germany on our own, even with the help of the Commonwealth nations.

The USA was a lifeline to this dear country of ours and we should never forget that. Without them, we and they could not have gained the freedom of the French, Belgians, Dutch, the Danes or Norwegians and I believe those nations too, and the whole free world, owe a substantial debt towards the USA which sometimes seems to be forgotten by some these days but which should be remembered by all of us for all time. I do not agree with everything the USA does or says – but I will never forget them.

It did not take long before the towns and cities of Britain began to fill with US soldiers. The British people welcomed them and apart from the kind of bigots you get in any section of the public everywhere, there were not as many problems as some had forecast.

The bombing of London continued meanwhile and I shall never forget that brilliant, clear and moonlit night in 1942-3 when a raid was in progress. I was standing in Cotton Street not far from the junction with the High Street. To my left, on the other side of the road, were dock warehouses going up in flames and with the moon above and the red light from the blazing warehouses it was a most unusual skyline. And then – one of our searchlights caught one of the bombers in its beam. In a flash other searchlights latched on to the German plane. The plane twisted and turned, diving this way and that – but still the searchlights kept on him. Now it was up to our anti-aircraft guns – and the noise they made was deafening. How many explosive shells they sent up there Goodness only knows – and even then they couldn't shoot the bugger down! Of course the plane escaped, no doubt counting his lucky stars – or being very thankful for the poor aim of our guns or their inability to reach that high which is probably more likely!

It was in June 1944 that the first of Hitler's V-weapons were unleashed towards Britain, especially towards London as the capital city. This was the V1, which was a pilotless aircraft made with just plywood and sheet steel, and apart from the engine, the rest of the construction was nothing more than a substantial bomb, a ton of explosives in fact. In the first instance these were sent from stations in France and there is no question that these flying bombs, which we nicknamed 'doodlebugs' were more than just a nuisance. However, the good thing about them, if one can use such a term, is that you could hear them and see them approaching; and then, quite suddenly, the engine would cut out and the machine would fall like a stone to the ground and explode. They were not at all accurate and so were liable to fall anywhere but with these flying bombs we did have a chance to take cover. Efforts were made to shoot them down and they were quite successful because they did not fly as high as ordinary planes Even more successful in preventing the V1s reaching the cities as time went on were the efforts of the RAF who found that by flying side by side to these flying bombs and then tipping the wing over it caused the machine to fall to the earth before it reached any heavily populated area. In total the Germans sent over 9,000 of these flying bombs towards Britain but it is estimated that less than 30% of them reached their targets. The RAF accounted for many and our anti-aircraft guns also scored.

So, for a while, we were bombarded by these V1s but when D-Day occurred on June 6th 1944 the situation began to change somewhat, for Germans defending the French coastal area saw a gigantic fleet of vessels approaching the Normandy beaches. Back in the East End we knew something would be happening shortly as we had watched liners leaving the docks fully laden with laughing and joking young American soldiers.

Over by the large bridge which separates Poplar from the Isle of Dogs we could stand just a few yards from where the liners were sailing gingerly out of the narrow docks estuary into the Thames, to rendezvous for the great invasion of Europe. They threw chewing gum and coins at us; they were joking and looked very happy. But they were about to go into Hell itself and many of those laughing boys we exchanged jokes with were never going to be coming back. And they were so young – just boys!

The landings, accompanied by inland air drops by paratroopers and glider troops, were successful although casualties were heavy, especially on the part of the American forces. The Supreme Commander was General Dwight Eisenhower but, under him, in charge of all land operations was our own General Montgomery. After a difficult period of time during which the Germans did their best to eliminate the beachheads, the Americans (being mainly in the general Cherbourg peninsula area) and the British and Canadian forces fighting Eastwards towards Caen, Bayeux and beyond, broke through and, despite heavy resistance from Hitler's Panzer divisions, forced them back.

Following the early battles Germany's so called 'invincible' Wermacht was almost decimated at the great battle of the Falaise Gap and after that they were in full retreat towards the Belgian border. The Allied forces chased after them, of course, but then, as far as the Northern sector was concerned, we stopped before the Belgian-Dutch border and we did not resume our attack for eight days. Those precious eight days gave the Germans an opportunity to re-group and make a formidable army from the bits and pieces and rabble that had retreated from the Falaise Gap, and they took advantage of our failure to keep up the pressure. In fact what the Germans, under the command of Field Marshal Model, achieved in those eight days was nothing short of miraculous. Later, one senior German officer was quoted as stating that after the battle of the Falaise Gap and the retreat to the Belgian-Dutch border, had our armies continued their offensive there was nothing to stop them slicing through Holland and into Germany itself. But those fatal eight days respite was given to the Germans and they took the fullest advantage of them. We were going to pay for that mistake later and it had a big effect on the failure of Operation Market Garden, the brave operation to end the war by the of 1944. I write more about that in due course as it was there, at Arnhem, where our childhood pal, Alfie Cowley, lost his life at the tender age of 19.

7

HITLER'S V2 WEAPON STRIKES, MY CHILDHOOD PAL, ALFIE, DIES NEAR ARNHEM, AND FINALLY THE WAR COMES TO AN END

Back home, we civilians listened to our radios at every opportunity for news of the progress being made through Normandy and beyond; we were relieved that our advancing armies were slowly limiting the ability of the Germans to continue to fire their terror weapons. The most important feature of concern and relief to us was that the Germans began to evacuate their flying bomb sites in France for fear of being overrun; however they had others in Belgium and Holland which could be made operative. Nevertheless, the flying bombs slowly diminished and then after a short lull, some mysterious explosions began to occur in London, about which the BBC was strangely silent. The first one was in North London, I believe, and then others followed.

Rumours started that they were gas explosions caused by earlier bombing nearby which had perhaps affected the gas supply equipment in some houses. But it was nothing of the sort. These explosions were the first of many to follow because they were in fact caused by Hitler's second terror weapon, the dreaded V2 rocket bomb, and the public were eventually informed. Now most people *did* regard these as terror weapons and I think it true to say that whilst we did not like the V1s at all, they did not frighten us as much as the V2 rockets because with the latter you didn't stand a chance. They could fall anywhere and at anytime without warning.

In the East End I do not think we were too badly affected by these rockets but I would like to relate an account of one rocket that did fall quite near to us in Prestage Street and the circumstances which I shall always regard as a lucky escape for me.

I should explain that eventually, when she realised I was going without lunch most days because of the shortage of money, my mother took pity upon me and suggested that I go to work by cycle and try to make it home for lunch. I tried this and used to padlock my bike to some railings opposite the offices where I worked, in Fenchurch Buildings. I found that I could indeed, within the space of one hour, get back to Poplar, have my lunch, and return in time – just!

So every day I left at about 1.00pm and was back by 2.00pm. On this particular day, however, for some reason which was not at all obvious to me, my immediate 'boss', Mr Thorn, told me I could go a few minutes early if I wished. I accepted this offer eagerly because I was a growing lad and always feeling in need of sustenance. So I went downstairs, unlocked my bike and proceeded along Fenchurch Street, into Aldgate, past my lovely Chop House there and down to Gardiner's Corner where I forked right into Commercial Road, past Berner Street, the scene of one of the Ripper murders (the first on the evening when he murdered two victims) and on through Stepney towards Poplar.

When I arrived at Poplar, I turned right at the junction between East India Dock Road and Cotton Street. Here I was usually held up for a few minutes by traffic lights but fortunately for me, not on this particular day. I then proceeded along Cotton Street, turned left at Poplar High Street, past the Queen's Theatre, into Blackwall Way and there was Prestage Street on the left. That day my mother had prepared one of my favourite meals, sausages and mashed potatoes with fried onions, and as soon as I arrived home that delicious smell greeted me.

I sat down at the table, my mother served my lunch immediately but before I could eat a single bite, a terrific explosion took place. The whole house shuddered and it seemed as though a bomb had dropped almost next door! I immediately got up, went to the front door and there, only 300 yards away, a big explosive cloud could be seen. I forgot my lunch and told my mother I would be back soon after I found out what had happened.

So I raced on my bicycle towards the explosion, into Blackwall Way, up to the Cotton Street junction, where I turned right – and there before me, mainly now on my left hand side, was a scene of utter mayhem and destruction. It was obviously one of Hitler's rockets. I was one of the first on the scene and the cloud of smoke and dust was still settling. You could hear the cries for help by those who were perhaps partially buried and trapped by the debris. Some men were on the piles of bricks trying to dig people out but the first official people on the scene were the Air Raid Wardens, God bless them, who cleared everyone away; they were followed by the Fire Service and then finally by the police – all arrived within minutes of each other. The Air Raid Wardens, or the ARP as we called them, were the only heroes who, in my opinion, have not been properly remembered in the great conflict we call World War II. Both my mother and my father were wardens and I do not believe they received any medals or recognition for what they did – at least neither my mother nor my father did to the best of my knowledge. But what brave and valiant work they carried out in the face of great danger.

Those members of the public who had arrived on the scene were ushered back by the police until we could only see what was going on from a distance of maybe sixty yards or so, perhaps a bit less. Then ambulances arrived and people with dogs that were specially trained to indicate where people might be buried.

It transpired that the rocket had landed right in the middle of a group of houses lying between Cotton Street and Bazely Street. But the outward blast had also destroyed much in the immediate vicinity including the pub (I think it was called either the Resolute or the Volunteer) on the corner of Cotton Street, a Nursing Home in Bazely Street,and damaged many properties including All Saints Church (where my wife and I were later married), the Pavilion Cinema and of course a large number of houses.

One of our opposite neighbours, a Mrs Reeves, who lived at 17 Prestage Buildings next to my grandmother, had been shopping at Chrisp Street market. On her way back she decided to stop off at the pub for a glass of stout – she was very partial to a drop of stout was Mrs Reeves. She was sitting there when the rocket landed and, of course, she perished. It was said that she was found three streets away, without a stitch of clothing on; Mrs Reeves was a very prim and proper lady and she would have been horror struck if she thought she might be found like that!

I shall always remember Mrs Reeves because when we were kids playing in the street, she was unsmiling and always complaining about whatever we were doing. She actually lived next door to my grandparents' flat – the same flat where my dear wife and I were destined to live following dear old Granny's death. But despite the fact that Mrs Reeves was a grumpy old lady, there was something about her which I respected and even rather liked. I recollect now that I never saw any relative or friend visit her – ever. I am sure, though, that she was one of those kind of people who, if you could only get close to her, would prove that she had a heart of gold and was probably a very nice person once she dropped her defensive, prim and proper guard. At the time I was very sad indeed that she suffered such a terrible death. The only thing is though – she couldn't have known anything about it. The rockets were silent and I am certain her death was instantaneous which, in those circumstances, is the best way to go.

Of course work went on for the remainder of that day and throughout the night, searching for possible survivors who might still be buried. I was one of those who was there to witness the Matron of the destroyed Nursing Home dug out, having been buried for 36 hours. The poor old soul was caked in a sort of yellow ochre dust and looked in a bad way as she was put into an ambulance and carried away to the hospital. But I am very pleased to say that she recovered fully from her ordeal – physically; whether one recovers from that kind of experience mentally one cannot be sure.

But looking at that incident as a whole, then purely from a personal point of view I will always regard it as a lucky escape because if I had been there at my normal time instead of a little early I could easily have been at that junction when the rocket fell. If that had happened then, for sure I would not be here now writing this narrative to you.

The rockets continued to fall but with the advance of our forces in Holland, and particularly the Canadian forces who figured prominently in the advance in that sector from where the rockets were being launched, these attacks on London occurred less and less; they even captured launching pads that the Germans never had the opportunity to use. If they had, then the number of rockets fired at us would have been much greater. But the attacks became fewer and fewer until they stopped altogether, to our great relief I have to say.

Many say that the tragic event of Operation Market Garden, a tremendous Allied paratroop and glider infantry attack in the Belgian border to Arnhem region, was pushed ahead with such an objective in mind, i.e., to eliminate those rocket launching bases. I will comment further on OMG later in this narrative because, as I have mentioned, I have a special interest in this particular military affair.

It should also be mentioned that Hitler even had a V3 terror weapon almost in place – this was a long range gun concealed underground, to avoid being bombed, and which could easily reach London and other targets in Southern England from French bases. This gun fired a barrage of multiple rocket projectiles. It is estimated that a series of 300 rockets or more per hour could have been fired if it had been possible to get this system into working order. But the rapidly advancing Allied forces made this impossible, thank God, because there is no doubt that this horrific weapon would have been a terribly destructive device and without doubt would have caused a large loss of life.

By the end of 1944 it was clear that between the Soviet forces in the East and the Allied forces in the West, Germany was being crushed and that we had all but won the war. In this time, we welcomed the fact that General Eisenhower, Supreme Commander of the Allied forces on the Continent, was being presented with the Freedom of the City of London at the Mansion House, traditional home of the Lord Mayor of London. I was one of that crowd numbering a few thousand who stood outside cheering Ike, as he was nicknamed, when he stood on the balcony to acknowledge the cheers. If I had known then what I know now I am not too sure that I would have been cheering quite so enthusiastically – but more of that later.

At around this time, I decided to leave my office job in the City. I was still only earning £1.10.0d per week but my National Service was looming and I needed to save some money, for I knew that a soldier's pay was minimal. On the recommendation of a boyhood pal, I applied for a job with a firm called Falkus Ltd, builders. They had been given a contract to repair bombed houses in Poplar and were looking for workers. I was of course quite unskilled but even as an ordinary labourer my wages went up immediately to £4.10.0d per week! And I have to say I did enjoy my brief time running around the roofs of London like a monkey. I liked the bonhomie and comradeship of the tea breaks in the mornings, when we were allowed fifteen minutes where we congregated at a cafe in Abbots Road and sat there munching thick slices of bread and beef dripping and drinking hot cups of tea. Very unhealthy but truly wonderful! It was really amazing what manual labour did for one's appetite! But of course there eventually came a time when all the bombed houses that could be repaired had been attended to and, in those circumstances, I was given a week's notice and so I was unemployed. But not for long, as I applied for a job at the Labour Exchange and they sent me over to Old Ford to a veneer factory. Frankly, I didn't care too much what I did then because it was only a matter of a few months until I would have to report for National Service.

And so the end of the war finally arrived. Hitler and Goebbels had committed suicide in Berlin and most of the other leading Nazis had been captured and were eventually placed on trial at Nuremburg. It was a period of much jubilation and celebration.

Almost every street had its VE Day party for which special extra rations were allowed, and so did we in Prestage Street. VE Day was declared after the war had ended so there were previous celebrations on the day war actually ended. Many of us went up to the West End, Trafalgar Square or the Mall and I was one of those who saw King George VI, Queen Elizabeth, the two Princesses, and good old Winston Churchill himself, appear on the balcony of Buckingham Palace. The crowd roared and sang and cheered again and again; they called for the King and then for 'Winnie' and again and again the crowds were rewarded as first the King and Queen came out, then the Princesses, and finally Winston. This happened a number of times and still it was not enough for the cheering crowd. That was a crazy, happy night which I shall never forget. What a wonderful atmosphere there was that day – people were almost delirious with joy for after six years of war, of battles, of bombing, of death, of blood, not to mention food shortages and rationing of almost everything, we lucky ones had survived to see this wonderful day and the public were showing how happy and relieved they were that it was all over. It is impossible to find words that could adequately describe our feelings at that time.

Of course, we had to remember too those who would not be coming back from the battlefields, as well as those who died at home or on the seas; it was estimated that around 46,000 were killed during the Blitz in London alone, and they represent the awful tragedy, stupidity, and madness of war.

Of course, in the Saloon Bar of the Ivy House, we spoke of the war and the fact that we had survived; we spoke of those who had suffered and those who had to move out of the street. Among them was the Cowley family who lived at No 1, next door to the Ivy House, and of course next door also to us. The Cowleys were poor like the rest of us but, somewhat like the Muller family house I have written about earlier, one got the impression that maybe they were rather poorer than most.

It was said that they had moved away of their own volition during the Blitz. Nobody seemed to know what happened to them or where they had gone to. But then someone said that he had heard one of the Cowley boys, Alfie, had died at Arnhem. This sparked my interest in Operation Market Garden at that time but it was not until much later in my life that

I had an opportunity to study OMG, not only through reading many accounts by historians and others but by reference to it via the Internet, which was a terrific source of information to me.

Having been in touch with so many people who had studied OMG, both in this country and abroad – especially Holland – I felt that I had become sufficiently knowledgeable on the subject and in fact I have written my own analysis of the main reasons why, in my opinion, this gallant and brave attempt to end the war by Christmas 1944 had failed.

I discovered that Alfie Cowley was in the 11th Battalion, 4th Brigade, of the 1st Airborne Division, that he was in the second drop on 18th September 1944 and that he was killed on Sunday, 24th September, just 150 meters from Hotel Tafelberg, Oosterbeek, formerly the HQ of Field Marshal Model, and only one day before the evacuation of the remnants of the 1st Airborne across the river. Alfie was aged just nineteen years – not old enough yet to find out what life was all about! Via the Internet I have even managed to obtain a photograph of his grave.

When I first learned what had happened to poor Alfie, I was not really in a position to easily find out the true story of Operation Market Garden and I hope the reader will not mind if I try, as briefly as I can, to recount what happened; I do this in memory of our childhood pal who certainly did not deserve to die so young.

I have already described how, in the Northern sector of the battlefront, our forces had beaten the Germans right back to the Belgian-Dutch border but stopped there for eight days – a military factor which some experts cannot understand even now, because there was virtually nothing ahead to stop us. Perhaps it was the vexed question of supplies which made us stop but therein lies the story of the error of bypassing ports rather than capturing them; this meant that all supplies still had to come all the way from Cherbourg which together with the artifical port made in the UK and established by Cherbourg were the only ports in operation – very far from the battlefront. However that maybe, without supply problems many feel that we could even have made it right through to the Arnhem bridge and beyond into Germany had we not stopped. In fact, a senior German officer went on record later to express his surprise at the halting of the Allied offensive on the Belgian-Dutch border; as he said, "We had nothing then to stop you".

Anyway, during this lull in activities, which the Germans appreciated very much indeed, they managed to perform absolute miracles in re-grouping and re-forming what was a defeated rabble into a strong fighting force. This 'rabble' included two Panzer Divisions which were in the process of refitting just North of Arnhem. This fact should have been known by our intelligence. Someone knew because their presence was reported to Monty's HQ and was discussed. However, the decision was made to continue on the basis that it was too late to call off the operation at that point.

On 1st September 1944, our General Montgomery was relieved of his overall command of land forces due to political and media pressure back in the USA as well as pressure from the American generals, Bradley and Patton. So he reverted to being in command of just the British and Canadian forces, and forces from other miscellaneous countries such as Poland and Czechoslovakia operating in the Northern sector of the battlefront. As a sop to him, Montgomery was promoted to Field Marshal but there is no doubt he was very unhappy with the decision to minimise his command because he was of the view that he had more experience of war than any of the American generals – including Eisenhower. Nevertheless, as a good soldier he accepted the decision and began to develop a plan in his mind which, if it had succeeded, would in his opinion shorten the war considerably and would save a lot of lives.

This involved a plan called Operation Comet and called for a double-pronged, joint Allied land and air attack, striking through Holland towards Arnhem and across the German border, sweeping across the North German plains and on to Berlin itself. Operation Comet was cancelled for a number of reasons, one of them was the fact that the Allied advance was so rapid. And so Operation Comet was replaced by Operation Market Garden (OMG), which was also a land and air attack; somewhat modified in some respects but expanded in others. However, one of its weaknesses was that it was now a single-pronged attack with the Americans being responsible for capturing the intervening bridges from the Belgian/Dutch border right through to Nijmegen by paratroop landings, thus allowing the British armour to forge ahead and link up with the British 1st Airborne Division who, in a separate operation, would be landing North of the River Rhine, with the object of capturing the vital last bridge at Arnhem from behind.

The supply situation of war materials, petrol, food etc. would only permit one major attack to be carried out and Monty pleaded for priority of supplies to allow OMG to go ahead. Eisenhower hesitated because he was under pressure from his other generals, Bradley and especially Patton, who were chafing at the bit and also wanted priority of supplies; he also realised that if OMG was successful and the British forces smashed their way clear through to Berlin, that would not make good reading to the public back home in the USA. However, eventually Eisenhower saw that OMG represented the best bet from the options before him, for it was in that sector that they believed the German forces were weakest. And so Ike agreed not only to priority of supplies but also, in conjunction with General Bradley, to render flank support to the advancing British armour, as well as the American paratroop divisions, whose task, as I have described, was to land and capture vital bridges (of which there were quite a few in this land of rivers and canals), thus facilitating the advance of the British armoured divisions.

That was the agreement; what happened in the event was somewhat different because, despite what he had agreed with Monty, Ike, who was well known for changing his mind, gave Bradley permission to launch an attack towards the Saar, knowing perfectly well that some supplies would have to be diverted away from the OMG forces to Bradley's sector and that furthermore, the promised flank support from General Bradley was in danger ,would doubtless be minimised or, in some localities, made virtually non-existent; we shall see the vital importance of that factor in due course.

When Monty knew what the situation was going to be, perhaps that was the time for him to reconsider and perhaps call off OMG or postpone it. But he considered that plans were too advanced and so he didn't; therefore the attack by the ground and air forces began on September 17th 1944 and simultaneously substantial air drops of American paratroops were made strategically along the single road which led through Holland and on to the vital Arnhem Bridge; their task was to capture the intervening bridges from the Belgian/Dutch border and thus allow the British armour to advance towards Arnhem.

Simultaneously, the British 1st Airborne Division would land North of the River Rhine with the object of capturing the all important Arnhem Bridge, for if a clear run for our armour advancing from the South could be gained across that bridge, then they would have had a choice either to swing the attack to the right and link up with Bradley's forces advancing Eastwards thus encircling the Saar, or to push straight ahead to Berlin itself. Monty's forecast was that if the plan succeeded then the war could be over by the end of 1944.

But sadly the plan did not succeed. The requirements of the plan were that (a) the American paratroopers should be successful in capturing the bridges over the rivers and canals, (b) that the advancing British armoured divisions should proceed forward and reach Arnhem in 48 hours, and that (c) the British 1st Airborne Division should capture the

Arnhem Bridge and hang on to it for those vital and very precious 48 hours until relieved by the advancing British armour.

Despite suffering very heavy losses the American forces did quite well – in some instances with a little help from the British; but the British armour could only advance along the single road towards their eventual target very slowly as the 'old men and young boys', reported by the intelligence that they would be facing, were nothing of the sort for now they represented a strong resistance due to the amazing organisational abilities of Field Marshal Model.

Here we come back to the question of the promised flank support for if those promises had been upheld and the Germans kept busy, especially on the right flank, then the attacks on the British armour would not have been so severe and so successful. As it was, the German forces could pick off our tanks and vehicles on the single road like sitting ducks. It should be borne in mind that the single road forged its way through a country full of dykes, ditches and canals, so once on the road there was nowhere else to go! The British armour did their very best to break through but their task to reach our chaps at Arnhem in 48 hours was too ambitious and was not achieved. The German forces were just too strong and so virtually without any, or very limited, flank support, the operation was doomed to failure.

Meanwhile, let us turn our attention to what was happening with the British 1st Airborne Division, aided and abetted by infantry transported by glider. The plan there, arguably a wrong plan, was to effect two drops. The first was also to be made on Sunday 17th September, to coincide with the landings of the US paratroops. That was duly carried out but our forces North of the Rhine landed some 8 km from the bridge itself. I did not see the air armada myself but the planes, either carrying paratroops or pulling gliders carrying infantry, flew over in their hundreds and to those watching, whether in Eastern England, Belgium or Holland, it must have been an amazing spectacle. However, the main point of an air attack is the element of surprise and, therefore, to split the attack over two days meant that 50% of that element of surprise had been lost.

Nevertheless, the British force comprising the first landing did not meet a great deal of opposition at first, because the element of surprise was effective, and one group under the command of Lt Colonel Frost covered the eight kilometres and actually reached the Arnhem Bridge without a great deal of resistance. Thus they were able to capture the Northern end of the bridge and a lot of the immediate surrounding area which they held on to for almost four days. We must remember that their original task was to hold it for just 48 hours. But they more than achieved this despite constant attacks from Germans troops, who by now had woken up to what was happening. They were hopelessly outnumbered and outgunned, for it must be remembered that airborne troops are of necessity only lightly armed whilst the defending land forces were equipped with tanks, heavy artillery, etc.

The following day, Monday 18th September, the second drop took place. By now the Germans, who realised that another drop was almost certainly planned, were gathered in force and the resistance was extremely heavy. The Germans had worked out what the British intentions were, i.e. to reach the bridge, relieve Lt Colonel Frost, and hold the bridge until the advancing British armoured divisions could reach them. They knew perfectly well that if that happened then in all probability the war was lost, for the Germans had very little to offer between Arnhem and Berlin. And so they placed a barrier of powerful forces between the landing sites West of Arnhem and the bridge, and many fierce battles were fought – the British were trying to battle their way through and come to the aid of Lt Colonel Frost with the Germans endeavouring to stop them. Casualties were heavy on both sides.

My childhood pal, Alfie Cowley, being in the 11th Battalion, formed part of this second drop. Their instructions were to track the Royal Staffordshire infantry who had landed simultaneously by glider.

They were to take the Northerly route and with the 11th Battalion following behind to protect their rear, try to reach and relieve Lt Colonel Frost and his men who were still holding on to one end of the bridge. But they had not travelled very far when they ran into a massive German ambush. The Staffordshires fought bravely and the 11th tried their best to help but again they were outnumbered and outgunned, with the result that this British force, comprising both paratroops and infantry, were almost decimated; of course, as a consequence, they failed in their mission.

Meanwhile Lt Colonel Frost was hanging on only by the skin of his teeth and the situation looked desperate as relief was unable to get through. The advancing armour had been seriously halted in the area south of the Rhine between Nijmegen and Arnhem. As precious time went by, it was realised that it was not going to be possible to reach Lt Colonel Frost in time. Colonel Frost, with so many of his soldiers wounded, with no food or water and very little ammunition, realised that he was in a hopeless situation and so, after an extremely brave battle, he and his men had no alternative but to surrender to the Germans. It must be said that the Germans treated Lt Colonel Frost and his troops with great respect and admiration for the courageous manner in which they had fought.

I return to my pal Alfie, because he is the main reason I am writing about OMG in this narrative. I know that despite the German ambush and the heavy losses of men that occurred on the 18th-19th September, he must have escaped with his life because the records show he was killed on the 24th September. We also know that all the remaining British forces were forced to congregate in a pocket around the town of Oosterbeek. Fortunately they held, and continued to hold, an area which gave them access to the river. Meanwhile, the advancing British forces from the south had at least got near enough to offer artillery support to the beleaguered troops in the pocket, which by now was completely surrounded by German troops, tanks, mortars, and artillery – except for part of the river bank which they continued to defend and hold. So the artillery support offered was welcomed by the surrounded troops holding out in the pocket and they were able to give guidance to the artillery by radio as to German positions; even so some shells landed among our own chaps and caused some deaths – such things happen in war.

Now there is no way I can prove it, but I believe it is possible that my pal Alfie *may* have been killed by so called 'friendly fire'. I write this because it is known that British shells did land in the pocket near to Hotel Tafelberg on Sunday 24th September. Alfie died 150 meters from the Hotel on that same day!! I admit that I may be putting two and two together and making five, but at least in terms of possibility I do not think I am being unreasonable in stating that as the date and place of Alfie's death coincide, it is at least possible that he died from our own guns.[3] But a very important factor I would like to add, and most historians agree, is that without that artillery support it is doubtful our boys, trapped in that Oosterbeek pocket as they were and almost surrounded by superior numbers of the enemy, could have held on for as long as they did.

Poor Alfie died only a day before the top brass recognised that the game was up and ordered the evacuation of the remaining troops across

---

[3]*Since writing the aforegoing I have, remarkably, been able to locate and be in touch with two of Alfie Cowley's brothers; Ed who now lives in Canada, and Bertie, who lives in Kent. I now have information from Ed that after the war and the return home of prisoners of war, Alfie's commander wrote to the Cowleys to tell them that Alfie in fact died from a bullet wound to the head and so my theory about 'friendly fire' is totally incorrect.*

the river on Monday, 25th September. In an attempt to carry out this evacuation and not alert the Germans, they went by night as quietly as possible down to the river's edge. Some troops went by the few boats available, whilst others tried to swim across; a number of these drowned but the attempted crossings were eventually spotted by the Germans and for most of the time they were fired upon by German forces. Therefore further losses were suffered from enemy fire. Overall not too many succeeded to reach the other side.

Afterwards, Field Marshal Montgomery described the action as a 90% success. It wasn't – it was a 100% failure and can be called by no other name than a defeat for the British Army. But nothing can take away the astounding courage of those boys who flew to Holland in an attempt to end the war earlier and who held out against overwhelming odds for so long. The Dutch people will seemingly never forget what happened in 1944 and every year they hold a commemoration of the event in memory of those who died fighting for their freedom. The graves of the boys who died are tended carefully by Dutch children.

To quote a few figures: Some 8969 British paratroops and glider troops took part in this airborne attack, of which 1174 (13%) were killed, 5903 (66%) were captured by the Germans, and only 1892 (21%) were evacuated safely. Of the glider pilots, 1262 took part, 219 were killed (17%) and 511 (40%) were captured. Of the Polish Brigade, 1689 took part, 92 were killed (5%), 111 (7%) were taken prisoner and 1486 (88%) returned to the Allied lines.

I have written on the subject of OMG at length because I am proud that a pal of mine took part in this operation and the story needs to be told to those who today enjoy a good life of plenty in a land of freedom. Well, Alfie and his fallen pals gave their lives so that we can live our lives as we do today and I believe this should be remembered by everybody who treasures freedom.

My description of OMG is very much abbreviated and there is much I could write about – in fact I could fill this whole book on the subject; especially on the main reasons why OMG failed, of which there are a number still argued about by historians today. And so this is not by any means an attempt to explain the whole story behind OMG, I have only dwelt upon it because it was important to me after discovering that my childhood pal, a hero of Prestage Street who was a next door neighbour, died there. Alfie was buried, very probably in a collective grave at first; his remains were exhumed and he now rests in the Oosterbeek War Cemetery.

On the subject of heroes, I believe we had yet another in Prestage Street and his name was Eddie Unwin. Eddie was a rascal when he was a boy but he was a very likeable chap. I am unsure to which regiment he belonged, nor of which particular award he won and so it is difficult now to check. But I shall continue to try.

In later years I crossed the Arnhem Bridge (now called the Colonel Frost Bridge by the Dutch) many times without realising what a historic spot it truly was and that not too far from there our Alfie had laid down his life. At that time, my full interest in OMG had not been completely aroused. That came later.

One final word about Alfie; he was a boy who was always in trouble and mostly for stealing. In other ways he was a quiet, inoffensive and likeable chap. Of course Alfie was punished for his misdemeanours and attended both the Court and the Probation Office on quite a regular basis. Alfie was a very skilful thief and I have often thought that if they had employed him as an agent to steal the secret war plans of the Germans, then the war would have been over much more quickly! I recall one occasion, around 1936 or so, when Alfie was on probation and he had to attend an appointment with the Probation Officer, who was a lady. Alfie asked me and a couple of others to go with him. Well, despite his reputation we younger boys looked up to Alfie, he was a little older than us, and we thought he was the bee's knees so we were very pleased to be asked to go with him.

At that time the Probation Office was housed in some council flats right at the top of Poplar High Street; and so we trudged up there in a small group and waited outside whilst Alfie was dealt with inside. After a half hour or so, out came Alfie with a big smile on his face. 'Quick!' he said 'I've got her purse!' He had actually stolen the Probation Officer's purse! In our innocence we little ones didn't realise the seriousness of what he had done. We all looked up to Alfie and never thought he could do wrong!

So following the instructions of Alfie we went quickly down the High Street and turned into the Recreation Ground through to East India Dock Road. Then Alfie had a brilliant idea – 'Let's all go up to Aldgate'. Well, to us smaller ones that was a great trip indeed, a terrific adventure, and so we enthusiastically joined him in the queue for a bus. One came along after some minutes and we clambered aboard, going upstairs which for some reason most kids preferred. We chatted away excitedly as boys do when they are engaged in an adventure and after a while the conductor came up to collect our fares. But when he came to us he said 'It's alright boys, that gentleman over there has paid your fares.' We looked over and there sat a jolly looking man who had evidently been amused by our antics. I can't recall what we did when we got to Aldgate. I am sure we adequately thanked the man who paid our fares.

Poor Alfie. Such a naughty boy – but he didn't deserve to die so young.

8

1946–1950, NATIONAL SERVICE AND MARRIAGE

And so the months passed by and soon the day to report for my Army service came around; I had passed my medical examination A1 some weeks previously over at a hall somewhere between East Ham and Romford. After that, in September, I was ordered to report to a barracks in Hounslow where I underwent six weeks' training with the Royal Fusiliers.

In this time the Sergeant asked if any of us played a musical instrument; I immediately put my hand up because I had taken my piano accordion with me. Anyway, it seemed we had just enough volunteers to form a small band and we were asked to play at a show they were putting on to mark the end of our training. How marvellous it was to be playing music instead of marching around the parade ground or learning about guns and how to kill people etc. And so we practised playing together – but none of us were any good at all and the sound we produced was awful. I took the lead because none of the others wanted to and I chose what we were going to play. All we had to do in practice is get it right. Instead we gradually became worse!

Anyway, I put a few tunes together and made up a kind of act. On the night of the show we did ourselves proud with white trousers and white shirts with painted black moustaches, i.e. Clark Gable style, we must have looked quite dashing or so we thought! But when the curtain went up everybody froze! We seemed to be in a panic as none of us had ever previously performed before an audience! Anyway, I decided to break the silence and launched forth into the 'March of the Toreadors' and soon the rest joined in and we were away. My recollection is that we were bad – we were even worse than during rehearsals, probably because of our nervousness! But with all the officers sitting in the front and the rest behind them the boys applauded us and seemed to appreciate the fact that at least we had made an effort no matter how bad it was. But I will never forget that awful din we kicked up – it was an apology for music!

After my training period had passed, I was then sent bag and baggage to Cirencester but during this long journey I found my jaw was becoming very swollen – the consequence of an infected tooth. By the time I arrived at Cirencester my jaw had swollen alarmingly and I was in quite a bad way. I made my way to the camp where I had to report and on arrival I had to go before the Officer Commanding to report. As soon as I entered his office and he saw my face he burst out laughing. I suppose I must have looked quite a picture with my one-sided swollen face. However, I was unable to join the officer in this supposedly hilarious situation for I was now in serious pain and felt quite unwell. When the officer saw the distress that must have been written on my face, and that I wasn't laughing, he curtailed his humour and ordered a car to take me to a dentist in town. I had the offending tooth extracted, which was agonising. Although they gave me a gas anaesthetic, they did not administer quite enough, and so I was in a state of semi-consciousness and actually felt the pain of the extraction as it happened. That was not at all a pleasant experience. I am not sure but I believe that officer paid for my private treatment from his own pocket – maybe he had a guilty conscience after laughing so much at my predicament.

The camp at Cirencester was a dispersement centre. You had to report and from there they posted you to a permanent camp. They also told you which part of the Army you had been allotted to; in my case it was the Royal Army Service Corps. Of course, there should be a simpler way of doing this than to send soldiers right across the country only to send them back again! Anyway, I found that I had been posted to a Food Supply Depot, near a village called Soulbury in Bedfordshire – a camp, incidentally, that the famous English running champion, Sydney Wooderson, had left only a short while before my arrival. So, with my still painful jaw, I travelled all the way back to Soulbury and reported there.

I was given an office job and helped a civilian employee to carry out her work. I suppose I must have worked diligently because not many months passed before I was told that I was being sent on a Non Commissioned Officers' Training course at Colchester. I consequently did so, passed, and was appointed to the rank of Lance Corporal. The rank of

Lance Corporal is only an appointment – not a promotion. The first rank of promotion is Corporal, which I attained somewhat later on.

This meant I left the communal soldiers' hut and instead shared a more private hut with another Lance Corporal. His name was Fairbrother and he was a bit of a peculiar chap; I could hardly make head nor tail of him. But I kept well in with him because as our camp was not large enough to have our own NAAFI canteen and shop, the shop we did have was run on a voluntary basis by one of the NCOs – and that was L/Cpl Fairbrother.

That was good thinking on my part because eventually Fairbrother was posted to another unit and he offered me the opportunity to run the NAAFI shop. I quickly learned that although this was an unpaid voluntary position, there were ways to make it pay for the chap running it! For example, as soldiers we were entitled to a ration of cheap cigarettes. Non-smoking soldiers didn't all take up their rations; however, the NCO in charge (that was now me) claimed their rations and sold them to the civilian lorry drivers who very often came to the camp to deliver goods, at shop prices. They were glad to buy them in view of the shortages of popular brands. I also found that I could indent for other items at cheaper prices from NAAFI as compared to normal shop prices. So in these ways the 'unpaid' position of NCO i/c wasn't really unpaid at all. And I made hay whilst the sun shone!

Furthermore, as this was a food depot I did a bit of exchanging of items which were in short supply, such as cigarettes for food which was of course still rationed at home. So when I came home on leave with my parcel of goodies, my mother was always very glad indeed to see me! Everybody was glad to see me! However, I had to be careful at the railway stations; I must have stood out by carrying not one, but two small attaché cases. If I had been stopped by the Military Police they would almost certainly have demanded to know what I was carrying and it would have been extremely difficult for me to explain away the goodies that I carried. So, when I saw a redcap I took appropriate action and performed my disappearing act!

But in the autumn of 1947, this splendid and rather profitable arrangement came to an abrupt end when I was called to the office, where I was told that I had an overseas posting. I imagined this would be Germany but when I asked where to – I was told 'Wales'! Somebody did not know their geography! I transferred the 'canteen shop' to another NCO, who jumped at the chance to take it over, taught him the ropes and the secrets of making money and soon I was on my way to Barry, South

Wales, to join No 1 Boat Supply Depot. This was quite a nice camp and I settled in well. It was very close to the Severn Estuary but where we were it was open sea where porpoises swam regularly. After I had been there some while and made new friends, we used to walk regularly along the coastline and gaze out to sea. On one never to be forgotten balmy summer moonlit night, we even went swimming. I was quite a good swimmer and was about 50-60 yards from the shore when something brushed my leg. I have no idea what it was but it terrified me and I broke all speed records getting back to the shore again.

Again I worked in the office and again, after some months, I must have done my work quite well because I was informed by the O.C. that as they had a vacancy for the rank of Corporal I had been selected for promotion. In fact the O.C. told me that if I was willing to sign on as a regular soldier, he would see to it that I was promoted immediately or after a suitable but short waiting period, to Sergeant and then, after that, who knows? But although I gave the idea some passing thought, I was not prepared to do that.

I can think of only two other incidents in this period; the first was that I gave up gambling! I was never really a gambler – just 2/6d here and there on the Derby or Grand National. But one time I came home on leave and went to see my older brother, Bill. He was sitting at a table in his flat looking quite pleased with himself and I asked him why. He looked at me, pointed to a pile of papers on the side and asked me to pick out any three copies and then turn to the dog racing section. They were copies of the *Sporting Life* and so I picked one near to the top, one from the middle, and one near to the bottom. Bill then asked me various questions about the going conditions, the weights of the dogs, and others which I cannot now recall; the *Sporting Life* gave all such information to prospective punters. Bill immediately proceeded to pick out a number of winning dogs and proudly announced to me his 'new' system for selecting winners.

Foolishly, I was greatly impressed and as I had ten days' leave and only £14 to spend, I met up with my pal, Sid Morris, who was also on leave at the same time and explained the system to him. He, too, was impressed and as we could both do with a little more money in order to enjoy our leave to the full, we decided there and then to go over to New Cross Dog Racing Stadium as there was a programme that night.

You will not be surprised to know, dear reader, that we came away from the stadium with hardly enough money to pay our bus fares home. Bill's new system didn't work and had let us down badly. So we were in a difficult situation with seven days' leave yet to enjoy but without any money. I do not know where Sid got more money, maybe from his father but in my case it was my dear old Mum who yet again came to my rescue. I decided then that I would never gamble again – I had learned my lesson. I didn't keep completely strictly to that vow but it was only on the odd occasion and never more than 2/6d, maybe 5/-, or so on the Derby, just for fun.

Another very pleasant experience I recall at this time occurred one Saturday evening when the lads in our hut and I decided to go into town to enjoy a couple of beers. We went to Cadoxton, a sort of suburb of Barry, a very picturesque place with lots of small valleys and hills. Nestling in one of these valleys was a pub which was called either the Three Bells or maybe The Bell.

Anyway we walked into this pub. It was absolutely full but we noticed that people were sitting there not smiling too much and not talking too much either. Well, we bought our beer and one of our lads spotted a piano. So he said 'Come on Mitch, give us a tune and let's liven this place up.' At first I was reluctant but you know what lads are like and I knew I wouldn't get any peace unless I played a few tunes. So I started to play some of the melodies that I used to play in the Ivy House back home.

After a couple of minutes a lady with a fine voice began to sing, then others joined her and soon everybody in that packed pub was singing his or her heart out and it seemed as though the very walls of the pub were reverberating. But this was not ordinary pub singing – I was in Wales, where they know how to sing and I have to say that although I have been in many pubs and heard many sing-songs, this was indeed something else. I have never heard such beautiful singing in a pub in my life. So, much encouraged now, I played and I played and people (in those days I had the energy to play non-stop for three hours or more) were buying me so much beer that it was impossible to drink it all; so I gave it to the lads who soon polished it off. The end of that very pleasant evening came and then someone took the beret from my head, passed it round the pub, and brought it back to me filled with money! So back to camp we went, rather inebriated and in my case a lot richer now than I was beforehand. What a great evening; that was a lovely experience and I shall never forget it.

And so 1947 went by and we were now in 1948. Another very important milestone occurred in my life in this period and I'll tell the story from the beginning. On this occasion, my brother Lenny, our pal Sid

Morris and I, the Three Musketeers as we were known, all arranged to be home on leave at the same time, around the middle of the year. As usual, we enjoyed many a glass of beer together; pubs were so different then for they were not just a place where neighbours met to chew the fat, they really were places of entertainment as well. Nearly every pub had its pianist and often you would find people willing to give a song. Some of them were mighty good too!

I recall it was the time that the great, never to be forgotten Al Jolson, one of the finest entertainers the theatre world has ever seen, was making a comeback after the great success of his film *The Jolson Story* and every pub had one or more customers who thought they were the bee's knees in imitating him; I knew every song he ever sang, which was just as well. Then there was the White Swan at Blackwall Stairs which, at that time, was frequented by a group of gay chaps. The excellent singing and comedy that went on there was really first class entertainment – and all for the price of a pint of beer which then was 1/- or 5p in today's money.

As a matter of fact, when one thinks about it, there were a whole variety of pubs around and each one had its own unique atmosphere and varying degrees or qualities of entertainment. But there we were on this particular Sunday, holding up the bar in the Ivy House and enjoying ourselves joking, laughing and drinking!

Now let me change the scene to a town in Northern England where a show called 'Laughing Room Only' had just finished their week there. This was a revue – one of many shows that were put together by impresarios or agents and appeared in provincial theatres all over the country. In the 1940s these theatres were still going strong – television had not yet hit them. The group in the show were told where the next venue was – the Queen's Theatre, Poplar. Travel arrangements were made by the management but generally it was left then for each member of the group to make their own way to the next venue.

Four of the girls who danced in the show decided to travel on the train together but when they compared notes they saw that they had all been given the same address for digs in Poplar, i.e. Mrs Boater at No 9 Prestage Street, which they thought was a little odd. After they arrived at Kings Cross Station, two of the girls decided they would like a cup of coffee; the other two said they would prefer not to stop and so they went on their way via tube and bus to Poplar.

Now in Prestage Street there were only two people registered at the Queen's providing digs for theatricals, i.e. my mother at No 2, and a Mrs

Boater who lived at No 9. And so the two girls who didn't stop for coffee arrived at Mrs Boater's first. The two who did stop for coffee arrived a little later. Mrs Boater, who had only room for two girls, was very puzzled and was wondering what to do.

Meanwhile, my mother was waiting patiently for her two girls to arrive and when someone told her that they had seen four girls enter Mrs Boater's house, she wasted no time but immediately marched down to No 9 to find out where her girls were! So a general discussion was held and it was agreed that the girls who had arrived at Mrs Boater's first would stay there and the two who had arrived later would go back to No 2 with my mother.

Lenny, Sid and I were in the Ivy House, unaware of the drama that was going on but then someone opened the door and said 'Hey Dave, two right smashers have gone into your house with your Mum!' Well, beer was momentarily forgotten – girls were much more important! So we piled out of the bar, into our house which was next door but one, and the three of us nearly fell down the stairs in a pile to the basement parlour where everybody was sitting. And there in a chair in the corner was Lynne. Her friend, whose name was Pat, was sitting at the table. I looked at Lynne, she looked at me and it was obvious that there was immediate eye attraction. Unfortunately, my mother had placed a vase of flowers in the middle of the table which blocked my view of Lynne somewhat, so I had to keep peeping round the flowers to see her.

I didn't know it then, but I had just met my future wife, my soulmate, my best friend and mother of my children! We enjoyed each other's company for the rest of that week but at the end of the week, Lynne had to go on to Bath which was the next venue for her show and I had to return to Barry and to camp. Lynne told me that when she arrived at Bath she sat down and cried, and when I arrived at Barry I roamed around the camp like lovesick young men do. Incidentally, when we met, Lynne had only recently turned eighteen and I was not quite twenty. But I think it is remarkable that it was just because of a cup of coffee that we met for if Lynne and her friend hadn't stopped and the four girls had arrived at Mrs Boater's house together then there is at least a 50% chance that I would never have met her. I wrote a short story about this event and one can maybe understand why I call it JUST A CUP OF COFFEE!

Of course, we continued to write to each other and then later on Lynne had a free week when there was no theatrical booking. So I tried to wangle a week's leave; I probably told my Captain some sob story – and he allowed it. Therefore, after speaking to my mother, we invited Lynne and her friend Pat to stay with us for that week and so we enjoyed a further week together.

About three to four months later, during which time we continued to write to each other, I was fortunate enough to win a one month course in Architecture before demobilisation; I think most soldiers had such an opportunity before returning to 'civvy street'. This was at the Welbeck Army College, a stately home owned by the Duke of Devonshire I believe, which was not very far away from Nottingham. So Lynne, whose show had come to the end of their bookings, and I were able to continue our relationship and this time I would have the opportunity to meet her mother and relatives. I thoroughly enjoyed my course at Welbeck College and even more I enjoyed being with Lynne once again.

By the end of that month I think we both knew that something quite serious was developing between us. But as my National Service was almost completed, I had to return to Barry to go through the motions of being discharged; then I went to the Demobilisation Centre and there I faced the task of choosing a suit and other items of clothing which the Army equipped you with when returning you to 'civvy street' – it's quite a performance really and the clothing they gave you was cheap and awful.

Meanwhile, Lynne had signed up for a new show, a pantomime in fact, at Leeds. It was 'Babes in the Woods' and starred Jewel & Warris, a well-known TV comedy act at that time. So she would be tied up from the end of November until the following February.

I eventually arrived home back in Poplar – at last a free man! But I moped around and didn't quite know what to do with myself during the long leave which they granted to those who had completed their National Service. In the Army I was always preoccupied with something or other and kept busy. I have to remark that I did enjoy my Army service; I think it did make a man out of me and encouraged me to think about things more seriously; it also taught me how to accept responsibility. I believe every chap should do a period of service like that – it straightens out a lot of things in a young man's mind and makes one take pride in oneself.

At around this time, I had a serious chat with my father. I told him I had enjoyed the course I had attended at Welbeck Army College and that I really would like to study to be an architect. But of course, I continued, I could not do that without the support of my family. He looked at me quizzically, laughed, told me not to be silly and that I should go out and get a proper job!

So there ended my ambition to be an architect. It is to be regretted that my father did not appear to have a great deal of confidence in me and I will quote another instance of this. He experienced a very bad accident in the docks; a gantry fell over and struck him. He was almost at death's door and I was granted compassionate leave to come home and see him. It was quite a shock because he was lying there in an oxygen tent, his face the colour of chalk; he really looked as if he was on his last legs. But he recovered in time, I am very pleased to say.

Then followed his claim for compensation. I had nothing to do with this but I believe his union, the TGW, fought his case for him. Anyway, the result of it all was that my father was awarded an amount of almost £5,000. Now for a working man in the 1940s who was by then probably earning around £6 per week or less, that was a huge sum and he was pressed by all to take advice as to what to do with this money.

He took the advice of his bank, which was that he should put a large chunk of the money into War Bonds paying, I believe, 2.5% per annum – a terrible piece of advice if ever I heard one and he lost heavily on this investment as the value of the bonds fell. When I was demobbed, I spoke to my father about buying a small confectionery and tobacconist shop that was for sale somewhere by North Street, on the main East India Docks Road by the traffic lights and close to a bus stop. I enthusiastically told him that within five years I would make the one shop into ten shops and that I would work my fingers to the bone to make a success of such a business.

But my father, who had already turned down my appeal to back me in studying architecture, now rejected me once again by refusing to even consider my idea. So what happened to his money? Well, some of it went on a disastrous decision to buy a car. He couldn't drive anyway and he was persuaded to hire it out, not realising that he needed a licence and insurance cover for such an activity. Inevitably, somebody who hired it had a crash. I think people were injured but I am unsure how it all ended up; I think he had a very lucky escape which could have cost him dearly. Then he was 'conned' by the son of the publican who ran the White Hart on the corner of Poplar High Street and Robin Hood Lane; fortunately in this instance the father repaid my father but in the act of so doing he described my poor old Dad as 'A VERY STUPID MAN'.

But he was only following the urgings of others. What a pity he didn't follow my urgings because instead of frittering the money away here and there, and quite a lot was also lost at West Ham Dog Stadium incidentally, I certainly would have made a success of the shop idea.

Instead I went on to make a great deal of money for other people and myself. When he died he left virtually nothing.

I do not blame my father; he was not used to having money and his ideas of how people like us should behave in this world were totally old fashioned. He thought responsibility was something to be completely avoided by working class people and that we should let the bosses do all that sort of thing, get on with any mundane job, and do not have ideas beyond our class; it would never have occurred to him that if he, or any of us, really tried maybe they too could be bosses!

I recall that when I gained my first directorship he tutt-tutted away at thirteen to the dozen, shaking his head all the time. And when we bought our first house for £3,250 – well, you would have thought the Heavens had fallen in! I was now earning £2,000 per annum and need not have done so but I told him that I had decided to take out a mortgage, just in case something happened in respect of my work position. My God! You would have thought I had committed some terrible act of irresponsibility. What a great pity it was that my father did not have more faith in me than he did; but I think that is perhaps a common fault among fathers and in many families one finds that they have more faith in others than in their own. I think my father thought I was too young to be regarded seriously. How glad I am that others didn't see me in that light also! Poor old Dad!

I missed Lynne a lot and tried to phone her at Leeds almost every evening. Then came Christmas 1948 and I wanted so desperately to spend it with her for I missed her greatly. For some reason I never did, however in our exchange of letters I made it clear to her that I wanted to be married to her and so I could not wait until February when her panto would end. She had agreed to come down to London to me rather than go home to Nottingham. Well, you see – true love conquers all in the end and this was IT with a great big capital 'I'!

The day when we would be together again duly arrived. I had ditched the awful suit they had given me when I was demobbed and visited a tailor in Stepney, who made a new suit for me in a lovely fawn, bird's eye material. I then also bought myself a raincoat with football buttons which I thought looked very sporting, very manly, rather dapper and smart. So I was of the opinion that I looked okay to meet my sweetheart at the station. I arrived early; it was a Sunday morning and I waited impatiently for Lynne's train to arrive. Eventually it did so and there she was, all bright and smiling and beautiful of course. We then made our way to the underground station and on to Prestage Street where my mother was waiting to greet us.

So we were together from early 1949 and the rest of that year just simply flew by. In that year we actually got officially engaged. We had a party at No 2 to celebrate, and Lynne's mother came down from Nottingham to join in. She was not too happy that Lynne had come to London instead of back to her at home; I think also she didn't really want Lynne to give up her career as a dancer. I am not even sure that Lynne knew herself in those early days what she truly wanted to do. But she eventually succumbed to my powers of persuasion, gave up the stage and stayed with me. In time, Lynne's mother came to realise that we loved each other very much and that our futures together had been irrevocably carved out. Nothing, but nothing, was going to stop us!

9

BACK IN CIVVY STREET AGAIN

Meanwhile, I had contacted the Soldiers, Sailors and Air Force Association, as had been recommended when I was discharged and they helped me to find a job. But what kind of job could I do? I had no skills and no qualifications whatsoever. However, I told the people there that I would like to try my hand at selling. So they fixed me up with a salesman's job selling stationery to offices and businesses in the locality. It was a commission-only kind of appointment in a small firm started up by two young ex-servicemen; I didn't mind this for I really did think I could sell! But when, at the end of my first week, I was told that I had earned just 2/6d it shook me to the roots. I was too inexperienced to realise that one needed time to develop good relations with customers and potential customers. But I was very disappointed with myself and thought that maybe I wasn't cut out to be a salesman after all! Reluctantly, and with a lot of humility, I told my 'bosses' that I thought it would be better if I tried my hand at something else because I somehow had to earn some money.

Safety first now was at the front of my mind and so, although the wages were poor, just £5 per week, I accepted a job as a Clerk in the Wages Office of St Luke's Printing Works, Old Street – this was part of the Bank of England and it was where all the 10/-, £1, £5, and £10 notes used to be printed. I always thought that notes were printed at the Mint, as many people did; but that is not so. The Mint produce only coins and it is the Bank of England that produces the notes.

The large office was ruled with a rod of iron by a man named Mr Guyatt; he was probably the most religious man I ever knew in my life. He was a member of the Pilgrims' Brethren, but he was a cruel, merciless and joyless man; I even witnessed him sacking someone just before Christmas Eve, sending the person home in tears. He had no sympathy and no mercy and yet he spoke of God, of forgiveness and so on – a true hypocrite of the type one often finds in religious circles.

But the sports facilities provided by the organisation for its employees were truly excellent and I played in their cricket, football and table tennis teams, along with my pal at work, Ken Shore. This side of working for the Bank of England was splendid. I enjoyed it very much and I took the fullest advantage of these sporting facilities for as long as I was there.

Lynne had bravely sought work and was given a position in a chemist shop in Roman Road, Bow. I say 'bravely' because it was quite a change for her after being on the stage and she faced up to it very well. But she had only been there a short time when an unfortunate accident occurred; she was asked to carry out the task of removing jars of malt on show in the window. So she began by taking the nearest jars first – it was a big mistake – with the result that the heavy jars counter-balanced and there was an almighty crash. Knowing her, she must have been mortified! Another thing she disliked was that she was sent to the bank every day with the takings. Sometimes these were quite substantial and she was sent alone, without any form of protection and it made her somewhat nervous. She was there for a couple of weeks or so and then decided she just couldn't go back there. So I phoned the firm on her behalf and made some kind of excuse to the company.

After that she broadened her horizons and obtained a position with Charles Butlers of Bond Street. They sold upmarket dresses etc., and a lot of celebrities shopped there. However, Charles Butler had a rule that none of their girls could stay on if they married. And so, although she liked this job very much, unfortunately she had to leave when we were married in May 1950. After that though, she did succeed in getting an office job with Initial Towel Co. (now absorbed by Rentokil I think). It was not very far from my place of work and so we were able to meet up for lunch – mostly it was poached egg on toast as I recall. But after a while we both realised it would be better for us to take advantage of our respective canteens where we could buy a subsidised lunch for just a shilling (if my memory serves me correctly) and so we stopped that habit after a while. Pity, for I enjoyed our lunchtime meetings very much indeed and looked forward to them.

I should explain at this point that meanwhile our house at No 2 Prestage Street had been condemned and we had been ordered to leave as soon as possible, as the structure of the house was not safe. After all the bombing in that area during the Blitz it was no wonder; for it had been shaken to its very foundations a number of times by the bombing during the war! My mother was offered various other possibilities but she liked none of them. However, time was pressing and when the offer of a pre-fabricated home was offered to her, and with all of us trying to persuade her, she chose that. It was situated on the Isle of Dogs in a street called Stewart Street. After the primitive conditions of Prestage Street this was Heaven. We had a bathroom, an inside loo and even a small refrigerator. My mother had never experienced any of these luxuries and I think she was very impressed. We moved into the pre-fab in the autumn of '49.

As I said, Lynne and I married in May 1950. My brother Lenny was all for it and urged us on but my childhood pal, Sid Morris, had some reservations. We had been the Three Musketeers for quite some time and Sid didn't want to break that up. Sid was not only a true Cockney but a Cockney comedian from the tips of his toes to the roots of his hair and a real East Ender. Sid made me laugh until the tears rolled down my face – especially when he mocked me for being 'posh'. He was very crude and rude and swore like a trooper. I tried very hard to refine him. I took him to the Tower of London to try to introduce some sense of history in him. As we waited in the queue, he tried to mimic what we might call a 'posh' or cut glass accent; it was really hilarious because he forgot himself now and then and lapsed back into his Cockney accent. I was doubled up with laughter for there was nothing funnier than poor old Sid trying to talk and act 'posh' and I wonder what those people in the queue thought of his performance?

I also took him to the Strand Corner House for lunch one day, which for us working class people at that time was quite an upmarket place to go to – it certainly was when compared to Vacari's Cafe on East India Dock Road. I tried to correct his table manners but he would provoke me in a humorous way by asking, for example, if it was alright if he mopped up his gravy with some bread. 'Absolutely not,' I said, 'not here.' He then pointed to a man sitting near to us and ... he was mopping up his gravy with bread! So what could I say or do with Sid?

In the end I gave up trying to change him. Sid was Sid and would remain so until the day he died which, sadly, was at a very young age. He was a big fellow and his heart gave out. I think Sid was only in his forties when he collapsed in a doctor's surgery but apparently nothing could be done for him as he was dead before he hit the floor.

Perhaps the reader will forgive me for telling one more story about Sid, for he was a true character of the East End. It was in the 1960s, so I am jumping ahead a little, and we had moved to our first house in Surrey a year earlier. Some time after that, we invited Sid to come and spend a Sunday with us. Now in my garden there was a mystery tree which grew there and we were not quite sure what it was. That year it had just one fruit on it. So I carefully nursed that one fruit and looked after it like a little baby. I asked everybody I knew what it was – but nobody could definitely say. The fruit itself looked delicious and I looked forward very much to eating it, which would be quite soon now. Well I proudly showed Sid my garden when he came to visit and I told him the story and how that one fruit had grown. He looked at it and with a flash of the hand he had picked it and popped it into his mouth! 'I fink it's a plum, Dave,' he said with a big grin all over his face! I was of course furious with him but you could not be angry with Sid for long because he would soon have me in stitches at the expressions he came out with. That evening we played cards – and Sid fleeced us! I'll always remember Sid and even now, years and years later, I think of him and start chuckling.

Anyway, despite Sid, Lynne and I did marry on 27th May 1950 at All Saints Church, Poplar. I must tell you that we had no money and, with our very low wages, precious little chance to save. Lynne came from a broken family and so we could not expect any help from her mother. But my mother, bless her heart, was determined that we were going to have a fabulous wedding in the family and so she came to our rescue. She organised the Co-Op to do the catering and although it was difficult managing in a pre-fab, the problem was solved by arranging two sittings.

Considering everything, it was a very good Wedding Breakfast and when everybody had finished eating the tables were taken down, the chairs placed back against the walls and then the fun could begin; and what a party it was! I think this was the last, and the very best, Cockney party I ever attended. We had a three piece band who started to play and very soon everyone was dancing and having a good time, for of course those were the days when if you held a party there were always guests who would like to sing a song or two. We had some very good singers and I recall one girl who sang 'Beware My Foolish Heart' – this girl could easily have sung professionally and the whole of the packed room was deadly quiet when she sang and applauded her loudly when she finished.

Whenever I hear that song I think of that magic day. The party went on all night; but as usual, we ran out of beer and so emergency supplies had to be obtained. I cannot recall now how that was managed but somehow it was!

As dawn arrived, Lynne and I had to prepare to leave, as it was necessary for us to get to Victoria Coach Station quite early to board our coach, which would take us to Looe in Cornwall for our honeymoon. But the party went on and on and my mother cooked eggs and bacon for all those who stayed. Danny, my brother-in-law, ran us to Victoria in his taxi; we boarded the coach and soon we were on our way. Back home we were told that after breakfast the party started up all over again!

The countryside looked very nice indeed as we travelled through the counties, never realising that one day, far into the future we would be living in Devon just off one of the actual roads we passed through. After what seemed a long, long, journey we eventually arrived at Looe. By asking locals, we managed to find the small chalet where we were to spend the following week; our landlady looked us up and down for I believe she thought we were too young to be married! Well, we did look like a couple of kids! In those days Looe was an unspoilt fishing village and in the evening we walked around exploring our new surroundings. I counted up our resources – we had £3 plus a little small change to last us the week!

No matter, our spirits were very high and we were deeply in love; we would manage somehow and so we did! We found a small family restaurant where the prices were very reasonable; I believe that fresh fish, caught there in Looe that very morning they said, and I believe them, and chips were either 1/- or maybe 1/6d. That little place was a Godsend to us with our very limited assets. Fortunately, we enjoyed excellent weather during the whole week and walked everywhere and in all directions. We especially enjoyed the cliff-top walks and we were amazed when we found new and beautiful views of small unreachable beaches and coves at each bend; from up high they looked very attractive places indeed.

Once we negotiated a bend on a cliff walk and there, far below us, was a small group of houses and bungalows – this was Talland. As we were very hungry and thirsty, we forgot about our meagre resources and decided to enjoy one of those proverbial Cornish cream teas. If my memory serves me correctly the bill was 2/6d (or 12.5p in decimalised currency) for us both! I wonder what Talland looks like these days and even more I wonder what a Cornish cream tea for two would cost today!

Another experience we had which is worth recalling was when we hired a little rowing boat for a very small amount. We rowed around, always making sure we did not go too far away from shore, when we saw a most peculiar black, grey hump protruding from the water about thirty yards from us. It was not moving but somehow it seemed to be alive; we looked at it for a couple of minutes, then looked at each other, and then broke all rowing speed records out of there PDQ and back to the beach! We spoke afterwards many times about what it might have been and we have come to the conclusion that it was very probably a basking shark. We knew that there were sharks of various types around the Cornish coast, and indeed we had seen a very large type of shark hauled up on a rope in the fishing port. It looked to us like a monster and we were given to understand that this was a potential man-eater! But all information about it had been hushed up because the locals did not want any kind of bad publicity of that sort spreading around in case it upset the tourist trade. I wonder how my dear Lynne, who could not swim, had the courage to go out on this boat with me!

Well, sadly our honeymoon, which we were enjoying so much, came to an end and it was time to return to London. We could only afford one week and that passed all too quickly. Again we enjoyed the countryside very much indeed on our way through. I reflected on the past week; our £3 had just about lasted us through the seven days but when we arrived home I had a very pleasant surprise; a small bet on a horse I had placed before leaving one week previously had come up and I had won a couple of pounds or perhaps a little more. And so, as we had a further week to go before resuming work we decided to go up to Nottingham, Lynne's hometown, and spend some days there. It was very nice meeting more of Lynne's relatives and they made us very welcome.

At this time my dear old Irish Granny was in St Andrews Hospital at Bow, a grim place if ever I saw one; I knew it very well. Poor old Granny was quite ill. My mother spoke with the doctors there and they thought there was no specific illness – she was just suffering from old age. Anyway, after some time Granny gave up the fight for life and she passed away. After her burial my mother gave some thought to the situation and came up with the idea that, as her grandson, I was entitled to take up the tenancy of her flat in Prestage Buildings. And to give her credit she fought tooth and nail and with great success! So there Lynne and I were, not having been married long and already we had a flat! How very lucky we were! Mind you, we had precious little to put in it! But we were over the moon because the number of people on the Council housing lists was huge and as we had such meagre resources, there was no possibility whatsoever of our buying a house or getting other accommodation. It wasn't much – just three rooms and a scullery and of course the usual outside toilet, no proper means of heating, no bathroom and even gaslight in two of the rooms. But when we moved in we were as happy as two young people can possibly be – it was our blue heaven for sure. So that is how Lynne and I returned to Prestage Street once more.

Somewhat later, perhaps a month or so, Lynne's mother came down from Nottingham to visit and at one point I found her visibly upset. I asked her what was the matter and she just said she was worried about Lynne being down in London and I, switching very quickly into my sympathetic mode, very foolishly asked her if she would like to come down too. I said she could occupy our spare room and she jumped at the invitation immediately. Lynne was wary and subsequently I realised I had been daft; it was a silly mistake on my part – but it was the tears! What man can resist the tears of a woman? Anyway, she eventually came down bringing her bits and pieces of furniture with her, which was just as well for, as I have said, we didn't have very much at all! She managed to get a job in the office of a small firm in Poplar. We all tried to make the arrangement work but it proved very difficult. Naturally, we, as two young people, wanted to be together and do our own thing but she seemed always to be there and I think that both Lynne and I grew to resent her a little which did not make for a very good atmosphere. In those circumstances then inevitably, there was friction from time to time.

It was in this period that I developed an interest in boxing – watching, not taking part, let me hasten to add. I preferred to maintain my 'cowardly' stance and watch others thump each other around the ring! On some occasions I would leave my place of work and instead of heading for home I would go to the old Mile End Arena – a historical boxing venue in the East End. It was an open air place and the price of a ticket was cheap. I think I used to pay 5/- (25p) for almost a ringside seat and quite often sat near to people like Jack Solomons, who was one of the big boxing promoters at that time; he was always on the lookout for new talent. I saw a number of up and coming new boys there and once again I have to emphasise the very special atmosphere that such places had. I did not go every week, of course – just now and then. Later on I used to go to the Albert Hall, Haringay, Earls Court, Poplar Baths, to see specific boxers.

10

THE EARLY 1950s –
MY NEW JOB IN BUSINESS

And so the year of 1950 rolled on and drew to a close and I began to think about the future. Working at the Bank of England Printing Works was very enjoyable from the sporting angle – but otherwise, to me, somewhat boring. I reasoned that I wouldn't want to condemn myself to being just a clerk all my life. I still had confidence in myself and I considered that despite my shortcomings in having no scholastic achievements or skills whatsoever, the cards were very much stacked against me. The chances of success were not very high. However, I nevertheless had the energy, the ability, the enthusiasm, the determination and the ambition to succeed. What I lacked in some respects, therefore, I realised I had to make up in others.

I was not a fool and so I knew that a tough fight lay ahead of me; but only I, myself, could do anything about it. All sorts of ideas came into my head; I even thought about joining the police in what was then Southern Rhodesia but had to forget about that – I just wasn't tall enough to begin with. But then, after seeing an advert in the *Evening News* or some evening paper I applied for a job as Assistant to Confectionery Sales Manager in the City – in Old Broad Street to be exact. I was granted an interview by Mr Andrews, the Sales Manager, and I got on rather well with him. To my surprise he offered me the position and I joined the company, Hale Hamilton & Co. Ltd, a firm of general importers, towards the end of 1950 at the princely sum of £6 per week. Well, I thought, we will not get very fat on that! On the other hand, it was 6d per week more than I was earning with the Bank and 6d was better than nothing! The main point was that I had broken into the business world and hopefully it was a step in the right direction; it was mainly a clerical position, with some sales possibilities and being a general dogsbody, i.e. wrapping up samples, running about here and there etc.

It was about this period that I decided – damn the expense! – I am going to take my lovely wife Lynne to somewhere very nice. I still felt a little uncomfortable somehow going to the West End – that was something instilled in me but for the life of me I had no idea why. I still didn't have a lot of money, but never mind – I didn't care. I wanted to show Lynne that we could enjoy nice places – and hopefully in the future plenty of them! So I proudly took her to the Trocadero in Leicester Square. It was quite a different place then to the brash kind of place it was the last time I went there. In those days it was a very upmarket restaurant and not at all cheap.

Never mind, I was determined we would enjoy places like this so we had better get used to them. So up to the West End we went and as we entered the Trocadero we walked down those deeply carpeted stairs to the main restaurant. The orchestra was playing soft music and it was a beautiful experience just walking in, never mind eating there. I was very proud that Lynne was by my side.

We were then shown to our table by the Maître D' who gave us each a very ornate Menu. I think it was all in French but we were able to decipher what was what (I believe there were English translations) and when the waiter came to take our order we thought we knew exactly what to ask for. He then asked us if we would like wine; well, I knew nothing about wine in those days and so I ordered a light ale and Lynne had a soft drink – that shows how ignorant we were or at least I was! But it was a very pleasant experience; we were a little out of our depth but it was a special occasion. In times to come we would go to places of that type, and even better, quite frequently – but by then we knew what we were doing! The Trocadero of those days cannot be compared with the Trocadero that exists today. But although I haven't been there since the late 1970s I can't imagine it is any better and certainly not as good as it once was.

When I joined Hale Hamilton I became very conscious of the fact that I would have to try my best to polish my accent and develop a better telephone manner. In those days such things mattered – today it seems not to matter at all. Following my two years in Windsor, which was an important learning period, I had tended to speak somewhat better than I did as a youngster but I never quite lost my Cockney accent. So I tried very hard and I think I succeeded to a reasonable degree (although you would always know that I was a Cockney). I didn't want to attempt a cut glass accent for that would sound quite ridiculous coming from me.

So I think I ended up as something in between! Best of all, I had the chance to prove myself and I came to the conclusion that the way to do this was to be the first one there in the morning and the last one to leave at night. I was so conscientious that I even took work home with me and Lynne helped me to enter orders etc., in the evenings. I couldn't afford a briefcase so I had to wrap my 'homework' in brown paper and tie it with string. In this new position I was given the opportunity at last to prove my ability to sell and I was very pleased with myself when I discovered that I could!

For example, there was an instance where the company was carrying a large stock, over 30 tons I seem to recall, of chocolate bars imported from Finland. For some reason the market had dried up on this product and our agents were just not selling. Fearful that the merchandise might deteriorate, and bearing in mind that confectionery was still on ration then, Mr Andrews applied to the Ministry of Food for permission to sell our stocks off-coupon, i.e. unrationed. The Ministry agreed but only allowed the sale to industrial canteens or to manufacturers for further processing. Without boasting, I was successful in selling quite a lot of these bars to Standard Telephones, a huge company at that time, for sale in their canteen. And then I sold to Daintee Confectionery Co. Ltd of Blackpool, for use as chocolate couverture used in manufacturing. Unfortunately, the goods were stored in a wharf in Lower Thames Street belonging to our Forwarding Agents, a firm called Baker Britt & Co. This was a very narrow thoroughfare. Daintee sent down these huge lorries to collect the goods, and they were unable to negotiate an entrance to the wharf. It was a problem and somehow it was resolved but I have completely forgotten how.

It was in this period that I was sent one day to the offices of Alex Kraus in Kingsway to collect some samples. It was the first time I had met Alex and I liked him immediately because he invited me in, asked me if I would like coffee, treated me with respect and really made me feel like a somebody instead of a nobody. Alex sent me a cut glass ash tray that Christmas which I appreciated very much indeed and I recall going home that evening clutching my gift from Alex to my chest; I still have that ash tray to this day and every time I look at it, I think of Alex. He was to become a very good friend in the years to come and I really appreciated his friendship.

Alex was a Slovakian Jew who taught religious studies, which eventually brought him to Prague to teach. But when the situation became ugly in 1938 and the Germans occupied the Sudetenland, Alex wisely saw that it was better to leave the country while he could – as did many Jewish people. He did not come to England immediately but ended up in the UK as part of the Free Czechoslovak Army, together with his friend Ladislav Sos who was also Jewish. Alex and Ladislav, who later also became a good friend of mine, were very good companions. If they had just 2/6d between them, it was always shared 50-50. If they had just one apple – it was half each. That was the strength of their relationship with each other.

Alex decided to stay on in England after the war and built up a good business in a variety of merchandise which included confectionery products. Some time after the end of the war, he learned that all the members of his family whom he had left behind in Slovakia had perished in the gas chambers at Auschwitz. From that moment Alex made a resolution that under no circumstances whatsoever would he ever visit or make any business transactions with Germany – or German companies. He kept to his word – and he never did!

Ladislav, however, returned to Slovakia where he became a pharmacist. However, being a part of the Free Czechoslovak Armed Forces, his life was not too good after the Communist coup in 1949. I eventually visited him at his home and met all his family.

After the Communist coup in Czechoslovakia, Alex was successful in applying for and obtaining the first UK agency for Czechoslovak confectionery products. He held this for several years before my future boss, Harold Frost, succeeded him. Alex eventually retired from business and went to live in Switzerland. I kept in touch with him throughout and we had some very interesting exchanges – especially in connection with Dr Tiso, a religious man who, after Hitler granted autonomy to Slovakia in 1938-9, became President of that new country.

During the 1980s I befriended a Dr Jan Guncaga, a Slovak medical doctor who had escaped from Czechoslovakia in the early 1950s. His country of residence was Switzerland, where he was professor at Zürich University, specialising in osteoarthritis. He also had a magnificent villa in Spain, maybe a couple of hundred yards or so down in the valley from where we lived. I played tennis often with Jan for he had a very nice, full size court. Afterwards we would sit down to rest and have a chat about this and that.

I had read something in the newspapers about the Slovaks commemorating Dr Tiso's birth or death – I cannot recall which. So when writing to Alex I queried this with him, for as far as I knew Dr Tiso was hung at the end of the war for collaboration with the Germans and was, therefore, a war criminal. Alex confirmed all the bad things I had read and heard about Tiso and then added something that I didn't know which was that Tiso actually paid the Germans to accept Slovakian Jews for slaughter in the gas chambers at Auschwitz. But when I spoke with Jan Guncaga I heard a quite different account about him. Jan evidently was of the view that Dr Tiso was a grossly misunderstood man and that against the threat of invasion by Hitler he had no choice but to dance to their tune.

I listened to both sides of the argument at length but found it impossible to decide who was right and who was wrong! Was Dr Tiso a good man doing the best he could under almost impossible conditions, as Jan said? Or was he a war criminal who willingly cooperated with the Germans and who sent a great many Jews, including Alex's relatives, to the gas chambers? I am afraid I still do not know for sure where the truth lies.

It is said that Alex lost the Czechoslovak confectionery agency because he was Jewish. In that period the Moscow line on those of the Jewish faith was very strongly anti. And so I thought it strange that they had disposed of one Jewish person and then given the agency to another Jewish man – Harold Frost! But there was some skullduggery; for Harold Frost, I knew, had bribed a certain someone to influence the people in Prague in his favour but that certain someone, with his strong Communist principles, did not hesitate to take his cut. I know because I was the chap who used to take the regular periodical envelopes to him!

As I have written already, I kept in close touch with Alex for years and years, and we both enjoyed our letter exchanges but one day I received a very sad letter from his Hungarian wife which advised me that Alex had passed away. Apparently, he had to fly to London on urgent business. He ordered a taxi, his wife attached a carnation to his lapel and when the taxi arrived, he went downstairs, walked towards the taxi and collapsed on the pavement before he could reach it. His wife's letter was extremely pitiful and she wrote about the tragedy of not knowing that when she kissed him Goodbye that was the 'last kiss'!

She asked me to continue to write to her, which I was happy to do but after two letters I had received no reply and so I made enquiries. I found that she had suffered a nervous breakdown following the death of Alex, which evidently hit her very hard. She was now in a mental hospital somewhere in Switzerland. Unfortunately I was unable to find out which hospital it was and so I do not know what finally happened to her. For the sake of Alex, I would certainly have maintained contact with her as she requested, if only it had been possible.

But to return to my narrative, it was now 1951. Lynne and I were quite adventurous when we were young. We wanted to go abroad to see what other folk were like and so we decided to go to gay Paris for a week. We didn't have a lot of money but one thing I insisted upon was that come what may, we would stay in a nice hotel – even if we couldn't really afford it. So all the plans were made for this adventure and then Frank Law, one of the directors, came to me and asked if I could postpone my holiday for a week or so as Mr Andrews was either indisposed or away on business (I can't recall now which). I explained that this would be very difficult as everything had been arranged but he offered to get everything changed for me and even phoned the hotel we were going to stay at. However, despite the postponement the day did come when we set forth to Paris.

We travelled by train from Victoria Station to Newhaven, where we boarded the boat for Dieppe. Once on board we made a beeline for the restaurant; yes, it was a bit expensive for us but I was determined to do things in style. So we sat at our table and the ship began to leave port; soon after, we were out at sea, which was decidedly choppy. As we went further out it got worse and worse. But we sat at our table and enjoyed our meal as if we did that sort of thing in fierce storms every day of the week. We tried to stretch out our lunch so that we could sit there in the restaurant a little longer, but eventually we were obliged to leave. When we did so, we found people being ill all over the place; not a nice experience after you have just enjoyed lunch but it did not seem to affect us at all. Soon we arrived at Dieppe, then on to a train, and we were on our way to Paris.

We arrived at the station, Gare du Nord I believe it was, walked out to the front and asked a taxi driver if he knew Hotel Madeleine de la Tronchet. 'Oui,' he said with a smile and opened the rear door for us. We travelled for about 10 minutes or so but later on we realised that in fact our hotel was just a short distance from the station and we could easily have walked it! On the short journey I practised in my mind 'Parlez vous anglais?' I repeated it over and over again in order to get word perfect. We arrived at the hotel but as they had a restaurant in the lower part, we had to walk up some stairs to Reception. I was still practising whilst walking up and as we approached the Reception Desk I said, 'Parlez vous francais?'! They looked at me as if I was crazy and replied 'Mais oui, Monsieur'! Of course I realised my mistake and covered my embarrassment by just laughing at myself with them.

We were shown to our very nice room which had a curtained bathroom attached. By now evening was rapidly approaching and so we decided to go out to get something to eat. Having enjoyed a good lunch we were not ravenous, so when we saw a small café we entered and I tried my best to ask for two ham sandwiches. I didn't use the word 'sandwich' because I thought that was only an English word. I tried all kinds of ways to make the chap there understand but I couldn't. So in desperation I said very slowly (why is it we think foreigners will understand us if we speak slowly?), 'Ha-a-m Sa-a-ndwich?' 'Ah,' the man said, 'sandwich jambon, oui Monsieur.' At last! So then he brought us not two ham sandwiches as we know them but two delicious baguettes with ham and salad which we enjoyed very much indeed.

I had booked to have breakfast served at the hotel, so that was covered and it was brought to our room each morning. We were conscious of the fact that our funds were very limited and so, as a help to our meagre financial resources and as we had one bread roll and one croissant each, we both decided to save one of these for our lunch – this enabled us to eat decently in the evenings.

So each morning, we set forth to explore Paris. I assure you, dear reader, that no two people could ever have walked further and explored more of Paris than we did. Lynne even wore out one pair of shoes in the process. We planned it very well, going from East to West and from North to South, taking the backstreets rather than the main thoroughfares but making sure we included all the sights such as the Eiffel Tower, Montmartre, the Moulin Rouge, the Tomb of Napoleon, the Bastille, Notre Dame, Champs Elysées.

On the Arc de Triomphe, we found an old Brownie camera that someone had evidently left behind; we waited around for a while but nobody came back to claim it, and so we had no alternative but to keep it because we were a bit suspicious that if we had given it to a policemen he would have kept it for himself! Now, I think that was certainly very wrong of us but I put it down to inexperience. I did have the film inside developed and printed to see if it would produce a clue to whomever it belonged – but it didn't.

On another evening we visited a garden restaurant and had a pleasant meal. But here, when asked which wine we would like, I ordered a bottle of Sauterne, but only because I had heard the name. I did not have a clue what it was like. It was a sweet wine and not at all a good choice to accompany our meal. We didn't like it and so we left most of the bottle there.

Frank Law at the office had advised us to spare one evening and go to a place called Lapin Agile (The Agile Rabbit); he explained it was an establishment frequented by artists and theatre people who were 'resting' or new, talented people who wished to get up on stage and show what they could do, so various people would often entertain. We found this venue and it certainly was unusual and, as I found out afterwards, very historical – it dates back to at least 1860 and people like Picasso, Toulouse Lautrec and many other famous artists, poets and musicians used to frequent the place. Mostly French songs were sung and each act was rewarded by a special clap which even we learned to do. They only served soft drinks or a special cherry brandy. I had the cherry brandy and Lynne had a soft drink. The cherries in the brandy were like little balls of dynamite – very potent. It was an excellent recommendation from Frank Law.

On another occasion we saw a man carrying publicity boards on which a restaurant was advertising a special price for steak meals. The price looked good and as funds were getting somewhat lower we decided to take advantage of this offer and enjoyed another good meal. What I found remarkable was that even with Lynne by my side the 'ladies of the night' were very cheeky towards me!

Finally came the day of our departure; this time we walked round the corner to the station and were in good time to board the train to Dieppe, where we were due to arrive about lunchtime. But then Lynne told me that she was extremely hungry and asked if we could get something to eat before boarding the ship. I searched in my pocket and all I had was an amount of change. I couldn't see my dear wife hungry and so I went into a café, showed the proprietor what I had, and indicated in my very poor French, that my wife would like something to eat. He peered at the change in my hand and said 'Omelette?' I said, 'Oui, merci.' So we sat there whilst Lynne tucked into her omelette which she said was very nice. Then we were presented with the bill. Horror of horrors, it was more than I had! So I again showed the proprietor my change, he looked again, and then looked quizzically at me, smiled, and said, 'OK – bon.' at which I was mightily relieved. I had visions of having to do all the washing up and missing our ship!

I would like to say something more about our trip to Paris. This was only six or so years after the end of the war and we met some interesting people. We didn't have the money to explore Paris properly or to visit any of the fine restaurants but, for example, we did meet an elderly, refined lady who was English and had stayed in France during the German occupation. We had a very interesting chat with her about her experiences from 1939-1945.

I am bound to say that we found the French attitude towards us very charming and kind – and rather different to our and my experiences on later visits. I certainly feel that the French attitude towards us British back then, in 1951, was warm and friendly but has grown much colder since. I feel that is a great pity. But back in 1951 it appeared that they still loved and respected us for helping to release them from the German occupation; the memory was then still alive. It is sad that those memories and sacrifices that were made in order to come to their rescue seem now to have been erased from their minds.

But, as far as Paris itself was concerned, when I look back and compare how it was in 1951 with the Paris of today, I believe that perhaps we experienced the last days of the old Paris and nobody, but nobody, could have seen more of that city than we did in the short time we were there. The Paris we had the good fortune to know and experience in 1951 cannot be compared to the modern Paris. But then, that probably applies to many cities all over the world; it certainly applies to London and Prague, that's for sure.

Back at work now at Hale Hamilton, I became conscious of the fact that I was regarded by the older personnel as a somewhat junior member of the staff. For example, from time to time the Managing Director, J.D. Hamilton, invited members of the senior staff to a luncheon paid for by the company and on other occasions, some were even sent to exotic places on the pretext that it was a business trip but it really was a holiday on the company. I was never once included when such luncheon occasions were arranged and certainly never received an offer of a paid holiday. Even when the Canned Goods Manager left the company and I was asked to take over – I was still not invited. So it seemed to me that I had to accept that in the eyes of those above I was definitely not one of them. I began to feel rather odd and out of place; it was not a good feeling. However, I continued to work very diligently and conscientiously.

I remember one occasion when we received a consignment of confectionery from overseas in which the manufacturer had failed to include price tickets. They offered to solve the problem by sending them in a parcel by air freight to Heathrow. Mr Andrews asked me to go there in order to pick up the urgently required price tickets so that they might be included when invoices were posted to customers. In those days it was not so easy to get to Heathrow as it is today but I managed to do so without too much difficulty. I was surprised to see that Heathrow, London's major airport, was nothing more than a collection of sheds!

I presented myself to the Customs Shed with my papers entitling me to collect but I was told they had not cleared Customs yet and would not be cleared for at least one or two hours.

I didn't know what to do with myself for one or two hours and when I spied a place where it looked as though I might get a cup of tea, I went there. It was no tea shop, it was a grand restaurant. However, I was there and I was hungry, for the evening had rolled on. And so when the waiter, who was dressed in a very grand manner just like a butler, came to me and asked if I would like afternoon tea, I said, 'Yes please.' After ten minutes, he came back with the full works; a pot of tea with milk and sugar, a plate of cakes, some bread and butter and a small dish of jam. It looked like a banquet to me but, as I say, I was hungry so I tucked in. Afterwards the waiter brought me the bill – it was 2/6d (or12.5p!!) That was a fortune to me and all I wanted was a cup of tea! I wondered what they would say back at the office when I submitted my expenses? But nothing was said! I do not believe there is quite such a place today at Heathrow where you can be served with afternoon tea as I was on that late afternoon; nowadays it seems more like a cafeteria service. I was finally able to obtain the release of the price tickets from HM Customs and arrived back at our flat in Prestage Buildings, Poplar, at about 10.00pm and very tired indeed – and hungry again!

Of that period I can recall two events: one was my being attracted to the idea of emigrating to Canada. I had read several articles about people who either were doing that or had done it, and it sounded very appealing. I discussed it with Lynne and she thought the idea was rather good. The trouble was, as always, the shortage of money. My idea was that I would go alone in the first instance, land in an Eastern port and work my way across the country until I came to a place where I considered it would be nice to live and where I could get a job. I was ready to do anything; dig ditches, chop down trees, pick fruit – anything. Well, that was the plan.

Not only was Lynne attracted to this idea but also my brother Lenny. So it was agreed that I would work my way across the country and when I had found a suitable place, I would send for them and they would follow me over. Berths on ships were not easy to get in those days and air travel was only for the very wealthy. So I registered my name with Canadian Pacific, who had offices in Trafalgar Square. Nothing was available for the foreseeable future; therefore I had to enter my name on a waiting list; and so we waited. Then, quite suddenly, I received a note from Canadian Pacific to say there had been a cancellation and that one berth was available in a few weeks' time. However, they said that it was necessary for me to come there with the fare no later than Tuesday of the next week. The passage one way was about £56 or so but the problem was I didn't have £56!

But then Lenny stepped in and offered to lend me £100, which would pay for the berth and something over for travelling expenses. On the Saturday, therefore, Lenny duly went to the Post Office to draw the money as none of us had bank accounts in those days – and he handed me the £100, which seemed to me to be a lot of money. Where to keep it for safety until Tuesday next? Well, between us we decided to keep it in an empty chocolate box which Lynne kept in her dressing table drawer. Monday arrived and we all went to work as usual. That evening I happened to be the first one to get home. I was pottering about when there was a knock on the door. A big chap stood there with a trilby hat on and asked me if we had had any visitors. I asked him what he meant and he told me that he was a Detective from Poplar Police Station and that next door had been burgled and ransacked. I invited him to look around and told him that we must have been lucky because, as he could see, all was in good order. So he asked me to close the door which I did; he put his shoulder against it and it flew open easily. He advised me to get the door fixed and I assured him I would. But then I began to be a little anxious and so I rushed to the bedroom, opened the drawer, opened the chocolate box, and there was ... nothing! Then Lynne arrived back and I told her the story. She couldn't accept it and so she also looked in her dressing table but it was a fact – our money had been stolen and when we carried out a check we found that Lynne's watch, my camera, and other things, even the rent which I had placed ready on the mantelpiece, had all gone!

It was of course a heartbreaking experience for us and in an angry mood I went around the pubs in the forlorn hope that I would see somebody unusually spending a lot of money. And everywhere I went they were playing the song 'Wheel of Fortune', which was popular at that time. Oh God! How I hate that song! It reminds me of a rather unhappy time in my life and even now, if I hear it being played, it brings back those unpleasant memories. We never did discover who was responsible for breaking into our flat; the only clue was that someone claimed to have seen a man wearing a trilby hat, accompanied by a woman, leaving the area at the back of the flat. But we couldn't match this limited description to anyone we knew.

Naturally, we had to abandon our plans as far as Canada was concerned. In any case, being unable to present myself at Canadian

Pacific on the following Tuesday and pay them £56 meant that I had lost the berth they were reserving for me. But, as we discovered, it would have been quite impossible for me to have gone anyway for, very shortly after this event, we found that Lynne was pregnant with our first baby. Therefore I would have had to cancel my plans in any case. Our initial disappointment about our plans was washed away immediately with the fantastic news that we were about to start our family. It also made me start thinking about how I could develop my career and earn a higher salary. Although I had a close affinity with the East End, I didn't want our children to grow up there as I had done; I wanted them to enjoy better conditions. I also realised that it would be very hard on Lynne to bring up babies in the somewhat primitive conditions in which we lived.

And then, out of the blue, either in the latter part of 1951 or the beginning of 1952, a chap named Larry Beale who also once worked for Hale Hamilton and whom I therefore knew, contacted me to tell me that his boss, Harold Frost, a canned goods merchant, had acquired the UK agency for Czechoslovak confectionery and allied products He was seeking someone with confectionery experience to administrate this new agency which now formed part of his business. And so, to cut a long story short, I arranged to go to Mr Frost's office in Rood Lane where I had a long chat with him. Harold Frost was Jewish and I had always got on very well with Jewish people. I had Jewish friends when I was younger and had sat and eaten unleavened bread with their families on Friday nights. And so it was with Mr Frost and he seemed to like me.

At the end of our discussion Mr Frost offered me the position as Sales Manager but of course I had nobody to manage except myself! It was just a title for there were only four people in the office: Mr and Mrs Frost, Larry Beale who assisted on the canned goods side and who gave me the tip about the position, and myself. Anyway, to my great surprise and pleasure, Mr Frost not only offered me the position but said that if I worked hard and succeeded I would share 25% of the net profits made through the confectionery agency and that I could begin by drawing £15 per week! That was a 50% increase on my salary at Hale Hamilton! I was extremely surprised by this offer but I was of course over the moon and couldn't wait to get home to tell Lynne – as I have said elsewhere, very few people living in poor districts had telephones back then. She was as delighted as I was but she insisted that she wanted to continue working for a while despite her pregnancy – and she did for some months – she knew we needed the money.

Back at Hale Hamilton, I informed my immediate boss, Mr Andrews, that I would be leaving the company and I told him the whole story. He wished me luck and said that he hoped I would remember the old firm when offers of good lines come from Czechoslovakia. The Managing Director, J.D. Hamilton, also wished me good luck and gave me a cheque for £50 for my services to the company and with that I left Old Broad Street for the last time. I never went back there but I did remain on friendly terms with Donald Andrews for many years to come.

Mr Frost's office was just two rooms. The main office consisted of a quite large room which began with an office counter, whilst over on the left sat Mrs Frost, who also acted as my secretary, a most unsatisfactory arrangement, and dealt with all incoming phone calls. My desk was going to be there against the far wall. The other room was not so large but it housed two large desks which faced each other. One of these was for Mr Frost himself and the other was for his Canned Goods sales assistant, at that time Larry Beale who sat opposite him.

During my first few days Mr Frost called me into his office and said that as I would be dealing with the Czechoslovak side of his business it would be necessary for me to be interviewed by the Commercial Delegate at the Czechoslovak Embassy who would like to ask me some questions.

This person was Karel Jiracek and I duly went to see him. He was a youngish man and I was due to have much to do with our friend Jiracek in the future. It was a quite pleasant interview and I think I said all the right things. But my first impression of him was that he was young, somewhat inexperienced, but trying very hard to show that he wasn't! This brought out a degree of arrogance in him which he never lost in all the years I knew him.

I knew very little about Communism or the Communist way of doing things at that time, so at that point I didn't know that following the Communist coup in Czechoslovakia in 1949, they followed a policy, no doubt dictated and influenced by Moscow, of discharging any person holding a position of importance, in any sphere, whose political persuasion was unfavourable towards Communism. Such people were replaced by a known Communist supporter – this was to ensure Communist loyalty throughout the country.

And so a ridiculous situation followed whereby a lot of square pegs were forced into a lot of round holes – just because they were good Communists. For example, I learned that the Managing Director of our particular government food export organisation, named Centrokomise, was a plumber – Mr Malik! He knew all about pipes and leaking taps etc.

but nothing at all about business. Therefore at every meeting he had to have a business expert (who may well have not been a Communist) at his elbow to help him along. Otherwise he would have been quite helpless when being asked commercial questions. The name of Mr Malik's right hand man was Mr Pavlacek, a nice man who unfortunately did not speak English but who knew a great deal about business. In time he became a good supporter of myself. I will write more about him and the management of Centrokomise later.

Of course this policy of putting loyal party members in positions of responsibility that they knew nothing about could not continue indefinitely, and so they quickly started a further policy of picking young people from the factories and elsewhere who came from good, loyal Communist families, sending them to special schools where education, commercial practices, details of commercial law, languages and general business experience were all forced into them over a relatively short period of time. The object was to give the Communist party good, loyal people who would uphold Communist principles; people who could be relied upon to follow party policies – for these would be the potential leaders of the future. And my interviewer, Karel Jiracek, was one of those chosen people!

I understand he was sweeping the floors of the Orion Confectionery Factory, near Prague, when he was selected – and now he was a Commercial Delegate in London! Of course he was a pumped-up, educated man now but in no way refined, and he was destined in later years to rise to the position of Commercial Counsellor no less, second only to the Ambassador in seniority at the Embassy, where he was, in fact, presented to the Queen at Buckingham Palace – more of that later. I have to admit that I admired him but Jiracek never lost his 'peasant-like' appearance and manner, even when dressed in top hat and tails. You can't make a silk purse out of a sow's ear!

During this interview with Jiracek, I had half expected a question or two about my own political views and I wondered how I would reply, because I was staunchly defensive of my political opinions. But he didn't ask, and not even when I worked for the Czechs in a more direct way, was I ever asked by anybody – the subject never arose, except with the close friends, mostly outside business, whom I developed over the years and who trusted me. It seemed to be accepted by them that if you come from England then you could not possibly be a Communist. But it was always important to know who you could trust if you lived in a Communist country or if you were working closely with them. No – I was never asked about my political persuasions. The Communists do not work in that way; they adopt more underhand methods, as I would find out in due course. I am certain that a file on me as thick as one's arm existed with the Czech Secret Police.

I soon found myself up to my neck in Czechoslovak confectionery matters. First of all I had to familiarise myself with the various factories that exported to the UK, and their products. Then I had to examine what business had been done and what might be pending or awaiting shipment. I found this to be a difficult task because very few informative documents existed and so one of my first jobs was to organise a card system for all the importer clients which I completed with all details of business done and transactions awaiting completion. In that way, anyone could look up who bought what and when, at what price and whether shipment had taken place or if awaited. Mr Frost was very impressed and I think I surprised myself, for I was showing a talent for office organisation that I didn't know I possessed!

I also made contact with all the importers to introduce myself and to discuss business possibilities with them. All of this took months rather than weeks but as the year rolled by, it was quite evident that we were going to have a good year. And then towards the end of that year, 1952, I had the shock of my life when Mr Frost told me that our principals in Prague wanted him to pay a visit there and that he would like me to accompany him! I was absolutely over the moon! I could hardly wait for Christmas and the New Year to arrive! But there was another reason to look forward to this period, a much more important one and that was the expected birth of our first child. She was in rather a hurry to join us and so arrived a little early – on December 28th 1952. I was very glad it happened then because I would have hated to be away on business when our little girl was born.

I remember that day so well; Lynne had begun to feel as though the birth was imminent and so, with the help of Danny, my brother-in-law, who was a taxi driver, we took her to the East London Maternity Hospital in Stepney. Danny returned home and I awaited events. But I was told that the birth was not as imminent as we thought and that I should go home; they promised to phone my sister, one of the few people who had a phone in our locality, should there be any development. I had to take Lynne's clothing, which I did; I felt very upset to leave her at the hospital all alone. I just didn't feel like getting on a bus so I walked home with her clothing under my arm for, unfortunately, I had not thought to bring a bag with me. And as I walked on, I just could not prevent the tears from trickling down my face – we had never been parted before and it had quite an emotional effect on me.

On the day of the birth, the 28th, my sister came across the road to our flat in Prestage Buildings to tell me she had received a call and that I should go immediately to the Maternity Hospital. I did so and there was Lynne looking rather wan and tired but very pleased to see me, and who announced that we had a baby girl. That was a marvellous moment in our lives. Mr and Mrs Frost had sent her a wonderful bouquet of flowers for which I was truly grateful – and so was Lynne.

11

MY INTRODUCTION TO COMMUNISM AND THE LATE 1950s

Our trip to Prague was to take place in January 1953 and I did feel rather guilty going away at this time, just after our baby daughter had arrived. But all arrangements had been made and it would have created a very difficult situation if I had said I could not go; in any case I had left Lynne in good hands and she would be taken care of by her mother. And I know she understood the situation quite well.

On arrival at Heathrow Airport we found the whole area submerged in a thick fog. Of course no planes could take off in those conditions. But this was 1953 and passengers were treated in a quite different manner to that which applies these days. We were looked after in every way. For those without accommodation, if the poor conditions continued the airline would find you a nice hotel room – and pay for it. Back then the airlines seemed to accept that any delay at all was their responsibility – rather different from today! In our case, the situation began to ease and the fog eventually began to lift; soon we were up in the sky and winging our way to Schipol Airport, Amsterdam. It was the very first time I had ever flown in an aircraft and so I found the experience quite exhilarating and exciting.

At this point let me explain that then there were no direct flights from London to Prague. I was told that this was due to the fact some Czechoslovak pilots had taken the opportunity to escape the clutches of Communism and had failed to report back after landing in London. But I somehow doubted the logic of this because these pilots could just as easily escape, if they wished, from the other transit cities such as Brussels, Paris or Zürich that the Czechoslovak Airlines used.

But anyway, here we were on a KLM flight to Amsterdam and very shortly after take off, the hostesses brought us a hot meal – and very good it was too! After that they came with trays of chocolate medallions, an apple and an orange and small bottles of various liqueurs which they distributed among the passengers. After a period of waiting at Schipol, we then boarded another plane going to Prague – and it all happened once again! Another nice meal, apples, oranges, chocolate medallions and small bottles of liqueur. So we arrived in Prague like a pair of Father Christmas figures! Of course we gave it all away to the people who we met in the course of the following week when we discovered how impossible it was for them to obtain such things.

Our principals met us at the airport and took us by car to our hotel. Of course I was watching and looking at every building as we swept through the outskirts of Prague on our way to the centre. I remember my overall impression was that everything looked very grim and depressing. After an hour or so we arrived at our hotel. This was Hotel Alcron in Ulice Stepanska, a street just off Vaclavske Namesti – better known to foreigners as Wenceslas Square. This was one of the two prime hotels used at that time for foreign visitors who in that period were few and far between. The other hotel used was the Hotel Esplanade, towards the top of the square and to the left. It wasn't easy for people from the West to obtain visas in the early 1950s and so it seemed that these two hotels were sufficient to house the meagre number of Western visitors.

The Alcron was a very comfortable hotel, even if rather old fashioned but it had a rather special atmosphere which I liked very much and came to know rather well in the coming years. At that time, I had a very limited experience of nice hotels and to me this was all too good to be true; I lapped up every minute, paid attention to every detail and appreciated it all – I especially appreciated Mr Frost's gesture in inviting me to accompany him. On the other hand, as our business discussions were filled with details of which Mr Frost knew little or nothing, I could see that my presence by his side was very necessary.

I cannot recall a great deal of what happened on that first day following our arrival but at some point we walked out of the hotel into Vaclavske Namesti and there before us was a blaze of red banners with hammers and sickles and Czech wording that of course I could not understand; they stretched all the way across the large square and gave an unmistakable air of forced propaganda to any visitor. Later I asked one of our Czech colleagues to translate one of these gigantic banners to me and it was:

WITH US IS STALIN – WITH US IS PEACE.

He translated others for me but I can only recall that one. Seeing all this kind of thing for the first time in my life was a shock to the system, for I had only known life in a free and ordinary country. If this is Communism, I thought, it does not appeal to me at all.

In the evening Mr Frost and I dined at the hotel. We walked from the large lounge into the dining area, where the Head Waiter showed us to a free table. On the right was a small stage with a four or five piece band playing melancholy melodies – even the kind of music they played was controlled by the Communists!. If they knew you were English they played 'Tipperary' or 'Roll Out The Barrel' or other tunes that they linked to us British but always very slowly as if they were playing funeral music. However, it should be noted that the wartime song, 'Roll Out The Barrel', much loved by British soldiers, is in fact a Czech composition called 'Skoda Laski', 'Pity For love' or probably more understandably 'Isn't Love A Pity'. It was written by a Mr Vavoda; I know this as his wife, Mrs Vavodova, used to serve my lunch in later years when I visited the Orion Factory at Modrany where she worked, just outside Prague. This happened frequently because this factory also housed Ceskoslovenske Cokoladovny which was the centralised HQ of the whole industry.

Later on, maybe 1965-6 when the harsher aspects of Communism began to soften a little making it easier for foreigners to obtain visas, many Germans started to visit Prague. The band changed their music and began playing Germanic tunes like 'Lili Marlene'; I thought this was a temporary change but I am afraid it became rather permanent and it was a change that I found difficult in bringing myself to understand. After all the Germans had done to them, I had to wonder how they could possibly adopt this rather friendly attitude. The Czechs explained it away by saying that Germany is their neighbour and so they must try to get on with them as they need them economically – despite anything that has happened in the past! I am not sure I could be so forgiving – but time is a great healer.

We sat at a corner table next to a life-size statue of a nude lady; I believe this statue became very famous and is now housed in one of the many museums in Prague. However, it is no longer to be seen at the now completely renovated and modernised Alcron. In subsequent visits, I always tried to obtain this table; I felt rather comfortable with my 'marble girl friend' by my side! Today, the Alcron is all new and sparkling – and mostly empty, perhaps because the cost of rooms there must be very high indeed! And so the old and very special, busy and bustling atmosphere it once had, as well as my 'marble girl friend', have gone.

But in 1953 all of this was quite novel to me; I had never experienced such luxury and elegance and I reflected how very fortunate I was to be enjoying all of this. It was a long, long, way from Prestage Buildings, Poplar, in the backstreets of London's East End Docklands. I thought, 'What would Lynne and my friends back home say if they could see me now?' I decided that I liked this style of living and would enjoy as much of it as I possibly could. And I did – for many years to come!

The next morning we were collected by car and whisked away to the offices of Centrokomise, the government food export agency. And now the discussions began in earnest. We were introduced to a bewildering number of different people and it was very difficult, especially with the funny sounding names, to remember everybody. As I have written earlier, Mr Frost did not know a great deal about the detail of the UK business. That, of course, is why I was there. We did not stop to go out for lunch; instead one of the female staff brought in a large silver platter laden with Prague Ham, salami, excellent liver sausage and a variety of cold meats and Russian eggs with Pilsner Urquell beer and delicious bread rolls; it was to me a banquet fit for a King! I grew to love those working lunches.

Each evening we were taken back to the hotel. Sometimes our Czech colleagues joined us for a drink but I noticed there always had to be two. If anyone was on his own, he would make some excuse and politely refrain from joining us at the bar. I learned later that it was forbidden for any Czechoslovak from the export office to be alone with any guest from the Western countries under any circumstances. But one evening, when sitting at our usual corner table having dinner, a gentleman approached us. We recognised him as one of those we had met at the offices of Centrokomise. He knew the regulations by which he was governed but evidently he was prepared to take the risk. He asked Mr Frost's permission to sit at our table and then began to pour his heart out. His name was Dr Knizek – the title was a scholastic or law doctorship, I forget which but it did indicate that he was a clever man. He was sitting next to Mr Frost and not only did he speak in very low tones but his head was turned away from me. Therefore, I could not hear everything that was said. I gathered that Dr Knizek's political reputation had taken a knock for some reason; he had either been reported as having said or done something not approved by those above, and he was pleading with Mr Frost, as an important man, to assist him by putting a good word in for him in the forlorn hope that it might help his situation. The poor man was almost in tears as he pleaded for help and Mr Frost clearly was placed in a very difficult position. He tried to pacify him by indicating that he would say a few nice words about him but he never did! It was very dangerous to get mixed up in such things and even I understood that. We, who live in a free country, cannot possibly understand these situations or how easily, and how serious, it was to fall foul of the Communist people who almost always occupied the top jobs and controlled everything below them; suspicion of, and gross exaggeration of, the most innocent happenings and occurrences was inherent in the Communist system. Nor could we understand how people were even prepared to ingratiate themselves with their Communist bosses by informing on others – and sometimes such accusations were completely without foundation! So if you bore a grudge against someone or perhaps if you coveted the work position of the one above you – just make an anonymous allegation against him or her and in the majority of cases the result you may have wished for would really happen. What a dirty business and what a way to live! It was a great opportunity for those with underhand and deceitful intentions towards others.

As far as Dr Knizek was concerned, I understand he was dismissed from his position at Centrokomise later and was very probably forced to accept some very ordinary job which belied his knowledge and experience in order that he and his family might live. I was to learn even more about Communism very shortly and to know that there were many such educated and clever people working in mundane jobs due to the fact that they did not toe the line and satisfy their Communist superiors. I know for a fact that two professors from the old Prague University were forced to become tram drivers because they refused to preach the Communist gospel. It was the only job they could get; it was that or nothing! This was the kind of treatment meted out to those who were not prepared to do as they were told under this ghastly system.

During this visit we had two appointments with the Director of Centrokomise, whose name it may be recalled, was Mr Malik – yes, Mr Malik the plumber! And of course, at his elbow was Mr Pavlacek, the proficient business expert, without whose help Mr Malik would be totally lost, as indeed would Mr Frost if I had not been there. I have tried to find out if Mr Pavlacek was a member of the Communist Party because when Centrokomise was absorbed into the larger State Foreign Trade

Corporation, which was called Koospol, Mr Pavlacek was also transferred and maintained a quite powerful position there. But after all this time nobody is available who might be able to answer such questions. However, in the course of my enquiries, I did hear a tragic but nevertheless fascinating story about the predecessor of Mr Malik, who was a certain Mr Gregor.

To tell the story in proper detail we have to go back some months, to the latter part of 1951. In Moscow they were carrying out one of their occasional pogroms against Jewish people – Russia was well known for that kind of activity. And what happened in Moscow on Monday was followed in Prague, Warsaw and Budapest on Tuesday or as soon as possible thereafter; the satellite Communist states always felt obliged to follow the Moscow line and they did so very enthusiastically – to show their Russian masters how loyal to the cause they were.

And so it happened that in 1952 a group of fourteen leading people in politics and business were arrested and accused of acting against the State; eleven of these people were members of the Jewish faith, and these even included Mr Rudolf Slansky, Deputy Prime Minister and former First Secretary to the Czechoslovak Communist Party no less!

It was about this time that Mr Gregor, who was also Jewish, disappeared. He was not seen or heard from for quite a long period of time; at first it was feared by some that he too had been executed, although his name was not officially included in the fourteen leading arrests, nor among the list of those subsequently executed; in fact it transpired that although he was charged with a number of serious offences against the State and could therefore have quite easily received the death sentence, he received instead a long prison sentence. I am quite sure he did not serve the whole sentence, for when matters began to improve he would have been semi-rehabilitated and then fully rehabilitated. I will explain the Communist system of 'rehabilitation' later in this narrative.

As far as Mr Slansky is concerned he had actually been out to dinner that evening with the President of the Republic and First Secretary of the Communist Party, Mr Gottwaldov. When they bade each other Goodnight, Mr Gottwaldov must have known perfectly well that the secret police were waiting for Mr Slansky to return home and that they would promptly arrest him.

Under questioning, Mr Slansky vigorously denied all accusations made against him i.e. of being an 'enemy of the State, conspiring against the State, and being in the pay of foreign capitalists' – the usual trumped up charges of which he was totally innocent – and at first he was very vehement in his denials. But over a period of time, they wore down his mental faculties by aggressive interviewing at one moment followed by kind gestures the next moment. Then they would ask him if he wanted to sleep and after hours and hours of questioning during both night and day he most certainly did want to sleep. But they only left him for ten minutes in a darkened room, then awoke him, and began aggressive questioning once again.

Using this form of mental torture, they wore down poor Mr Slansky's mental resistance until they decided the right moment had come to make propositions to him. They promised him that if he would stand in Court and admit to his 'crimes', they would see to it that he would only receive a short prison sentence and that the pension rights of his family would be protected. Mr Slansky must have been in a state of mental exhaustion by this time and we can only suppose that he thought the matter over, if he was really capable of doing so by then, and decided, for the sake of his family, to go along with these demands. And so it happened. I have seen the film taken of the trial. Mr Slansky appeared in Court, stood smartly to attention with his arms by his side and said everything he was instructed to say. But he was a broken man and in fact confessed to being an enemy of the State, involved in a conspiracy against the State and that he had received payments from USA spy organisations. None of this was true – but he wanted desperately not only to do his best to save his own neck but also to protect the financial situation of his family. Most unfortunately, he believed the words and promises made to him by his captors. The Communist judge promptly sentenced him to death and he was hung within days. Not only that, his family were deprived of their pension rights! Mr Slansky made the great mistake of trusting in Communist promises.

We can safely presume that Mr Gregor underwent the same kind of cruel questioning to that meted out to Mr Slansky. However, he was lucky – he only went to jail. Of the fourteen people arrested, eleven were executed and three were sentenced to life in prison.

Of course, in later years when the evil influence of the power-corrupted leaders of Communism began to waver and weaken somewhat, there were many discussions about these infamous trials. I believe that Mr Slansky and maybe some, or all, of the other people who were executed with him were 'rehabilitated' – which is the Communist way of saying they may have been wrong and that they were sorry – you see, the word 'sorry' does not exist in the Communist vocabulary! Learning all of this as I did in later years, it gave me a look into the very heart of Communism.

I do not necessarily claim that it was Communism which was at fault, for every system has some good points but it was the power of life and death that Communism gave to the State and to its party leaders which became so corrupted and misused.

Well, Friday arrived and it was time to go back to London. Since I didn't know if I would ever visit there again, I asked Mr Frost that as we had had no time to see the sights, would he mind if I stayed over the weekend and return to London on Monday – and he agreed! Well, the head of the confectionery department at Centrokomise, a gentleman named Bedrich Zboril, a very nice man who spoke absolutely perfect English and with whom we cooperated, promised to take me under his wing and show me something of Prague. And so on Saturday morning he phoned me at the hotel. He asked me to walk from the hotel to Vaclavske Namesti where I would find a bookshop on the corner. I was to wait there for him. I did so and in a few minutes he arrived. We then caught a tram, went for a few stops, then took another tram and a few more stops; I am sure that when we finished these journeys we were not far away from where we had started! I didn't realise it then but we were enacting the kind of precautions one had to take to avoid being followed. Mr Zboril was taking quite a risk and he was merely trying to protect himself. But that day he really did show me a lot. He took me to Hradcany, the castle and seat of government, then to the lovely St Vitus Cathedral, Charles Bridge, the quaint Old Town, and finally to a church in a side street not far from the river Vltava, which runs through Prague.

He explained that in 1942, SS Führer Reinhard Heydrich was appointed Reich Protektor by Hitler for Bohemia and Moravia. Slovakia had been separated from the rest of Czechoslovakia, was independent and now operated almost as an ally of the Germans (although some Slovaks would dispute this) and ruled the area with a rod of iron. Heydrich was one of Hitler's favourites and a very cruel man. It was Heydrich who invented the term 'The Final Solution'. He was present at the infamous conference at Wannsee, just outside Berlin, where head Nazis (including the infamous Adolf Eichmann and a number of concentration camp officials) thoroughly discussed the Final Solution and issued instructions which sent millions of Jews and others to their death in the gas chambers at Auschwitz and other death camps.

It is said that Churchill was not at all happy with the limited efforts of the Czech underground and thought that much more could be done to disrupt the German occupation in that country. Furthermore it was also said that Heydrich had a plan to enlist young Czech men into the German army.

And so the Free Czechoslovak Forces in the UK decided to do something to solve both problems. They therefore ordered a group of Czech men to train as commandos, mainly in Scotland, with the object of dropping them by parachute into Bohemia, where they would organise and encourage more underground activity and also deal with Heydrich. Altogether seven parachutists were dropped – mostly in the wrong area but they managed to rendezvous.

However, one of them decided that before he did anything else he would visit his girlfriend whom he had not seen since the outbreak of war and whom he missed very much. Perhaps because of her influence he became reluctant, and, it could be said, even grew more afraid to get deeply involved with unpleasant business like sabotage and underground work. And so he, in the first days and weeks, became more and more uncomfortable about the whole affair. One wonders why he volunteered in the first place, for they were all volunteers.

However, two of the parachutists whose names were Gabcik and Kubis, were more active and enthusiastic about the reasons for which they had returned to Czechoslovakia; their prime objective was to deal with Heydrich who, besides his plan to arrange enlistment of young Czech men into the Wehrmacht, had other unpleasant plans for the people of Bohemia and Moravia. What they sought was a plan which, if possible, would put him out of action.

So they did some reconnoitering to see if they could determine some of the habits and movements of their intended victim. They discovered that he came from his villa outside Prague where he and his family lived, to his offices at Hradcany Castle by the same route every day – and without any protective escort to ensure his safety! Hitler had earlier berated him for taking such unnecessary risks. Heydrich promised Hitler that he would arrange protection during his journeys but on this particular day he had to fly to Berlin for discussions after attending to urgent matters at his office at Hradcany Castle, and maybe he thought he would leave the matter of protection until his return. Meanwhile, Gabcik and Kubis had discovered a hairpin bend on the outskirts of Prague which was on Heydrich's route, where his car would have to slow down almost to walking pace. This, they decided, would be an excellent place where they could attack him.

On this day, therefore, Heydrich left his villa, sat by his driver and off they sped towards Prague. Gabcik and Kubis waited patiently on the bend and then saw Heydrich's car coming down the hill. One of them (I think it was Gabcik) had a Sten gun in his brief case and Kubis was armed with a hand grenade. As the car approached the bend, Gabcik took the

Sten gun out and then ... disaster! The gun locked and would not fire – a common fault with Sten guns apparently! Kubis took his hand grenade and lobbed it into the back of the car but it landed towards the rear wheel. Heydrich drew his gun and prepared to exit the car just as the hand grenade exploded. Both Gabcik and Kubis ran for their lives with the driver following and shooting at them. Heydrich got out of his car and also tried to take aim at the escaping men. But he had been wounded by the explosion; it did not seem at first as though his injuries were all that serious. The two parachutists meanwhile had made good their escape, leaving their briefcase and Sten gun behind. Now Heydrich began to wince and it was obvious that he was in agony.

A passing milk cart was stopped and used to take him to a nearby hospital; he lay in the back of the cart with his legs dangling over the end. In the hospital, they found that tiny fragments of the hand grenade had passed through his seat and entered his spine, carrying small pieces of fibre. These had caused an immediate infection. Penicillin had not been discovered then and so he lingered for a few days, and although Hitler sent top specialists from Berlin to assist in his recovery, Heydrich passed away.

His corpse was taken to Hradcany first of all, to lie in state, and then slowly transported down from the castle in a procession which went across the well-known Charles Bridge and a part of Prague and then flown to Berlin, where he was given a state funeral by Hitler.

Terrible occurrences now began to take place throughout the country. Let us go back to Gabcik and Kubis. Having made good their escape from the scene of the attempted assassination, they returned to the apartment of a Prague family who supported the underground movement and whose apartment was used as a rendezvous point and safe house. The two men had left a briefcase at the scene of the assassination as well as a bicycle. Pictures of them were widely shown in all newspapers in the hope that someone might identify them. It was impossible to stay in that apartment for very long as the search for them by the Germans had started in earnest and nobody knew who would be knocking on the door or when. So it was arranged by agreement with the priest in charge who sympathised with their activities, that they would be hidden in his church not far from the river, where a crypt lay under the main part of the building. This was the very church I was taken to by Mr Zboril.

All of the six parachutists were eventually to congregate and hide there. But now we must return to the seventh man whose heart and soul was not in this operation. He agonised with his girlfriend as to what he should do; he had heard about the church refuge idea whilst visiting the apartment but did not know exactly where it was. He was in a nervous state because by now the search for the culprits had reached a high and intensive level; nowhere was safe, for the Germans were determined to capture the assassins. So he came to the conclusion that he did not want anything more to do with his six colleagues or their underground work. After hesitating a number of times, he made the drastic and dramatic decision to go to the Gestapo headquarters in Prague, to make a confession pleading that he had no connection with the assassination of Heydrich and offer to help them find the remaining six parachutists. His reward for his treachery was one million Czech Crowns, paid to him by the Germans. Yet another 'reward' awaited him in the form of just retribution, for after the war he was captured and hung.

The traitor did not realise the importance of the church, for it had only been mentioned in passing. But he was able to give the Gestapo the address of the Prague family whose apartment had been used as a so called 'safe house' or rendezvous point; within a short time the flat was raided and all the family, including a young man and a young girl, were arrested. All of the occupants were interrogated. The Gestapo specially worked on the young man and girl, convincing them that they knew all about the church and that therefore, no useful purpose could be served by holding back about this.

Almost certainly, promises were made that in return for their cooperation the security people would see to it that any sentence passed upon them would only be very light. Unfortunately, the young ones fell for this ruse and thinking the Gestapo were fully informed anyway, spoke openly of the church where the six remaining parachutists were hidden. In this skilful but brutal and deceptive way the Gestapo had gained the information they were seeking – i.e. where the parachutists were hidden.

In a very short while the church was completely surrounded by German troops; the parachutists, having been alerted by the sounds of activity outside realised they were trapped and tried to plan their reaction accordingly. Two men were placed in the upstairs gallery of the church, two in the main church at floor level and Gabcik and Kubis in the crypt down below. A fierce battle ensued but against overwhelming numbers they had no chance. One by one the parachutists in the upper parts of the church were killed or committed suicide – but they did not die cheaply and caused widespread casualties among the Germans.

This now left the two survivors down in the crypt. Many assaults were made by the Germans. They tried every means to attack the two

Czechs, but there were two features to the crypt; firstly it had been used as a burial sanctum many years previously and so one side was almost completely catacombed – but emptied of corpses of course. It was therefore easy to take refuge from the explosions caused by hand grenades lobbed into the crypt. However, there was also an air opening high in the crypt, reachable from the pavement. It measured about two feet long by one foot in depth and was about nine feet above the pavement. This was a danger point for the men inside and the Germans considered it as the only way to eliminate them.

First of all, the Germans called the fire brigade to assist them. Attempts were made to insert a fire hose through this gap. But the two Czechs fortunately had a ladder inside the crypt and so were able to climb up and push the hose out every time the firemen pushed it in. However, eventually one of the firemen (or a German soldier) managed to put his arm through the gap, grab the top rung of the ladder, and pull it out on to the pavement.

Now they could insert the hose once more, and slowly the water in the crypt began to rise. The two brave Czechs realised that they now had no chance – they were trapped; pitifully, they had even tried to dig through the crypt wall, hoping they might strike the sewers and escape that way but without success. So each of them climbed into a catacomb, said their last farewells, pressed their pistols to their heads and fired simultaneously.

Afterwards, the Germans laid the corpses out on the pavement and called for the seventh parachutist to come to the scene in order to identify his fallen comrades for the Gestapo. Of course, the Germans were not satisfied with just killing those who had committed this crime and they took further terrible retribution. They wanted vengeance and they made doubly certain they would get it.

First of all, the entire family, young and old occupying the rendezvous flat were summarily executed, as was anyone who had anything to do with them. The doctor who assisted them, the priest of the church where they had taken refuge – all were executed without trial. Even before the discovery of the parachutists in the church, the Germans had begun to select prisoners from the jail and people from the streets who were guilty of any minor offence; even many who had committed no offence. They were executed in their thousands, including members of their families, no matter how innocent they were. Even that did not satisfy the Germans, for they surrounded a small village near Prague named Lidice, arrested all men and boys from the age of 15 upwards, placed them against the wall of a barn and shot them. I believe some 147 villagers lost their lives on that day. All the women and children were taken away, the women to concentration camps, while some of the children were sent to German families for adoption. Then the Germans pounded the village with artillery until every building had been destroyed.

Today, where part of the old Lidice stood, a commemoration centre and museum has been constructed and is visited by many tourists.

I am not sure about the family of Kubis although we can be quite sure they suffered but I know that the whole family of Gabcik was wiped out. Mother, father, brothers, sisters, uncle and aunts, and even cousins – all were executed. I think it is quite certain that the fate of the Kubis family was the same. I am sure that neither Gabcik nor Kubis ever thought about this and what might happen afterwards but I cannot help but wonder whether they would have proceeded with this action against Heydrich if they had known what the consequences concerning their respective families would be.

In the aftermath of this terrible tragedy and loss of so many innocent lives, there were a lot of questions. Many people wondered if the assassination of Heydrich, brave action though it had been, was worth the awful retribution of the Germans.

I apologise to the reader for taking up a lot of space relating this wartime historical occurrence. I am sure some will find it fascinating; others may wonder why I have included it. I do so only because in the first place it is an interesting and factual part of war history and secondly because it was an important part of my first ever visit to Prague and an experience which had a deep and lasting effect upon me. I had never before been present where such terrible things had actually happened and apart from visiting the church, I have also stood on the very spot where Heydrich was mortally wounded.

Well, I returned to my hotel and Mr Zboril returned to his home. He said he would like to meet with me again that evening and as I had nothing else to do, I gladly accepted. Once again I had to meet him on the corner of Stepanska and Vaclavske Namesti by the bookshop, at 6.00pm. I was again there first but he arrived only a few minutes later. We then crossed over the large square and then boarded a tram. After a few stops we alighted and then boarded another. Again, after some stops we alighted, walked for a bit and there, in a dark side road, was his little, old car. He was one of the very few people lucky to have a car in those days. We drove for ten minutes or so. When we stopped, Mr Zboril turned to me and told me we were going to his apartment, and warned me that when entering the building I should be very careful not to say a word. He would explain later. I did exactly as I was told and after taking the lift to the third floor, we arrived at his flat. I then met his wife and two small children – but they were packed off to bed very shortly.

As to why I had to be silent when entering the building, Mr Zboril explained that as a person employed in a government foreign trade organisation, he would have to report that he had received a foreign visitor in his flat. Furthermore, each building had a kind of caretaker, appointed by the Communists of course, who kept a book in which the name of any foreigner entering the building had to be recorded. If an entry was made at any time, there would be many questions at his office. The whole system really tested his levels of patience to a considerable extent. The book kept by the caretaker was regularly inspected by the police and once again there would be many questions, such as what was the name of the visitor, how long did he/she stay, what did you talk about and so on. So in my case, as I was from the West, it was better to avoid all that and I completely understood. I was learning about Communism very fast!

Mr Zboril then announced that we would have something to eat and, very proudly, told me that we would be enjoying the very last tin of sardines that they possessed! This is what the Czech people had come to – they even treasured a tin of sardines as a luxury! Later I was made aware just how many simple things which we took for granted every day were either in extremely short supply or could not be purchased for love nor money. And where some goods did become available spasmodically, a queue quickly formed. So it was quite common to see queues in the Prague of that period – in fact some people joined queues, if they saw one, and only then would they enquire what the queue was for – queuing became a habit!

In later years, when I stayed at the International Hotel in a district called Dejvice, there was a butcher's shop opposite where you would see queues all the time. As this hotel was used for people in transit and other Westerners like myself, the Communist authorities eventually came to the conclusion that this was bad publicity as the hotel guests saw the queues every day. Therefore they closed the shop down!

After dinner, Mr Zboril asked if I minded that one of his friends and his English wife would join us for a cup of coffee and a chat; I of course welcomed the suggestion and after some minutes the couple duly arrived. He was introduced to me as Otto Sik and his wife as Mrs Sikova. I cannot tell all that we discussed that evening, it would take too long, but briefly Mr Sik told me that he was formerly a member of the Czech division of the Royal Air Force during the war and fought during the Battle of Britain. He could have stayed in Britain but decided to return to Czechoslovakia with his English bride. Of course he was unaware that later there would be a Communist government and therefore such people as him (i.e. with links to the original Free Czechoslovak Government and the West) were regarded by the Communists as highly questionable, untrustworthy and many were suspected of being capitalist plants or spies; this applied to anybody who had served in the Free Czechoslovak Forces in England – and so such people were therefore watched and controlled very closely.

The Communists seemed to be paranoid about such things and were always imagining situations which were completely without foundation and which existed only in their minds. In so many cases, if no crime had been committed, they simply made one up! The object, seemingly always, was to find the person being investigated guilty of something – even if they were not!

After the Communist coup in 1947-8, Otto told me he lost his somewhat important position in an organisation which, like everything else, was nationalised and a loyal Communist installed at the top. But losing his job was not the only act of persecution, for they visited his flat at stupid hours, creating havoc and searching for God knows what; he and his family were also harassed in many other ways. They never found anything incriminating – but they kept returning, expecting or hoping to find something.

His wife joined in to tell me that whilst she did receive letters from her relatives in England, they were so mutilated by censorship that they were often unreadable. I asked her if she sometimes visited her parents back home and she told me that although she would love to do so, it was impossible. Although she, but she alone, could leave at any time as she had a British passport, she was very afraid that they would not let her return to her husband and her two children so she was really trapped there in Czechoslovakia. She began to ask me about various places like Oxford Street, Piccadilly Circus, etc., and especially if it was all lit up now, what kind of things are shown in the windows etc., and as I described these places to her, the tears ran down her face uncontrollably and I felt very sad for her.

Just a further note on Otto Sik – things did improve later in the 1960s and the harassment became considerably less, as did the control over what work he could do. The Communist way of treating these people, like Otto Sik whom they had dealt with so badly, was very peculiar. As I have mentioned previously, they could not bring themselves to admit that they had made mistakes; instead they announced that some people would be semi-rehabilitated and then, after a further period of time, they were fully rehabilitated!

Later, Otto even became the official representative in Prague of the then British European Airways and had offices in the same street as Hotel Alcron. I believe I met him once after our initial meeting in 1953 but eventually he became a well known agent in Czechoslovakia, arranging contracts for Czech footballers with foreign clubs and was quite a wealthy and famous man in the sports world.

The weekend soon passed and on Monday morning it was time for me to return to London. I came to Reception at the hotel, but they directed me to a room on the 1st floor as apparently I had to report to the police who occupied this room for the purpose of vetting foreigners who were leaving; in fact they held all the passports of such people. It was only a formality; they asked a few questions, gave me my passport and then I was allowed to leave the hotel en route to the airport, where I arrived in plenty of time to catch my plane to either Brussels or Amsterdam and then on to London, where I went straight to the office to report to Mr Frost that I had safely arrived.

At home in Prestage Buildings, Lynne welcomed me. I was very glad to see her again and our new baby, Jackie. As I have written already, I must confess that I felt a little guilty at staying over the weekend in Prague but she was in good hands with her mother caring for her, and Lynne fully understood the difficult situation I was in. Naturally, all my family were very curious to hear about my adventures in Prague but when I told them, I do believe they thought I was grossly exaggerating about Communist control and cruelty, how people were suffering and the low standard of living in Czechoslovakia. They eventually discovered that my descriptions of life under the Communist regime were in fact quite true.

Well, the months went by. Business was so good that we oversold our permitted confectionery quota by the summer. After discussions with the Commercial Delegate at the Embassy we succeeded in obtaining part of a Miscellaneous Quota which the Trade Agreement provided for but within a short time, we had sold that too! It was certainly a successful period but it was also a lot of work which mainly fell upon my shoulders. Mr Frost was earning quite a lot of money but not a word was spoken about the arrangement agreed when I joined the company that I would be entitled to 25% of the profits! Looking back, I am the first to admit that I should have spoken up about the matter but for reasons I cannot really

DAVID MITCHELL

explain – I didn't. I suppose I made the mistake of trusting his word, for had it not been Mr Frost himself who, shortly after I joined him, took me to the London Commodity Exchange, opened the door and pointed out the various gentlemen who were standing in groups talking to each other and, apparently, making deals? From time to time they shook hands with each other, brought out a small notebook, made an entry and then moved on to speak with somebody else – probably to make a new deal or perhaps even to sell what he had just bought! Mr Frost urged me to pay attention to how they were doing business and told me that deals totalling millions of pounds were made there every day without immediate contracts – all was done by word of mouth and every man there kept his word no matter what. 'That, Mitchell,' Mr Frost said to me, 'is the City of London – a place where one's word is one's bond.'

I was very impressed by this and so I formed the opinion that Mr Frost was surely a man one could trust; maybe that is why I did not raise the subject. After the end of our first year, when I received no share of any profits, perhaps that is when I should have raised the subject, because as time went by, the problem was exacerbated and it must have reached the point when, under this agreement, Mr Frost would have to pay me thousands of pounds. It was the same in our second very successful year and still I said nothing. My problem was that Mr Frost had been quite kind to me in small ways and I didn't want to spoil our relationship by raising an agreement which he almost certainly now regretted ever having made. But on the other hand, he was indeed earning a great deal of money from the excellent business we were achieving and mostly that was my work.

Well, in the latter part of that year, 1953, there were some problems which needed sorting out in Prague and so this necessitated another visit. To my delight, Mr Frost again asked me to accompany him – but as I have already stated, he didn't have a lot of choice because discussions in Prague were always about the detail of the business and I dealt with that. Without me to refer to and ask questions of, I think Mr Frost would have been completely lost and would have shown his ignorance of what was actually going on.

In September we flew to Prague and once more it was necessary to go via an alternative airport. Of course we were received there with much praise for what we had achieved that year and they rowed the boat out in every respect. Firstly, we were taken by Mr Zboril, who continued to head the confectionery export department, to a wonderful, famous but small, restaurant quite near to Centrokomise called the Didek Grill. I believe it only had about eight tables and a grand piano and was frequented a lot by diplomatic people. It was very ornate and even a majestic kind of place; very expensive and they had everything you could possibly want.

In ordinary restaurants it was very common to ask for something only to be told that, sorry, they didn't have any. But this did not apply to the Didek Grill – they had everything one could possibly want. Once again, we noticed that a fourth person had to join us because it was not allowed for Mr Zboril to be alone with us. It was a lady and she was very pleasant company. However, as she eventually married a man from the confectionery department who became a good friend of mine in later years, I happen to know that she was a member of the Communist Party and therefore trusted to keep an eye on us. However, my recollection is that she spoke very poor English then and so I wonder just how much of what we spoke was understood by her. The meal was truly magnificent – one of the finest and most memorable I have ever had. Mr Zboril was a fine host and ensured that we had only the very best.

On one of the days, Mr Zboril, still continuing to spoil us because of the excellent results we had enjoyed during 1953, invited us to lunch at a restaurant just outside Prague. I can remember we went by car down to the river, continued along the embankment and then turned right over a bridge. We then continued in the general direction of the Barandov Film Studios and somewhere there we turned left into a wooded area. We climbed a hill through this forested area and there, in a clearing, was the restaurant. And very impressive it was too, almost like a Swiss chalet. I understand that once again this place was used a lot by diplomats from the various embassies. I also recall it specialised in extremely large ash trays, coveted by Mr Frost. Thanks to Mr Zboril, an arrangement was entered into whereby Mr Frost took one home with him. Once more we enjoyed a fabulous meal and once more we had to be accompanied by a fourth person.

As the conversation went on, I took the opportunity to look around the restaurant. My attention was drawn to two people sitting at a corner table. They looked very English but seemed to be behaving in a rather strange manner. They spoke with their heads close to each other as if they didn't want anyone to overhear what they were saying and continued to glance furtively from side to side. It was a highly suspicious way to behave and if they wanted to avoid attention it seemed to me they were going the wrong way about it. At the time I did not think a great deal more about it, except to mention it to Mr Frost afterwards but he had not noticed this couple especially. Later on, when I read the complete story of Philby and the warning he gave of the impending arrest of McLean for passing secret information to the Russian KGB, I knew that Burgess decided quite voluntarily to accompany McLean. An act which he later lived to regret very deeply.

I was aware that both of these traitors, Burgess and McLean, went first of all to Paris and on to Prague in 1953, where they stayed for some time before finally turning up in Moscow! I cannot be 100% certain but when I subsequently saw pictures of this pair in the newspapers, I was almost sure that those two suspicious people in that restaurant were, in fact, them!

One note on these two is that it appears, despite everything that the MoD knew about what both of them had been up to, they did not possess absolute evidence of their misdemeanours. MI5 did not have any realistic basis on which to prosecute either of them – and especially Burgess! So although the British government made a lot of noises when either of these people made entreaties to be allowed at least to visit the UK – we now know that there is little that could have been done even if they had set foot once again in Britain. So it was all bluff on the part of the British authorities but neither Burgess or McLean were aware of this!

The week was very productive despite the lunches and dinners and quite a number of problems were dealt with. During the discussions, our principals asked us to give sales forecasts for the forthcoming year – 1954. Mr Frost diplomatically requested that they let us ponder over this and render our estimates the following day. He had little idea how to respond to this question; it was left to me to retire a little early and work out the estimates in my room which I was quite happy to do. I rendered a very optimistic estimate which I first of all discussed with Mr Frost over breakfast and which pleased the Czechs.

With all business matters achieved it was time to fly home. Once again we had to report to the police in their room to collect our passports and went by car to Ruzyne (Prague) Airport. I was always amused when, even after all the bureaucratic control we had been through, there was one last hurdle when boarding the plane. The steps up into the plane were guarded very strictly, usually by a plump woman, a member of the People's Militia armed with a revolver and with a red arm band. She stood right in front of the steps and would allow nobody to board the plane without once more inspecting one's passport. But as soon as she allowed one person to climb the steps she immediately blocked them once again with her unusually large presence until the next person's passport had been thoroughly scrutinised. I found the whole performance to be at once comical but also sad, that the Communists mistrusted people so much and went to such lengths to prevent anyone escaping from that grim country.

And so the year 1954 went by and my optimistic estimates were not misplaced. I believe it was the year when the British government announced that confectionery was to be de-rationed. After years of rationing control, the public went mad and, quite frankly, I could and did sell any type of confectionery for which the factories in Czechoslovakia had spare production capacity. When they saw the chaos that ensued, the government soon backtracked and once again confectionery was rationed until the supply situation could be sorted out. I believe that period was a bad one for the Czechoslovak confectionery industry because the demand from Britain was so frantic that we sold a number of quite unsuitable lines on the market which, despite the shortages, proved difficult to sell and this reflected poorly on the future reputation of confectionery products emanating from Czechoslovakia.

However, the good times were about to come to an end for us. We had heard that the negotiations between the Board of Trade and the Czechoslovak trade negotiators were in some difficulties and then – disaster! It was announced that the two parties had been unable to come to an agreement, had broken up and there were no plans for a resumption of talks! This meant that when the existing Trade Agreement came to an end, which was very shortly, no further business could be transacted between the two countries.

It is worthwhile to study for a moment how this situation came about. It seems that the BoT was lobbied very strongly by the London Chamber of Commerce, which had a number of members holding shares in various Czechoslovak companies. These were of course nationalised by the Communists after they came to power – without compensation! Of special interest was the heavy investment by British investors in the Skoda complex. On the one side the BoT fought very hard but were seemingly unable to persuade the Czechs to compensate the former investors. Their political attitudes in regard to capitalism, shares, private ownership etc., simply did not allow them to give way; furthermore they made the claim that the Skoda in which there was a heavy British investment had been bombed and destroyed by the RAF in the war and what existed now had been built by themselves.

Unfortunately the only weapon the BoT could use to exert pressure during these negotiations was to delay signing the new Trade Agreement which was probably of more importance to Czechoslovakia due to their dire need to earn foreign currencies. And so, like children quarrelling in the school playground as they found they could not reach agreement, they decided not to speak with each other!

Mr Frost, never a patient man, was beside himself with anger and frustration with what was going on and so began a period when he started to make himself very unpopular in Prague. Mr Frost was of the view that it was not his fault that no business could be transacted and that therefore Prague should subsidise him financially so that he could continue to pay his expenses and exist. But he went about it in a demanding and blustering manner – even thumping the desk when on the phone to the people in Prague and also when the Commercial Delegate at the Embassy had the misfortune to call upon us – the point was that everybody knew that Mr Frost was a Canned Goods Merchant and had no extra expenses whatsoever to pay out in connection with his Czech agency, except me and I was paid £20 per week – just a flea bite when one considers what he had earned over the last three years or so! If he had been patient and not been so unpleasant in his negotiations with the Czechs, maybe matters would have resulted in a different conclusion as far as he was concerned. But as we shall discover, his loss was my gain.

In the interim period, I had suggested to Mr Frost that I try to establish connections with confectionery manufacturers in other countries. He agreed and so I made contact with the Commercial Sections of a number of European countries, obtained lists of such manufacturers from them, and got busy writing to them all, offering our services as sales agents in the UK. Quite a number of them replied and others sent samples.

Some of these I thought were quite interesting but it was as well I had greatly improved my maths, as some of the calculations I had to make were quite complicated. I never offered any item at all without costing it out fully beforehand so that we, i.e. the buyer and myself, knew exactly what we were discussing. For example, 10 Deutschmarks per kilo, at an exchange rate of DM 8.57 per £, plus landing costs, storage, various duties, and final delivery costs – how much per lb in Sterling? Bearing in mind that the rates of exchange varied quite a lot in those days, I was kept very busy with such calculations – and without the machines that calculate so easily for us now! All I had was a pencil and a piece of paper! And so as time went by I managed to build up a very good list of items which we sold to various importer clients. Therefore I was much more than earning my keep – I was showing a profit net of all expenses to Mr Frost and I think he was quite pleased with me. This factor was also known to the Czechs.

But business is all about using one's common sense. I recall one instance when Mr and Mrs Frost went to the Continent on holiday – they loved the Italian Riveria. Larry Beale, who assisted Mr Frost on the canned goods side of his business, had been long gone to work somewhere else and eventually to start his own business. So I was alone in the office. One day the phone went; I answered it and the chap on the other end wanted to know if he could purchase a further 500 cases of solid pack apples, catering size, in addition to some he had bought a little while ago from Mr Frost. I asked the gentleman if I could phone him back. I of course knew absolutely nothing about the canned goods side of the business but after rummaging around I found a file cover of recent invoices, found the document covering the previous sale to this particular customer and from that I could trace from whom the goods had been bought. I phoned them, was told that they had just 550 cases left; I then asked them to put a ring round that quantity for ten minutes, phoned the buyer who agreed to take the lot, but then I had to explain to the Sellers that I could not give a cheque for the goods as Mr Frost was away. I assured the Seller that payment would be effected immediately on Mr Frost's return and he accepted those terms. In that way I did the deal and when Mr Frost did return he was very impressed with me. In fact he bought and gave me two tickets to a musical in the West End called *Wedding in Paris* with the unforgettable Evelyn Laye and a hero of mine of earlier years, Anton Walbrook, who of course starred in *Dangerous Moonlight* – this was a reward for using my business instincts and I appreciated such recognition very much.

And so, for the moment, things were going well. I had developed our new business to quite a good level but Mr Frost's mind still rankled about the Czech business. And then, after some months had gone by, the news came through that, after all, the Board of Trade and their Czechoslovak negotiators were to meet again and take up where they ceased. I have no idea what broke the ice or which side gave way; I only know we were all pleased that things seemed to be taking a turn for the better and so Mr Frost tried to make contact with Prague and the London based Commercial Delegate at the Embassy. But on each occasion his attempts did not meet with a lot of success.

One morning the phone rang in the office; Mrs Frost, who also manipulated the small switchboard, told me that there was a call for me – from the Czech Embassy! It was the Commercial Delegate, Jiri Stepan, a gentleman who was destined to become a life long friend of mine – I will tell his story later – and he asked if I could come to the Embassy for a chat the following day. Of course I was quite taken aback – why had he not spoken to Mr Frost? I, of course, had an inkling that this might be to do with his unpopularity in Prague after his behaviour but I was not absolutely sure what to expect. I spoke with Mr Frost and he simply said that I had better get along there and see what they wanted.

And so with that I made arrangements to go to the Embassy at the appointed hour whereupon Mr Stepan informed me that Prague had decided not to renew their agency agreement with Mr Frost. They recognised the hard work I had done over the past several years and would like to offer me the UK Directorship and the responsibility for establishing a new London office.

I asked Mr Stepan if he would be so kind as to allow me a day or so to think the matter over, to which he agreed. But the moment I left the Embassy and even though my head was spinning, I began to imagine the tremendous opportunities that lay before me and already I had ideas floating in my mind which was already made up.

But how to break this to Mr Frost? It would be a delicate discussion. I reasoned that it would certainly be best to face up to the task before me and get on with it. After all, what could Mr Frost do to me? No point in sacking me – I was quite sure that I would accept this wonderful appointment which presented me with such tremendous opportunities and so I was going anyway.

12

GOING UP IN THE WORLD –
THE LATE 1950s AND THE EARLY 1960s

Before entering the office I tried to rehearse what I was going to say to Mr Frost. Since I didn't quite know what his attitude would be it was a little difficult to do that. I just plucked up courage, went into the main office, knocked on Mr Frost's door and went in. He, of course, was very interested to learn what had been said to me at the Embassy and I just told him everything – just as it had been said – and held nothing back. Mr Frost was quiet for a moment and then said that it was certainly a great opportunity for me, that he was reluctant to see me go and he would like me to stay. He continued that if I did he would offer me a directorship of his agency company, Harold Frost (Agencies) Ltd, on an agreed profit sharing basis. I told him that I would think it all over and let him know in a day or so. Then I went home to consider it all and talk it over with Lynne. But I had already made my decision just seconds after Mr Stepan made me the offer and Lynne fully agreed with me.

The new business with other European countries was going well but I gave Mr Frost's offer only fleeting thought; he had not honoured our first profit sharing agreement, so why should I believe that he would honour this one? He had the view that his word was his bond and that paper contracts, therefore, simply threw doubt upon his given word. How much credence, therefore, could I place upon these new promises? In any case, the enormous scope that I had with the Czech offer far outshone the one Mr Frost had placed before me. And so the very next day, I informed Mr Frost of what I had decided. He was very understanding, very reasonable, for I think he had anticipated my answer. I was very surprised at how easily this potentially difficult and delicate problem was resolved.

But it would be true to say that I did have pangs of some degree of guilt. Wasn't it true that Mr Frost had given me my first real chance to show what capabilities I had in business? And when Lynne gave birth to our first baby at the East London Maternity Hospital, wasn't it Mr and Mrs Frost who sent her the most beautiful bouquet of flowers. Didn't Mr Frost lend me the money to buy my first car? Hadn't he been kind to me in other ways? All these things were running through my mind but then I remembered that although Mr Frost had earned a lot of money in the good years, it was me who had carried out the vast bulk of the work involved. And the fact that he had failed to keep to his agreement with me on profit sharing rankled with me most of all. Nobody likes to be let down and I considered that Mr Frost had in fact disappointed me – but I have to say, in all fairness, only in that one respect.

I should have explained before now that during the time that profits were being made I had recommended that part of them should be invested in shops – confectionery and tobacconist shops – and that we could without doubt build a chain of such establishments, develop a wholesale warehouse to supply them and other shops too, and perhaps even one day start a small manufacturing company. I argued that having control over distribution, manufacturing, wholesaling and retailing was the way to maximise profits from the confectionery trade. I must have persuaded him with my ideas, for he agreed with my suggestion. I found our first shop in a street off Primrose Hill, Hampstead. It was very near to where Mr and Mrs Frost lived – but very far from where I now lived (which was Clapham, SW London). However, I now had a car and I left the office in the City most evenings and, instead of going home like everyone else, I went up to Hampstead to supervise and check that the running of the shop was going well. Mr Frost had appointed me as a director of the company, which was called Leslie James Ltd; I was then twenty-five years old and this was my first directorship; he offered me shares in this company, which I took up but for which I had to pay £150.

Knowing now that I was leaving the company he did not hesitate to put the shop on the market and very quickly he found a buyer as that venture had been built up and was quite profitable. In my own time I joined him one weekend to help carry out a complete stock valuation, for on his own he would not know where to start. The job was done and frankly I was glad to see the back of the shop as it involved a lot of my time and travelling many evenings from the City to NW London and then home to South London.

Mr Frost asked me to come to his office during the following week as he wanted to give me a cheque for my involvement with Leslie James Ltd. I did so and he handed me the cheque in an envelope. When I got outside I opened it eagerly to see how much he had given me – it was a cheque for £150, exactly what I had paid for my shares in the first place! So all the hard work I had done over the past two years and the many late evenings home had apparently counted for nothing! At that point I knew that I had made the right decision to leave Mr Frost and join the Czechs.

I now had to think very deeply and very carefully as to my plans. In the first instance I had no choice but to work under the name of the Pilsner Beer Company which, although a Czech company, was of course a ridiculous name for a confectionery company. So my first task was to either think of a more suitable name or purchase a defunct company with a name more allied to confectionery. My second task was to agree with the Commercial Delegate my terms, i.e. salary, how to go on regarding expenses etc., for in my wild enthusiasm to get cracking in my new position I had not had the opportunity to tie things down in detail. As for office space, I had to be satisfied with a corner in the offices of Mr Purdy in Eastcheap. Mr Purdy was a Scottish communist, which probably explains why he was appointed UK agent for a number of Czechoslovak foods including Prague Ham (a ham with a special and wonderful flavour – Sour-Sweet Gherkins – the best ever in my view, especially when served with Prague Ham), various cheeses and other items. He operated out of offices in Eastcheap under the name of Inter-Allied Exports Ltd. This company was later absorbed into the Pilsner Beer group of companies of which mine would, in time, also become an associate company.

I had no choice but to accept this most unsatisfactory beginning but I knew quite well that I would soon sort out these teething problems. Mr Purdy loaned me a desk and a chair to sit on and Mr Stepan, the Commercial Delegate, borrowed on my behalf an old typewriter from the cellars of the Czechoslovak Embassy. I am sure this typewriter was older than me! In the Czech language they have a saying: *Zacatek je vdycky velmi tezky*, which roughly translated means 'The beginning is always very difficult' and Oh Boy! That saying certainly applied in my case!

After pressurising Mr Stepan, he agreed with me that we had to have a name which meant something in the confectionery world and that a beer title was quite unsuitable. He therefore searched in the Commercial Section of the Embassy since he knew that some defunct companies were taken over from Czech nationals in earlier years. He discovered several but the only one that came anywhere near to suitability was Sugosa Ltd., a company started pre-war by a Czech lady by the name of Mrs Marie Bernkoff (I am amazed that I can I recall these details after over half a century) which, as the name suggests, dealt in sugar in the late 1930s. For some reason Mrs Bernkoff was unable to continue the business and that was very probably connected with the outbreak of war and the resultant supply restrictions. Possibly because Mrs Bernkoff had no family, the Embassy took over all papers and rights to the company sometime after that. This happened with a number of other companies owned by former Czech nationals.

Well, at last we had a better name. I was appointed director of this company and Mr Stepan was the other director but in a completely non-executive role – the work of developing Sugosa into a successful confectionery company was down to me. That was the first step achieved. My next task was to find alternative premises of our own but that was not quite as easy and so I had no other choice but to continue occupying that corner in Mr Purdy's office. I had some very peculiar experiences there. One day Mr Purdy called me into his office and told me among other things that I should conduct myself in such a manner that whatever the situation, and whatever the circumstances, I should always proclaim that Koospol, the Foreign Trade Export Office in Prague and therefore the Principals of both him and me, were correct no matter what.

I did not like his manner, which was rather overbearing and condescending and he attempted to talk down to me; I told him frankly that I will run the confectionery business as I see fit, that it is my responsibility, and that if at any time I believed that Koospol were doing, or wanted to do something which I considered to be wrong, then I would tell them so in a very frank and open manner. I continued that I would not be carrying out my responsibilities in a proper manner if I did not. Mr Purdy did not like that at all.

Also I could hardly help but note that from time to time he had meetings of his political cronies and fellow communists in his office and they would play games just like children when they pretended that they were the government of the day. From my corner I could hear Mr Purdy saying, 'Well, you be the Foreign Minister today, you be the Chancellor, you be the Home Secretary and I'll be the Prime Minister.' At first I thought this was humorous and that they were playing games but then I must admit I eventually found it all to be somewhat alarming. I therefore resolved to get out of there as soon as possible.

Once the circumstances were right, it was not long before I found an office which had become vacant in Mark Lane. It was on the third floor of a nice building named Marlon House and consisted of four rooms; they were formerly the offices of a tea importing company. The room I chose for my office was a corner position and through the windows, which were on two sides of the room, I had an excellent view of Mark Lane where it connects with Fenchurch Street.

And so Sugosa was established there and I *did* build it up into a successful business. Of course, it was necessary for me to obtain a secretary and as luck would have it, one of our importers told me that they had a girl surplus to their requirements who was an excellent shorthand typist. Her name was Joan Gloster; I interviewed her, found her to be suitable and so I employed her. She developed into an absolutely first class secretary and without her I do not know on many occasions how I would have managed. She was very loyal to me, quick and very protective in times of stress. I owe her a great deal.

I do not want to bore the reader with a lot of details as to how the business developed but very quickly I ran into troubles. It is very difficult to explain fully why exclusivity, i.e. the granting of sole distribution rights to a buyer if there is such a word in the English language, was so important and necessary. But one can appreciate the problems posed by selling the same item to a number of different importers because, as I had experienced before when with Mr Frost, such a policy often resulted in chaos if a weak buyer decided to offload his stock at cheap prices because of lack of sales; that invariably meant that other stock holders of the same item were forced to follow suit and in all probability lose money.

But unfortunately, before I took up the reins, Mr Stepan was acting as a kind of 'caretaker' for the business and had sold an item from the Marysa factory in Moravia to a number of different importers. It was an Easter Cabinet with a half milk chocolate egg filled with chocolates in the upper part and a tray of chocolates in the lower part. A very nice line – but unfortunately, too many had been sold to too many different people; there was competition in prices among them therefore and sales had become difficult. In that kind of situation it only needed one stock holder to weaken and then the situation usually ended in price cutting. At that point the wholesalers did not quite know where they were and mostly opted to leave the item alone; in some cases the buyers probably felt that if they waited long enough, they would be able to buy at quite cheap prices.

One large buyer had a shipment en route and they advised me that some of their wholesale customers were complaining that when the tray was pulled out the chocolates were scraped by the upper part of the cabinet and that did not look nice. They informed me that they would not therefore be accepting the next shipment when it arrived. Of course the reason the Seller gave for rejecting the merchandise was not the real reason at all; he was rejecting the goods because he was experiencing difficulty in selling them, for as I have earlier indicated, too many had been sold to too many different buyers and they were all calling upon the same wholesalers. So my new position began with headaches but I knew that I not only had to get used to such experiences but I also had to learn how to overcome them.

But my beginning was not all bad news. For example, Mr Stepan passed me an enquiry he had received at the Commercial Section concerning lollipops. This potential buyer was up in Fleetwood and was in fact a seaside rock manufacturer himself. His name was Freddy Greenwood and what a character he was; a fellow who had also come from either a poor or an ordinary background, had made a lot of money during the war by discovering that you could buy an item called Sweetened Fat off ration – if you could get it – and that this commodity had a very high sugar content. Sugar of course was very strictly rationed but Sweetened Fat wasn't. So Freddy experimented and found he could make a very acceptable standard of ice cream using Sweetened Fat as a base and he made a fortune.

However, he was a gambler who had a small string of racehorses and he gambled with a lot of quite famous people. He told me that, for example, he had gambled with Jeanette McDonald the famous singer and film actress who, by all accounts, liked betting and gambling. Anyhow, he lost much of his money but not before having developed a taste for the high life. I first met Freddy at the Strand Palace Hotel. This was back in the days when the Strand Palace was one of the nicest hotels you could ever wish to stay at and when a man in top hat and an immaculate brown uniform stood outside and opened your car door for you when you drew up; if it was raining he would protect you with a large umbrella. It bears no relationship to the Strand Palace of today which, in my opinion, has been completely spoiled – they call it modernisation but in so doing, they have totally destroyed the character of this once fine hotel! Anyway, Freddy was accompanied by another gentleman; he was an accountant and, knowing later what I didn't know at the time, I subsequently discovered that this accountant was attached to Freddy for most of the time and represented his creditors to whom he still owed money – all of this was unknown to us.

The accountant's task was to watch Freddy and see that he didn't spend money recklessly. But the charm of Freddy soon overcame the accountant and it was quite evident that he too enjoyed nice hotels, good food, etc.; but he frowned upon some of Freddy's activities, particularly those concerning the opposite sex. However I heard from a reliable authority that on occasions he also succumbed in that respect! In other words, looking back, Freddy had the accountant just where he wanted him but, as time went, by I learned a lot from the accountant about Freddy; he told me things which he should not have and whilst not wishing to stand in the way of business, my knowledge of these factors did put me on my guard.

Freddy's interest in Czechoslovak confectionery lay principally in the product of one of our factories in Slovakia, in a town called Trnava where they produced lollipops which had pictures of assorted varieties of flowers in them. The Director of this factory was a man called Mr Sloboda. Now Freddy was still manufacturing seaside rock up in Fleetwood/Blackpool and as a manufacturer, he marvelled at the skill with which these picture lollies were made. He wanted to buy the whole capacity of the factory. But by this time, although not wanting to pass over an opportunity to begin my new position not just with troubles but with a nice fat contract, I was already more than just a little wary. Somehow, I reasoned, we had to have a safety clause and I had to get this man to buy on a basis whereby he will agree to put down a percentage of the value of the goods as a deposit with us before despatch from the factory – just as a precaution. Well Freddy was so desperate to obtain exclusive rights for the picture lollipops that he therefore agreed with our somewhat severe terms.

So this is what we were negotiating at the Strand Palace Hotel that evening. As time went on, we were all getting rather thirsty and hungry and so Freddy suggested we adjourn to get something to eat and drink. To my great surprise, Freddy took us across the road – to the Savoy Grill no less! Wasn't this the favourite restaurant of Winston Churchill himself? And Vivien Leigh and Laurence Olivier, too? And innumerable other famous people? To say I was thrilled to bits to be going there to dine would be an understatement. In terms of actual miles it was not all that far from the Strand to the East End Docklands but to me, such establishments were a million miles away and never did I ever dream that I would one day frequent such exotic places. I had better get used to it, I thought, which I most certainly did, because possibly these kinds of very nice experiences were going to happen quite a lot in the coming years. I was not wrong about that!

Somewhat later on, I received a request from Prague to the effect that Mr Sloboda, the Director of the factory that produced these picture lollipops, would like to pay a visit to the UK, that he would like to visit Blackpool, the world's centre for lettered rock, in order to see how the experts put the lettering in this very popular type of confection. This was one of the skills not yet developed at Trnava and he wanted to see if this might be achieved at his factory in Slovakia; I too was very interested in this type of development as I had other new line ideas where lettering would be necessary. And so I immediately contacted Freddy Greenwood who responded enthusiastically and said that Mr Sloboda could see and learn everything he wanted to in his factory.

And so Mr Sloboda duly arrived in London and we, i.e. Mr Stepan and myself, took him up to Blackpool where Freddy was the perfect host – he was very good at hospitality was Freddy. Anyway, Mr Sloboda was shown everything he wanted to see, noted carefully how the sugar mass was prepared, then rolled on to a large table and how the confectionery technicians placed the required lettering very carefully, then equally carefully, rolled the mass up into a quite long sausage-like shape and the whole was then placed in a special machine which was thick at one end and thin at the other and which revolved, thus pushing the rock forward and persuading the mass towards the point where another technician, and this requires an awful lot of skill and experience, plucks the thin end and pulls it. Thus the machine extrudes the rock which is now only 1.5 inches in diameter. Perfect! Watching rock being produced from a basic lump of sugar mass to the finished product is a very interesting experience.

Mr Sloboda was enthralled by the lettering procedure and afterwards thanked Freddy, and us, profusely as he had learned a lot. For the remainder of his visit we looked after Mr Sloboda, showed him all the sights and visited a few nice restaurants; I am sure he had a good time. I was sure that our treatment of Mr Sloboda and his obvious enjoyment of his visit to the UK would stand us in good stead at some time in the future – and I will explain later in this narrative that it did!

I mentioned earlier that after the birth of our first child I was determined to increase my efforts to get us out of the East End. Both Lynne and myself wanted our children to grow up in a better atmosphere than that. Furthermore, to look after a baby with all that that entails, was not at all easy for Lynne living in a three-room flat with extremely limited facilities and I was very conscious of that too and determined to do something about it. But although my income had increased since leaving Hale Hamilton, I didn't think it was the right time to consider buying a property.

I had to accept that, for the time being, we were reliant completely on obtaining a move via the Council and it seemed a pretty hopeless task before me. But then, in 1953, a stroke of luck occurred – it so happened that a friend of Lynne's mother had a friend who worked for the London County Council and when she heard about us, she promised to see what she could do. Imagine, therefore, our great surprise and pleasure to receive a letter from the Council stating that we had been approved for a new flat on a new estate in Clapham. We went to see the flat, which to us was amazing, and we were given to understand that the Council was trying to preserve this estate for the well behaved type of council tenant. The flat had only two bedrooms but a spacious lounge, a kitchen of course, and that luxury we did not have back at Prestage Buildings – a bathroom!

For us it was a heavenly change for the better; the only snag was that Lynne's mother, who was partly responsible for us obtaining this flat, had to come with us – what alternative did we have? At that time we had only the one child and so Lynne's mother slept in the second bedroom with her. However, despite the fact that we were eternally grateful to Lynne's mother for her help, we did gently suggest to her, after a suitable period, that it might be a good idea if she started to look for a small place for herself. After all, I had never intended that this arrangement would last for ever.

From time to time we tried to encourage her, pointing out how better it would be for her to be independent. But no matter what we said, it was clear that she really had no intention of even trying. Matters came to a head in the latter part of 1953 when Lynne became pregnant again with our second child, Philip. We were not at all happy with an arrangement where by she would sleep in the second bedroom with two children and so we became more and more urgent in our entreaties to her to make an effort. Lynne and I even looked ourselves – but there was no sign of her budging and the situation remained like that until the bubble burst just before I was due to fly to Prague for the third and last visit in the company of Mr Frost.

I was forced to give Lynne's mother an ultimatum and told her that if she was still in our flat by the time I came back, I personally would go straight to a hotel and that unless she wanted to ruin a very happy marriage, she knew what she had to do. I did not want to do this; it is not my style. But something had to be done and I could think of no other way to force the issue. By the time I returned from Prague she had found a flat not too far away from us; she had not physically moved there but all was in hand and in a matter of a week or two, she did. We of course told her we would keep a close eye on her and that any time she wanted to come and visit, our door would always be open for her. It was a long journey for her to travel back to Poplar each day but she wanted to keep her job as book-keeper to this firm in Poplar; eventually they offered her a flat in Moness Street, Poplar, which belonged to them. Moness Street, incidentally, was the same street where years before I had almost been struck by shrapnel during a heavy raid. It was a great relief to both Lynne and myself to have extricated ourselves from this very difficult situation.

Back to business – I was not able to deal with the problem of Easter Cabinets I had inherited when taking over in a manner to my own satisfaction; the rejected goods had to be returned to Czechoslovakia and any further shipments halted. But in other respects, business was going well. However, I had been very foolish in retrospect in plunging in without negotiating and obtaining a clear contractual situation with Mr Stepan as far as my personal arrangements were concerned. We had agreed that I would begin by drawing the same salary as I was drawing with Harold Frost which was just £20 per week. However, it was never intended, certainly not on my part, that this was my final income status.

But somehow we never seemed to get the time or the opportunity to sit down quietly and discuss the matter. It is true that Prague had sent a proposal giving me an incentive arrangement but bearing in mind that the whole business had to be started up from scratch again, their proposals were far too ambitious, even unrealistic, and their terms too vague. I resolved to discuss this in Prague at some future opportunity. But once again we found ourselves always so busy we never seemed to find the right time to talk about it. Looking back, I think my reluctance to raise the matter was from my own inexperience. I should have tackled it with more determination and much sooner with Mr Stepan. But he was such a nice person, I felt that it would be a great pity if we came to a disagreement in the course of negotiations to spoil the excellent relationship I had with him. I am afraid this reluctance to fight for myself followed me all the way during my career – until I started my own business and worked for myself. I was a better 'Boss' to me than any of those I had before!

Well as time went by the business developed to an extent but my business brain started to work. It seemed to me that acting simply as selling agents and working on a commission only basis, thus leaving the efficiency of sales and distribution of our products to the various importers, was not the best system. And it was often very frustrating when

I had a good line to offer but was turned down because the importers were able to buy something similar from an alternative source. Also there was the profit factor to bear in mind; Sugosa was, as I have indicated, earning only a small commission on sales – the main profits were, of course, being earned by the importers. I thought about this situation continually and the more I thought about it, the more I became convinced that we should control the sale and distribution of our products ourselves. I therefore was of the view that we should make Sugosa a direct selling and distribution unit. I began to make noises in Prague but it took a long time before they thought about my proposals and I was asked to put forward a plan, and a financial estimate that could be considered, complete with details of anticipated costs, turnover, gross and net profits, etc. I had never formulated such a plan before, nor had I carried out such calculations and forecasts previously in my life. But when needs must I found I could do so – and did! I realised that I was asking Prague to place an enormous amount of confidence in my abilities to organise, institute, and control both sales and distribution of all products throughout the whole UK. But there I had to leave the matter for a while and not press too hard – otherwise I might get rejected.

Meanwhile, Mr Stepan had to return to Prague and he was replaced in London by our old friend Karel Jiracek ! I was not at all sure that this appointment would eventually work well for me. I had experienced many a difficulty with Karel, sometimes called 'Charlie', but all in all it was not as bad as I thought it might have been. He was a changeable sort of chap; sometimes nice and affable and at other times, difficult and impossible. A real Dr Jekyll and Mr Hyde situation.

However, the case of Jiri Stepan needs some comment, for after his return to Prague he was given a managerial post in the Sugar Department at Koospol but, as in the case of all those people engaged in foreign appointments, their behaviour and attitude was always subject to scrutiny in the communist system.

Looking back, I think that almost certainly someone who probably had some kind of a grudge against him had lodged certain allegations about Jiri Stepan – and I have a feeling that I know who that 'someone' was. Jiri was therefore ordered to appear before the usual committee to explain himself. These committees were almost always comprised stalwart communists – and maybe others, who, fearing for their own positions, could be relied upon to follow the lead of the rest. So my good friend made his appearance and was accused of improper behaviour whilst in London by making too many friendships with English people.

This was of course a preposterous accusation. Did they think that Jiri could do his job efficiently by making enemies?

But in the communist world, once you have been accused it is very difficult to wipe the slate clean. The committee refused to accept Jiri's absolute denials of any impropriety or accusations of having developed relationships in England which were unhealthily close, and consequently he was told that he may no longer work in foreign trade. So poor old Jiri, one of the finest diplomats and gentlemen ever to grace the steps at the London Embassy, lost his job which was really a serious situation for him.

Once again, I have to explain that in the communist system, every person's working record is documented and follows that person around. Therefore it was perfectly clear to any other government department or nationalised company – nothing private was allowed to exist – why the person in question had left or was discharged from his previous position. And there were a great many managers and directors who just would not take the risk of employing a person with a record of so called 'improper political behaviour'; under communism it is very dangerous to make the wrong move for you, too, could be accused 'by association'. So Jiri's situation was dire and it was diabolical that this clever man, a fine gentleman if ever I met one and a man who spoke several languages, could not obtain employment.

One wonders what might have happened to Jiri (whom I called 'George' by the way) and his family had it not been for Mr Novy, who was Commercial Attaché to the UK during the time Jiri was Commercial Delegate in London. Mr Novy was now back in Prague and had been appointed Director of Cedok, the government organisation which controlled all travel, hotels, etc., throughout the whole country. Mr Novy knew that Jiri was totally innocent of the charges made against him and he also knew he was a clever and hard working man. So Mr Novy called him to his office for a talk.

You may wonder, dear reader, why Mr Novy should be prepared to take such a risk and the answer lies in the fact that everybody's situation in that strange world of communism depended on your position either in, or with, the Communist Party. Mr Novy's position was extremely strong and he need not fear anyone; very few would want to cross Mr Novy. So Mr Novy asked Jiri how he would fancy working at one of the hotels that he controlled. Jiri, by now somewhat depressed and without a job, jumped at the chance and that is how he became Reception Manager of the Hotel International – a huge hotel built in the Russian style. Built originally for the military as a school for officers, it was subsequently changed into a hotel. It partly catered for people in transit, as it was not too far from Ruzyne Airport, and partly, of course, for normal guests – like me, if I can be allowed to include myself in that category. So for Jiri things had turned out not too badly after all. He liked his job at the International and I stayed there many times and kept my relationship with him on a close level. He always made sure that the rooms I occupied there were the best and I am not sure about this but I do believe that when he could he charged me the rate applicable to Czechoslovak citizens not the rate for foreign guests which was considerably higher! I only know that my excellent accommodation there was extraordinarily cheap.

Jiri stayed at Hotel International for quite a number of years but eventually, after years of service, had to leave because something happened at the hotel concerning foreign currency and Jiri became implicated in this quite innocently. Foreign currency was in very short supply right up to the time almost of the Velvet Revolution in 1989, when finally the communists were thrown out of power; this time the Russians did not intervene being quite occupied with their own problems at home! But at almost every hotel visited by foreigners, especially those from the Western countries, one would be asked if you wished to exchange some dollars or pounds or Deutschmarks for Czechoslovak crowns – and very often this would involve staff working at the hotel – especially the waiters.

If you wanted to get involved in that sort of thing, which could be quite dangerous if discovered, you could get a much better rate of exchange than in the bank – sometimes even 100% higher!. Thus most people throughout the country became involved in currency arrangements. For ordinary people the possession of foreign currency was very important because it then enabled them to go to the special Tuzex shops where they could buy many items which were quite unobtainable in normal shops. Anyway, it so happened that there was quite a scandal at Hotel International over foreign currency dealings and *all* the managerial staff were obliged to leave their jobs whether they were directly involved or not. Everybody was summarily dismissed and replaced with others – the innocent as well as the guilty. And that is why Jiri had to leave his job at Hotel International.

Unfortunately, his good friend and mentor, Mr Novy, had moved on from the earlier position and so was not there to protect Jiri. For a short while he worked in the offices of Cedok, the state travel organisation, but at a very ordinary clerical level and for a man of his intelligence and experience it was a ridiculous situation. However it was not for ever and later on, a friend who was employed in the State Bank recommended his name as a suitable candidate for the position as Personal Assistant to the Director of the bank. This was a much better position, for he had to organise everything for not only his direct boss but also to look after the various financial guests, including eminent people such as Ministers of Finance from various countries. He did his job well and so stayed at the Bank until his retirement and now spends his time between Prague and Zeleznice in Northern Bohemia where he has a cottage. He and his wife, Jarka, have become very dear friends of ours.

Back to London: and so, as Jiri Stepan had been replaced at the Embassy by Karel Jiracek, it was he I had to deal with, for the Commercial Delegate also took the positions as Managing Director of the Pilsner Beer Group controlling the three Czech companies dealing with foods, beer, sugars, etc., which had now been amalgamated. I viewed this prospect with some misgivings, for Karel Jiracek and I didn't see eye to eye on many things; I found his swaggering, somewhat arrogant, style difficult to handle. But now, having at last received the go ahead from Prague in respect of my revolutionary idea to change the function of Sugosa, it was my task to put my massive plan into operation.

However, I had made it clear from the very beginning that knowing the creation of a national sales and distribution organisation and developing it successfully, was going to take not only a lot of effort on my part but a lot of midnight candle burning, travelling and absence from family and home, as well as a big responsibility on my young shoulders; I would insist on being properly rewarded for my efforts. This time I did stick up for myself because I could clearly see that in such a set up, nobody else would fight for me – except me! However, when Jiracek replaced Jiri Stepan I felt it was advisable to restate details of my stipulation so that all would be clear to everybody. And so I spoke with Jiracek about the agreed salary basis which would mean that from the beginning of the new plan being put into operation my salary would be increased to £2,000 per annum which, I admit, was a very good salary for those days when the national average wage was not much above £500 per annum, perhaps even less. But I was absolutely certain that I would have to work very hard in order to ensure success and would, therefore, earn and be entitled to such a salary.

Jiracek paused when I spoke about this and then said that was OK but my salary should be increased only in instalments! This was totally contrary to what I had already agreed earlier and I am afraid I showed my great displeasure by telling Jiracek that he could find somebody else to do the job because I was fed up with my low salary basis which was not commensurate with the degree of responsibility my position entailed and I most certainly would not be prepared to work in an extraordinary manner at all hours of God's night and day for a very ordinary level of financial reward. I therefore insisted on the full salary increase originally agreed with his predecessor – and without any conditions. Jiracek saw that I was in a very determined and somewhat angry mood and backtracked immediately; that subject was never raised again!

As to the UK sales organisation I put together, I will not bore you, dear reader, with all of the details. But by early 1959 I had managed to appoint twelve sales agents who would represent us in every part of the UK, including Northern Ireland. This meant many miles of travelling for me, lots of discussions, much humping of my large sample range in and out of hotels and to be quite honest, I was glad to get home now and then to feel a little more normal. But at last the task was achieved and we could get started with our new operation.

As a rather pleasant aside, I would however like to mention that one of the agents I appointed was a chap called Bert Dance who lived in Birkenhead. Bert had acted as an agent to one of our importers in earlier years and I had no hesitation in appointing him our agent for Lancashire including Cheshire and N. Wales. I visited Bert, as well as our other agents, as often as I could and occasionally Bert's daughter, Jean, would bring us tea. Jean sometimes helped her father in his business. She was a beautiful girl and once told me that she aspired to be an actress and that she was joining the Liverpool Repertory Theatre very shortly. I remember wishing her lots of luck and saying to her that I was sure she would be a big success. Well, I was correct, for that young girl eventually became Jean Boht of television fame and her name became well known by a great many people when she played the part of Nellie Boswell in the popular TV programme, *Bread*!

Meanwhile, one thing happened which will show what kind of a person Jiracek was and what I had to contend with. In all my travels building up our sales organisation I was using my own car, bought with my own money and for which I received no allowance whatsoever, except petrol usage whilst on business – another gross error of mine – and during a trip somewhere in the North Western part of England, I broke down right on a roundabout. I think someone helped me to push the car to the side of the road and I walked to find the nearest garage.

They examined my car, which was a Ford Prefect, and announced that one or some teeth of the gear change had broken off and would need to be renewed. However, the spare parts would not arrive until the following day and so I had to find somewhere to sleep for the night. I did so in the small village nearby and a very nice and attractive little inn it was too. The next day I collected my car and paid the repair bill which was £14 something – what such a repair would cost these days I have absolutely no idea, but a great deal more than £14! As I was on my way back to London, I went to my office before going home for a well earned rest; whilst I was there Jiracek called in and he asked me about my tour and I gave him a good report as to what I had achieved. I mentioned the mishap with my car and the £14 bill and, only because I was always very conscious of the fact that, although I was the Director of Sugosa, it was not my money and so whenever items of expenditure or expenses arose, I always made a point of discussing it with my Czech co-director out of respect.

I told Jiracek that I proposed claiming this item on my expense sheet as I was travelling on company business but on this day Jiracek was in one of his argumentative moods and said that such a mishap could have occurred anywhere, anytime and that as it was my personal car, I should pay the bill myself and not claim it as a legitimate expense. Well we had a little quarrel about this too but he would not budge; I became exasperated with the conversation. I have never in my life begged for money and was not about to begin so doing and therefore I ended the discussion – I was much too proud for situations like this and so I paid the bill from my own pocket; for the use of my car I claimed not a penny – just petrol expenses for which I provided the bills. How foolish can one be?

From a personal point of view our business was going quite well and with my increased income, we began to go places. Our family had been added to by a son, Philip, and many were the Sundays when we all jumped into my car and visited one seaside place or another returning in the evening sunburned and looking well whilst the London area was either soaked with rain or covered with thick clouds. We always found it amazing when sometimes we would leave the cloudy or rainy London area behind us but found brilliant blue skies and sunshine when we reached the coast! I have to say that motoring in the late 50s and early 60s was as different to these days as chalk is to cheese. Leaving our flat in Clapham we could be by the sea well within two hours travelling at only moderate speeds; so with an early start we could be walking along the seafront by 9.00am, looking for somewhere to enjoy breakfast. The return journey was not quite as good; I suppose that more people co-ordinated their time of departure than they did their time of arrival and that of course led to a slightly heavier traffic level when returning. But in general it was very pleasant motoring and not to be compared with the traffic snarl-ups that are commonplace these days and which spoil so many family outings or indeed the level of crowds at the resorts. Today, wherever one goes in the UK it is crowded and places that were once quiet areas and country pubs where you used to find maybe ten people are now packed, and this, sadly, has led to a deterioration in quality and service standards in my opinion. Back in the 1950-60s it was all so very different and much more pleasant; we enjoyed some wonderful Sundays at various places like Dymchurch, Bognor Regis, Brighton, Eastbourne, etc.

But it was about this time when one day our children, just Jackie and Philip then, came in from play and quite innocently began to use bad words. In their innocence they had no idea of the meaning of the words they were using – they had just picked them up from other children. Well, that was the last straw for Lynne and I. We had noticed that this lovely estate had been deteriorating for some while and one wonders why it is that people destroy such nice places by their behaviour and actions. Also, when taking into account my salary increase to £2,000 per annum, a high salary for that time, this placed me in a somewhat different situation and so Lynne and I decided it was time for us to consider buying our first house. Therefore at the weekends we started to look at houses rather than go to the coast. For us, Surrey was an obvious area to look at and to cut a long story short, we found a detached three-bedroom house with garage in a place not too far from London but almost looked as though it was somewhere in the countryside.

This was Old Coulsdon which lies between Caterham and Coulsdon. The price was £3,250! Yes – £3,250! It wasn't quite what I had in mind; I thought it was a bit too small and offered little opportunity to extend or improve the property. But, we considered, we could buy this house and move into the area; this would place us within the locality we liked and we could keep our eyes open for a property that suited us rather more. In the event, we stayed there for eight years!

Before that we had viewed a very large property near to Epsom which was owned by an Indian gentleman and previously owned by Commander Campbell, formerly of BBC fame. The property was quite considerable with a big house of obvious quality, a number of outhouses, shed, stables etc., and what looked like a substantial area of ground, too. The price was £11, 500 and looking back what a fool I was not to have bought it, for today it must be worth well over £1 million – perhaps even £2 million! With a salary of £2,000 p.a. it was a purchase not totally beyond my means but my cautious inner self, who had never liked owing money to anybody, would not allow me. And so we bought the house in Old Coulsdon and lived there happily for the next eight years.

I would also like to mention at this point the Lyons Corner Houses which in my opinion were truly wonderful places for those who liked entertainment together with eating a very acceptable standard of food etc., but did not want to spend a fortune doing so. I think one of our early visits to the Strand Corner House was New Year's Eve 1949. It was a Grand Dinner and Ball; a three-course dinner would be served followed by a cabaret show and then followed by dancing to the orchestra. The price per person? It is hardly believable now but it was 17/6d! Or 87½p! And if you wanted a bottle of good wine with your meal – that was five shillings. Or 25p! So for 22/6d, or £1.12p in present money, you had a complete evening of enjoyable entertainment. We started to go regularly every New Year's Eve with our friends, Jean and Ken Shore, and if I remember correctly, the price went from 17/6d to £1.00, then £1.5.0d and then a big jump to £1.17.6d!

But quite apart from the New Year's Eve Balls, we would sometimes take the children there. On one occasion I had received tickets from Enid Blyton's agent for the Noddy show in a London theatre; more about Enid Blyton and Noddy later on. So it was an ideal opportunity to take our children to the Corner House. We walked downstairs to the Brasserie; it was a lovely entrance, all thickly carpeted, and as you descended you could hear the strains of the so called 'gypsy' orchestra playing. You were then shown to your table by a girl dressed in black and white frilly uniform if you were there in the day, or a man with a long white apron during the evenings. They all spoke to you in a very nice way and, most importantly, they were properly trained in their jobs. The menu was quite extensive and very reasonable as far as price was concerned.

In those days one could mention quietly, as I did on one occasion, that my daughter was enjoying her birthday treat; he would ask her name and age and then go away. After ten minutes or so he would return with a small round cake with just one candle on it and simultaneously the band would strike up with 'Happy birthday to you, happy birthday to you, happy birthday dear Jackie, happy birthday to you.' Of course everybody joined in and the picture on my darling daughter's face should have been captured on camera – but I didn't have one with me. There was no extra charge for this additional treat incidentally! It was a lovely gesture – gratis, free!

These were very nice experiences and I cannot finish this part of the narrative without also mentioning that later Lyons began what they called

'Showboat'. This was also held in the old Brasserie and you paid an entrance fee of a sum but I cannot now recall what it was – but let's say £5 per person. For this you had a three-course meal served by the men in long white aprons, then followed an excellent cabaret and then dancing to the orchestra. At that time the 'Talk of the Town' was indeed the talk of the town and everybody wanted to go there. We went there on a number of occasions, the last being the farewell appearance of the extremely popular group at that time, The Seekers. I cannot now remember what the prices there were but it was considerably more than Showboat at the Strand Corner House – and, in my humble opinion, it was not as good as Showboat when considering the quality of food served, the service, etc.! It is true that the level of the entertainment was not of the standard of Talk of the Town but it was very good considering the difference in price. I used to entertain a lot of Czechs there at the Showboat from time to time when they were visiting London and they were very satisfied when being taken there.

Alas! The Corner Houses are no more; at least not as they were. Lyons was taken over and the new management evidently saw things rather differently. They embarked on a programme to modernise the Corner Houses and in so doing they killed off a landmark and a special feature of entertainment in London of particular interest to those who wanted to feel that they had 'been out' but without spending more than they could afford in doing so. The last time I visited the Strand Corner House, I was very sad indeed to see what it had become when compared to the old days. It was more like a hamburger and pizza joint. What a tragedy – and all in the name of progress of course!

It was the same with the Strand Palace Hotel, which was also owned by Lyons and, as I have related earlier, was once regarded as one of the top London hotels and what a lovely hotel it used to be. The entrance was quite impressive; I accommodated a lot of people there when they were visiting from the factories in Czechoslovakia and I knew it very well. From the foyer you went downstairs to the Exeter Bar and after a drink or two there, you wandered into the Exeter Room which was a first class restaurant. I ate and drank there many times. Today it is but a shadow of the fine hotel it once was.

I once heard that the present management intended to bring back the Corner Houses but as I live now in Devon I have no idea if that is true. But what I do know is that it was a tragedy to end the days of the Corner Houses in the way they did because to a great many people, the Corner Houses had become part of London – a place where ordinary people could go for good food and entertainment at very reasonable prices and where you knew you would never be ripped off.

Searching for a good place to entertain my staff for a Christmas do when I had my own business, I did make some enquiries to the new management of Lyons one year, perhaps late 1970s or so, and the lady I spoke to told me that I was just one of so many people who call with the same enquiry about the Corner Houses. She intimated that this had been noted by the management and they were considering how they might bring them back as once they were. I heard no more, although the lady promised to keep me advised of developments. I am afraid the Corner Houses of the 1949-1960 era that we knew have gone forever – and as I have said before, all in the name of progress of course!

But now, in this period of the end of the 1950s and beginning of the 1960s I found that those importer clients we were still dealing with always wanted to be the first to be considered whenever new lines were offered on the British market; I was of course the person responsible for deciding to whom I would offer such lines. As a consequence, I and sometimes my wife Lynne, were being invited to all kinds of wonderful places to either lunch or dine. I recall Simpsons of the Strand which served the finest roast lunches and dinners in London and where the tradition was that you tipped the man who carved your meat with 2/6d – no more, no less. Then I had lunch at the Savoy Hotel; I had already been introduced to the Savoy Grill by Freddy Greenwood and it was very interesting to compare the two. Then, as I have said, in those days The Strand Palace was very good and I often ate in their Exeter Room. Then there was the Caprice and so many others that I can't remember them all – it seems such a long time ago.

But I do recall that never to be forgotten evening when Lynne and I were guests of honour at the Dorchester Hotel on the occasion of the Candy Queen Ball in 1960. This only arose because as UK Director I was also responsible for the advertisement of our products. I was given a budget to stick to but it was up to me mainly where and what kind of advertising we invested in and I cooperated closely with RAPID, the State Advertising Organisation in Prague, and their agents in London. And so I was able to book the double page centre spread of the *Confectionery Journal*, our main trade magazine, for every issue for the whole year. As the journal was organising this particular Ball, and I was then an important customer, I suppose they thought it would be a good idea to invite Lynne and I as guests of honour. To this day I do not know what obligations this had cast upon me. Would I be required to make a speech? Would I help choose the Candy Queen?

I was never to know because whilst having a pre-dinner drink in the bar I was called urgently to the phone. My father had suffered a heart attack and was in a critical condition at St Andrews Hospital, Bow. I was advised it would be better to come there immediately. And so, without further ado, Lynne and I left the Dorchester and raced to the hospital.

My father looked very poorly indeed. Nobody knew what was going to happen but it did seem that nothing was going to occur imminently. So Lynne, in all her finery, went home with my mother to keep her company and my childhood pal, Sid Morris, stayed with me at the hospital. In fact we stayed all night long; I suppose that in evening dress I must have looked like a waiter who had come straight from the restaurant! My father did regain consciousness during the night and asked for a cup of tea which the nurse was glad to get for him. At round about dawn Sid and I decided to return home as my father appeared to be sleeping peacefully. I collected Lynne, went home to our flat at Clapham, changed my clothing, and then we returned to the hospital where we found the condition of my father had worsened. He passed away later that morning and I felt that he knew he was leaving us because the last thing he did was to pull down the head of my eldest brother, Bill, kiss him, and tell him he loved him. It is always a sad and terrible time when a loved one passes away and this was no exception. Our dear old Dad had left us. I never went to the Dorchester again after that and I never wanted to – that place had unhappy memories for me.

In the planning and execution of our business it was of course necessary for me to go not only to Prague quite often but also to the main factories, which were situated all over the country and were involved in exports or were instructed to involve themselves in exports. Those factories had their plans too but if the targets they were set for exports were achieved, then there were a number of rewards granted to them. For example, they would be given an allocation of foreign currency with which to purchase spare parts for their old, even archaic machinery; in addition, they would be granted an amount in Czech crowns to maybe purchase a country residence where workers could go free of charge for a weekend or even a short holiday at little or no cost if they had carried out their duties in an exemplary manner. Or perhaps even a coach to take the workers on trips. And so the factory managements were very keen on exports – as long as it was convenient to them! This was a much better plan than the earlier ones when quantity targets ruled the day, resulting in huge quantities of easily made but unwanted stocks in all the factory warehouses.

I believe the first factory I ever visited was called Marysa in a small town, Jihimoravska in Moravia. On my first visits we always were accompanied by two people who changed on every trip and whom I did not know from Adam. Later I was informed very quietly that one person was from the Trade Union and the other from some department responsible for security. After several visits, when they saw I was a serious and responsible person who would not, for example, preach to anybody in the factories about any supposed superiority of the capitalist system or even make a lot of noise telling people how much better we live in the West, my visits were allowed to the factories without these special people accompanying us.

We went by night train as I recall and during the journey slept in bunk beds. But the conditions on Czechoslovak trains were rather primitive and not to be compared with the sleeper services on our trains in Britain. We arrived at our destination very early in the morning – before even the crack of dawn! I recall standing in the outer room of the factory, waiting for the Director's meeting to finish so that we could enter when the lady standing next to me began to shiver – she was the Trade Union representative. And so, wanting to demonstrate my rapidly developing knowledge of the Czech language I said to her, 'Vy ste studene?' – which I thought meant 'Are you cold?', and she began to laugh at me. I was quite puzzled at this and later on I asked Mirek, one of our colleagues from Koospol, about this. He asked me to repeat my question, which I did, and then he started to laugh! Wishing to be put out of my misery I asked Mirek if I had said something funny. 'Yes David, it was incorrect. You should have said simply "Jste zima?",' Mirek replied, which according to my Czech lessons, means 'Are you wintry?' but is the way to ask someone if they are cold! What I had actually asked the lady originally was 'Are you frigid?'. Well, no wonder she laughed at me! Hard to understand the difference? Me too! But although in the end I conquered many of these differences I continued to make errors when speaking Czech and I still do. However, I do not let this stop me in any way from talking in Czech and if I make an error, I laugh along with the others – I never get embarrassed!

A further feature of these factory visits was that every factory was guarded at the entrance by a person and once again it was a fat lady wearing a red armband, a uniform very like an army uniform and a pistol belt around her waist – just like at the airport. Obviously I had to use my discretion and not ask directly but in a roundabout way I enquired about these fierce looking ladies and was told that they were members of the

People's Militia and had the responsibility of guarding factories. This amused me for who would want to steal the most valuable secrets of a confectionery factory? But this was the communist way – suspicious about everything and everybody!

Another thing I noticed was that every time we entered the Managing Director's office there were always probably three bottles of Slivovice (plum brandy) on his conference table. So no matter what time of day it was the first point was to drink a glass of that horrible drink which over many years of sampling I never came to like. I, not knowing Slivovice at all, just sipped at my glass when the Director raised his glass. But he noticed that and said something to me in Czech which one of our colleagues from Koospol, the Foreign Trade Organisation, translated – because at that time I spoke only a little conversational Czech, although I was getting better and better. Apparently he was gently chiding me for sipping my drink and was recommending me to drink in the Moravian style – bottoms up and down the hatch! Well, I was quite unused to strong drink and try as I may, I could not do that.

Another point which I observed was that when glasses needed refilling they did not use the partially consumed bottle – they opened a new one. Much later I discovered why – the Director and his colleagues shared out what was left afterwards and took them home! And it was the same with lunches and dinners – I needed only to talk to several people in the factory, i.e. the Director himself, the Export Manager, the Packaging Manager and the Production Manager. But when the talking broke up and we all went to lunch or to dinner, depending on the time of day, we usually went to a nearby hotel or restaurant. However, when we got there a great, long, table had been prepared with floral decorations etc., and it looked very nice indeed but I was surprised to see that already seated at this table were a number of additional people from the factory that I did not know. It seemed that the Director had invited half the factory and, I do not doubt, a few of his personal friends, to this meal which was more like a banquet – and all in my honour! As smoking was not frowned upon in those days there was even a packet of cigarettes placed at each person's place. At first I have to admit that I was very appreciative of these gestures but as time went on, I began to wish that there were not so many lunches and dinners – my constitution, and the shape of my figure, were both suffering as I went from factory to factory and in any case I had work to get on with! I also learned, when I became more experienced, that the factories used my visits as excuses to drink Slivovice, and take it home as I have said, and have grand lunches or dinners to which they also invited their cronies – but really they were entertaining themselves and using my visits as justification for such occasions and to charge the costs against expenses. Now why does anyone think that may only happen in communist Czechoslovakia?

On one early visit, in 1958, I was forewarned that the question of packaging and design suitable for export was going to come up and so I purchased a number of English boxes and packets to demonstrate what was needed for the British market and equipped myself with an extra suitcase in which to place them. It was just as well, for when I arrived in Prague I was told that a meeting of all the artists used by the HQ, called Ceskeslovenske Cokoladovny, had been arranged and they requested that I address them and speak about designs for the UK and explain what it was that I needed to help me carry out my work back home in a better manner. I suppose there were about twelve or so of these artists and although I was quite unaccustomed to giving lectures, I did so and at the end of what I had to say they clapped me and said they had learned something about the requirements of the British market which would be very helpful to them. We had a coffee break about halfway through and during that time one of the artists approached me; he introduced himself as Jiri Trnka. He then asked me if I played golf and I very enthusiastically told him that I did. He asked where did I play and we discussed various courses in Britain, some of which he knew as he had read about them in golf magazines he was fortunate enough to get hold of. He told me that he played mostly at Marianske Lazne and sometimes at Karlovy Vary.

Well, it so happened that in my brief-case I had a pack of six new golf balls and I offered them to him. You would have thought I was offering him the Crown Jewels! He explained that golf is somewhat frowned upon by the authorities, i.e., it was considered to be a very bourgeois game and was mainly for the rich people. In other words, they thought it was a decadent form of sport and, with the shortage of foreign currency, imports of golf accessories were considered as being of low priority and therefore few and far between. So when he explained this to me I then appreciated why he was so very pleased at my small gift. I was a little surprised that he was so frank and open with me; perhaps he thought I had a trustworthy face! Anyway, that was the first time I met Jiri, I subsequently called him 'Georgie', and we became very close friends over the next 30 years or more.

Also in these early factory visits the subject of hunting came up very frequently. Many times I was asked if I liked hunting and if I would like to try it. Wanting to be friendly and to show what a man I was, I nodded when the subject came up and so I was taken out into the country to sit aloft in a tree hide for what seemed ages and ages until I had corns on my rear – and didn't see a thing! But at least I demonstrated my willingness. However, even on such occasions it was difficult to escape unwanted hospitality and I remember one occasion in a large town called Olomouc, in Moravia. Mr Valka, the Director of the Zora Confectionery Factory situated there, had insisted I go with his chauffeur, Zdenek, in the evening to experience hunting. I found it difficult to refuse and so off we went by car to a spot about five kilometres outside Olomouc. There we climbed up to a hide in the tree and we sat there and watched, and watched, and watched. I soon learned that in hunting you need a great deal of patience. I think we sat there until dawn and in that time we heard what sounded like a small herd of buffalo charging through the forest – Zdenek told me they were wild boar but we didn't actually see them. We did see a fine roe deer, a buck, and that was another thing I learned about hunting – you do not shoot fine, healthy, specimens unless they are specially selected for culling purposes. You select those with poor trophies for it is they who are sick and it is better that they are removed in order to protect the genetic quality of the herd.

Anyway, came dawn and so we climbed down from the hide and we walked for about one or maybe two kilometres and came to a farmhouse. Zdenek didn't speak English, by the way, but with my limited Czech and using signs we managed to understand each other most of the time. So he invited me in and inside the farmhouse was an old gentleman who I gathered was the grandfather and that it was his birthday. Out came the traditional bottle of Slivovice and a dish of cold duck. Of course I had no choice but to toast the old boy on his birthday and eat some of this duck which looked, and in fact was, very tasty indeed. I have to say that drinking plum brandy at 6.00am and eating cold duck is something I did not relish but I noticed the Slivovice was white and tasted very much better than the commercial type I had been offered in the Director's office. I queried this with Zdenek and he explained that their Slivovice was home made on the farm and that it was far superior to the commercially made type – to which I agreed wholeheartedly. I praised it so much that they gave me a bottle to take home with me! But I didn't really want it; I wanted to save the bottle I was allowed to bring in by Customs back home to choose either a good Cognac or Whisky or Gin. I can't recall now but I believe I gave the Slivovice away to somebody in Prague who would no doubt appreciate it much more than me.

I also recall another occasion in Olomouc that I would like to include in this narrative whilst I remember it. It occurred around 1964 I think when I was returning from Slovakia and had agreed to call in to see Mr Valka at Zora Factory whom I knew quite well by now. It was a Friday and my intention was to sleep over in Olomouc on the Friday night and then go to Prague the following day but Mr Valka told me there was a message for me from Mirek Kudlacek from HQ, asking me to stay there and he would join me there on Monday morning. But when enjoying a glass of wine at a vinarna there with Mr Valka, one of his friends joined us at our table and when he heard that I had to stay at Olomouc over the weekend asked me if I would care to join a small walking party which would be going up almost to the top of a mountain called Praded in the Jeseniky range the following day, sleeping overnight in a mountain cabin and returning to town on the Sunday. Well, I thought, it was a very friendly gesture and would certainly be more interesting than sitting in the hotel by myself plus it would be yet another new experience. So I enthusiastically agreed to join this small party which, as I discovered, consisted of three men including me, and two ladies – yes, I was the gooseberry! We went in two cars in a northerly direction towards the Polish border and I think these Jeseniky mountains represents the border between the two countries – I believe they are part of the Carpathians although I must confess ignorance on that point. We stopped at a car parking area at the foot of the mountains; they lent me a small knapsack into which I put everything I might need and off we trudged, in a constant upward direction of course, to get to the top of Praded. Near to the top I saw for the first time in my life a large bird we call capercaille – it also exists in very small numbers in the highlands of Scotland but they are quite rare and so it was rather special to see one in the wild. Finally, as dusk began to fall, we reached the cabin.

I was quite surprised when I saw the mountain cabin. It was spacious, neat, clean and had an enclosed stove fire in the centre which warmed us through completely once it was lit. We were all given little jobs to do; my task was to collect some more wood whilst one of the other men chopped it so that it would fit in the fire. By now we were all feeling hungry and at that point one of the men began to prepare what he called a 'gypsy' meal; it had a special name which I cannot now remember but it was 'Ciganske' something or other. He took some slices of sausage, some slices of salami, peppers and other vegetables. He then cut the pieces into a bite size and laid them alternately on a piece of what looked like greaseproof paper. First a piece of sausage, then a piece of pepper, than a piece of salami, a piece of vegetable and so on until he had a long sausage like shape. He then made it into a roll and twisted the ends. When he had finished this preparation, he then placed the long roll on top of the metal fire. 'Won't it burn?' I asked, and he smiled and said I should wait and see. But actually it didn't burn despite the fact that it was very hot on the top of the stove, also the fat was showing through the paper; occasionally a flame or two would lick this 'Gypsy' meal and finally it was ready! The smell was wonderful; I just watched and was absolutely fascinated.

And so then our good friend, the cook, took the preparation off the stove and opened it. It both looked and tasted really delicious and we all tucked in hungrily. In my knapsack I had cunningly secreted a bottle of Beaujolais, for I knew that an occasion like this would probably occur and I offered this to my new friends. Glasses were there in the cabin and these were brought to the small table around which we were sitting and we drank each other's heath. They liked Beaujolais very much and said they had never tasted French wine before *and* that such a wine had never been drunk in this cabin previously. They insisted that this be entered in the Journal which is kept in every mountain cabin. So my name and especially the bottle of Beaujolais is recorded in that Journal for all eternity.

During the conversation that followed whilst sitting around the stove, I enquired what these friends did for a living and the man who prepared the 'Gyspy' meal told me a story which I shall now relate. After the war had ended he started a shirt factory in Karlovy Vary (Carlsbad) over in Western Bohemia and part of the Sudetenland. He had good staff, he treated them fairly and they seemed very contented. But when the communist coup took place in 1949 there were lots and lots of stories flying around as to what may or may not happen. He then heard a whisper that his factory was about to be confiscated by the State. So he held a meeting of his staff and told them of the rumour he had heard and with one voice they roared their support for him and shouted how they would reject any moves by the communists. They told him that the politicians will never take this place from you, we shall protect you and support you come what may, and so on.

With this response the factory owner was much encouraged and very pleased. He left the factory later in the morning for a business appointment and was unable to return to his factory that afternoon; so he was unaware that a few political commissars had arrived there during that time and held their own meeting with his staff. The commissars told them that the days of working for the capitalists are over, that no longer will they be exploited, that the factory belongs to the workers and they promised the earth, moon, and stars, all of which had a devastating effect on all the staff. When the owner came to his factory the next morning he found the gates locked against him and his workers refused adamantly to let him in! He pleaded with them and reminded them of their words of support spoken only the day before but they still refused to let him in, saying in effect, 'This is our factory now!'

Our friend said that it took him a long time to believe in the goodness of human nature once again – but he did eventually. Of course he lost his factory without a penny compensation; the factory was ruled by a political appointee and none of the good things they were promised ever came to pass; in fact it would be true to say that their standards of pay and therefore of living, were much lower than before. It was a very interesting story to hear – but not uncommon in the crazy world of communism.

But now it was time to sleep and I wondered how this would be arranged. Then I saw that there were six bunks – enough for all. None of us undressed – we just remained in our normal day dress. The next day we had to go down below of course where we had started our climb and that was worse than going up. When I reached the bottom some hours later I remember that my leg muscles ached so much that I could only walk in a Charlie Chaplin style for a couple of days. It was a great trip, a nice experience, excellent company and I was very glad that I took part in it.

During my earlier visit in 1958, I had to put the finishing touches to the agreement that Sugosa would convert from an agency to a direct import, sale and distribution organisation and, as I have related earlier, I had to appoint the necessary agents throughout the country. Before doing that, there was the unpleasant task ahead of me when I returned to London to inform our importers that from the 1st September of the following year, we would no longer be able to supply them as Sugosa would be taking over all sales and distribution of Czechoslovak confectionery goods in the UK.

We linked this task with the forthcoming visit to London of Edouard Hlavin, the current gentleman from Koospol with whom I was cooperating then – such changes went on all the time. And so, after his arrival, Mr Hlavin and I duly made appointments with all our customers to give them this news. Naturally, we had expected something of a furore with every customer and our expectations were not wrong. All of them were up in arms and we received a lot of flak. Perhaps the worst instance involved one client threatening to protest to the Board of Trade; it appeared they had earlier experienced a similar occurrence with imports of Russian matches and on that occasion they had won the day. After seeing most of our clients, Edouard Hlavin and I retired to lick our wounds and to discuss the various reactions we had received.

My own modified view was that perhaps we should consider some form of compromise which would enable Sugosa to carry out its new duties whilst allowing the importers to purchase some selected items from us. I thought very carefully about this complex problem and I came up with the idea of separating the various distribution channels of the market as a whole and offering to supply certain importers on the basis that they would only offer our goods via the channels allocated to them. Mr Hlavin, who was also worried about the importer's reactions and was no doubt wondering what they would say back in Prague, agreed with my proposals and they were presented to our clients. The result of these new negotiations meant that two importers, who did not clash with each other, looked after chain stores, two looked after the grocery trade and two looked after the retail trade. This left the wholesale confectionery sector open for Sugosa to act freely through the twelve agents I had appointed. I considered that this was a fair division of trade outlets. This was never a perfect solution to the problem but it was the only way I could overcome the impasse we had reached.

And so this is how we managed to overcome what could have been a very tricky situation. We were delighted when our proposals were accepted by our most important customers, however I fully realised that it would be a difficult system and that perhaps somebody would sell outside their allocated channel and then there would be trouble; it would of course be my job to calm troubled waters. Little did I realise when nursing these reservations that the culprit who would break the agreement and sell outside their allocated channel, would be me ! Unwittingly, unknowingly and innocently – yes. But it was me! This involved us in a legal situation and Court action was threatened; thank goodness commonsense prevailed before it got that far and I managed to sort out the problem to everybody's satisfaction.

And so we launched forth with our new programme and Sugosa forged ahead with its newly won freedom from restrictive obligations within the wholesale confectionery sector. Of course looking after, corresponding, and phoning twelve agents and visiting them from time to time throughout the country was not easy; in fact it was a lot of work for me in particular, and in many instances such contact could only be made during the evenings, but I relished it because it opened up a million business possibilities for me to explore.

I had remained on friendly terms with Mr Frost and as my office in Mark Lane was only five minutes' walk away from his office in Rood Lane, I popped in occasionally to see him and have a chat. When I told him what I had persuaded Prague to agree to, he congratulated me and said that he didn't think anybody would ever be able to get them to agree with such a substantial change.

And now let us return to our old friend, Freddy Greenwood, and our contract with him for flower lollipops. First of all let me remind you, dear reader, of the kind of character Freddy was. I have already related how he took me to the Savoy Grill and that was not the last of such invitations. His preferred HQ whilst in London was a hotel which was then called the Washington Hotel in Mayfair. I met him there on a number of occasions and it was there that Freddy introduced me to his favourite dish, bananas fried in butter and flambed in Cointreau. Naughty – but very nice!

And then one day he phoned me to invite me to the FA Cup match at Wembley Stadium. What a day that was! First we met at the Washington Hotel where a reception for about forty people was being held. All kinds of people were there, including members of the CID from Blackpool. We were then taken by car to Wembley to see the match. Afterwards we returned to the Washington for further drinks, after which most of Freddy's guests slowly diminished. And then Freddy suggested to me that I go home and bring my wife, Lynne, back with me and, together with his current lady friend we would have a night out. I thought this was an excellent idea and so I did. Lynne of course was very surprised when I phoned her and asked her to prepare herself for an evening out but miraculously she was ready by the time I reached our flat in Clapham. We returned to the Washington and by this time Freddy and his lady friend were alone and waiting for us. That evening we went to the theatre and saw a play with, I think, Bonar Colleano and Bernard Bresslau. And then to end the evening, we went to Edmundo Ros's nightclub for a meal.

With that it ended a whirl of a day – but that was the kind of person Freddy Greenwood was; I mean, who could obtain forty-odd tickets for the FA Cup except Freddy? I am only human and at first I must admit I enjoyed all this entertainment and being taken to the kind of places I had only dreamed of before; however, I was sensible enough to keep my guard up and not be taken in by his generosity of hospitality. I should remark that in the various times I was with him, he did often suggest that I should relax the stipulation that he should put down a deposit before each shipment of lollipops was despatched. Although I had the authority to cancel the arrangement, I never did and, sure enough, came the day when a shipment arrived, and for which the usual deposit had been placed, when our bank phoned me to say that documents covering the shipment had not been taken up by Freddy's firm and no further payment had been made. I of course contacted Freddy immediately who explained to me that sales of the lollipops had not been as prolific as he thought they would be and he was therefore unable to take up any further shipments for the time being. He even had the cheek to ask me to arrange for the return of his deposit. I of course refused in as pleasant a manner as I could muster and told him that we would have to ship the goods back to Czechoslovakia and that I would be deducting the full costs of so doing plus any other expenses involved, and that eventually, I would return to him any balance of his deposit left over. He was quite angry and seemed oblivious to the fact that he was in the wrong. He threatened legal action against my firm, Sugosa. I told him he was in breach of contract and that he would not stand a chance in a Court of Law. I believe we did receive one very strong letter from his solicitors but I ignored it, organised the return of the rejected shipment, deducted the costs, and refunded the balance to Freddy. I didn't hear any more from Freddy and I never saw him again except once at Heathrow Airport; I didn't approach him but he looked OK and he had a glamorous girl on his arm as usual; no doubt flying off to some exotic resort for a romantic sojourn. I don't think Freddy will ever change but by now he is, of course, an old man or maybe is no longer with us for all I know.

13

CONTINUING TO DEVELOP SUGOSA AND OUR FIRST TRIP TO CZECHOSLOVAKIA BY CAR

Well the business of Sugosa, with freedom now to explore much wider possibilities throughout the whole of the wholesale confectionery sector and via our own efforts, went ahead. I would not say we set the country alight but we were not doing too badly for what was, after all, a massive change in our activities. It takes time, of course, to develop a new business system. One of our big difficulties was trying to persuade the factories to produce new lines which are most certainly the life blood of the confectionery industry. I used every effort and I believed that the friendly relations that I had developed over the past few years with all the factories exporting to the UK would bear fruit. The main problem was that few factories, if any, had a department with full knowledge of each factory's total manufacturing capabilities with the specific responsibility for the production of new lines. I made a lot of noise on this anomaly in planning and eventually something was done about it and such a department was set up in the course of time.

And I should mention the favours the factory directors, and others, asked me to do for them; it is hard for anyone to realise just how many everyday types of items were almost unobtainable in Czechoslovakia back then – especially medicines but also a wide variety of items and I had very many requests to bring this or that on my next visit. I did so to the best of my ability but it was difficult for me to carry out all requests as everything had to be bought from my own pocket and not only that – some of these requested drugs and medicines were only available on prescription; somehow I mostly managed to overcome this problem. There was no way, however, that I could, or would even try, to claim recompense from the company of which I was Director, for such expenditure was not a legitimate expense. Nevertheless, as a consequence of these requests quite a few people in the factories owed me some favours and as time passed it proved to be a good investment even though it was my money!

Despite this situation, however, I once again have to come back to the strange and silly Communist system of control and how this inhibited business. Every factory was given targets by their respective Ministry and various rewards were offered if those targets were reached but as I have indicated in the previous chapter, the targets in themselves gave only quantity targets – not quality targets. The results of such policies may have suited some industries but certainly did not suit the confectionery industry or indeed any industry producing perishable goods, because the factories then tended to produce large quantities of simple confections that were easy to manufacture, in order to reach and exceed their targets but they were invariably products which few wanted! So whilst it was very nice for the directors and managers in the factories to be awarded red banners, medals and certificates for being Heroes of the People for having reached, and sometimes exceeded their targets, the unwanted surplus confections lay in the store until someone realised that they would deteriorate if not disposed of. They were eventually disposed of but at cheap and sometimes ridiculous prices. Believe me, one needed the patience of a saint when coming face to face with such problems. In time one got used to them and found ways of overcoming them mostly – but not always. Eventually, of course, they began to realise that their economic policies were not best suited to any trade dealing with perishable commodities and they changed such policies.

One year, around 1964-5 or so, our supermarket programme was going with a swing and sales were very buoyant. We had a few problems to iron out and so I prepared for another trip to Prague and to the factories concerned. But about a week before my departure, I received a telex from Prague saying that they had hit a very serious problem for the factory in North Bohemia, in a small town called Velky Cenov, where the printing of boxes and cartons for our supermarket range took place, the HQ had informed of their inability to produce the printed boxes required for the supermarket programme until early September.

This was indeed serious because we had to start shipments in late August and they would continue right up to the last moment. For this to happen we needed those printed boxes in the factories producing the confectionery contents not later than the end of July. On this occasion I travelled by car and after I arrived in Prague I went directly to the Ceskoslovenske Cokaladovny HQ at Modrany, an outskirt of Prague. My colleagues there were very worried indeed for they told me that they had done everything possible with the printing factory but totally without success. They had sent people there to plead with the management, they had even asked the Ministry of Foreign Trade to intervene – all without result. I then responded by saying that as the problem was at the printing factory then that is obviously where we must go to see what can be done. They shook their heads and said it would be a waste of time but I felt it necessary to insist. As I said, one last attempt to solve a most important problem cannot be wasted.

So we went to Velky Cenov and as we travelled along we were all very glum for we realised what a disaster, even a catastrophe, this situation would be for everybody if we were unsuccessful. The supermarket business by now represented by far the greatest part of our annual turnover – it had become our backbone – and it was very hard to know what would happen unless our assignment succeeded. Should we fail in our mission it truly would have been a disaster and I hesitate to imagine, even now, what the consequences may have been.

So we set off from Prague in my car to Velky Cenov, arrived at the printing factory and were immediately shown into a large room where they evidently held their daily meetings and there we all sat at a large, round table – there were about ten people taking part and all were looking very glum indeed.. I made a point of sitting next to the Director of the factory. Well, the discussions went ahead which was only a repetition and explanation on their side why the printing of our boxes could not be achieved before early September. After two hours of this it seemed as if we had reached stalemate and the talking stopped for a cup of coffee. In this break I began to talk with the Director – in Czech as my knowledge of the language was getting better all the time.

He was a nice man and he explained in an apologetic tone to me that if he could possibly change the situation he would – but unfortunately it really was not possible. So we began to talk about English football and the Director spoke eagerly with me on that subject. He said that his son was a great fan of English football clubs and he mentioned a few to me. Now in my brief case would be found a lot of weird and wonderful things, something like a lady's handbag – sometimes I didn't know myself what was in there! But I did recall that I had a velvet covered piece of cardboard to which was attached the club badges of every English First Division Clubs. This was, of course, before the days of the Premiership.

So I presented this to the Director for his son and he was terribly appreciative and thanked me several times; in fact he couldn't thank me enough. And then I had another idea and asked the Director if he had ever tasted Scotch Whisky and Dry Ginger Ale. He said he had not and others said they had never heard of mixing whisky with beer! I explained that Ginger Ale was not a beer. It was hard to explain Dry Ginger Ale and anyway I did not know the Czech word for 'ginger' so I went to my car just outside and took a bottle of Dry Ginger Ale and my small travelling bar that I took everywhere with me. This was a case containing two bottles of whatever, plus some glasses, a small towel, bottle opener, etc.

I brought this in and asked if everybody would like to taste it. They all nodded enthusiastically and so the Director ordered his secretary to bring some glasses which she did very promptly. With great care I poured ten glasses of whisky and added a small quantity of Ginger Ale and we all toasted each other with 'Na zdravy' (on your health) and sipped it. We all looked at one another and they began to nod to each other as if to say, 'that is very nice indeed'; after some fifteen minutes, our short break came to an end and it was necessary to resume our discussions.

But then, to the surprise of everyone the Director began to talk directly to his staff and after much shaking of heads, which changed to smiling nods, the Director made an announcement. It was amazing; the whole atmosphere had changed and so we listened to what the Director had to say very carefully. The Director, now also with a smiling face, announced that they had spoken of some reorganisation of priorities which they will bring into effect urgently and that these changes, which although very difficult for them indeed, would after all allow them to print our boxes for them to be ready during the second half of July! We had won the day!

Our group, three people from HQ who accompanied me in my car, drove back to Prague in an extremely satisfied and delighted mood because we all knew that had we not succeeded – then only disaster lay before us. The supermarket section of our business was now the backbone of our entire annual programme. I have to rate that occasion as one of the biggest successes I had during my reign as 'Colonel-in-Chief' of the London office. And it just shows how important a card of football badges and a glass of Whisky & Ginger can be when you need them!

During that trip I also had a very interesting experience with fishing. As I have explained I always mixed business with pleasure and when in Marianske Lazne, my friend, Slavek, would always arrange something for me on those weekends when I could get away. On this occasion Slavek told me had arranged for me to fish for trout in waters that were reserved for the top people. He and his friend, who had arranged the permission, took me to the stream, left me there and they vanished – probably they went to the pub! Anyway, I caught six very nice fish. Somewhat later, our two friends returned – yes, they had been to the pub as I could see! So we headed back to Marianske Lazne where Slavek's wife, Jarka, prepared the fish by wrapping then in bacon and baking them. They were truly delicious.

During the lunch, Slavek's friend spoke more about fishing – especially fishing for carp. Unfortunately I cannot recall his name but I do recall he came from Melnik, a small town to the north of Prague which has an attractive castle where you can eat fish freshly caught from the rich waters in the vicinity of the castle. I had never fished for carp and remarked what a difficult fish it was to catch – at least that is what I had always understood. He immediately responded by saying he could take me to a lake where I would catch a carp within ten minutes! I was astounded at this and challenged him to do so.

So when we had finished lunch, the three of us set off in the direction of the other famous spa town, Karlovy Vary, (Carlsbad). We arrived at the lake after about 45 minutes; I prepared my rods and whilst I was doing that, the friend from Melnik told me I was standing on the exact spot that Juri Gagarin, the first man ever in space, had fished when he too was the guest of the Forest Organisation some little while before. I was very intrigued to know that and hoped I would be as successful as they told me he was. Well, within ten minutes, and he was perfectly correct about this, I had landed a lovely 8-9 lb carp! I could hardly believe it! Within minutes yet another followed – this time a little heavier.

To cut a long story short, we took the carp back to Slavek's flat, where the hard pressed Jarka was waiting for us. She was pleased I had been successful and the dear girl offered to cook the fish for supper that evening to which we all agreed. Dear Jarka – she always carried out these duties with a smile on her face and with evident pleasure. I never heard her complain once. What a lovely and nice person she was. Anyway it proved that one fish was enough; Jarka sliced the carp and fried the slices in butter. It was truly delicious. There is no taste quite like freshly caught, cooked fish – and Jarka knew how to cook them perfectly.

There is a sequel to this story because the next day I had to return to Prague and Slavek handed me a parcel just before I set off. He told me it was the other carp and that I should take it with me to Prague and give it to my friends there. So I duly took the fish to Prague and my first call was to my artist friend 'Georgie' at his studio in Ulice Revolucni. He was very pleased to see me and I handed him the parcel. He enquired as to its contents and when I told him he was horrified. He said that his wife was away, that he had no idea how to cook it, and that I must give it to somebody else.

Well, later that day in the afternoon after finishing work, I had agreed to play for the Orion Confectionery Factory who were playing against a sewing machine factory at a small stadium somewhere in the northern part of Prague. So Georgie, who had agreed to accompany me and show me where the stadium was, had the brilliant idea of taking the fish with us. We did so and as luck would have it, outside the stadium was a row of benches where the old folk sat to watch the world go by. Georgie told me that one of those old folk would be very pleased to take the fish from me.

I should have mentioned that this was late June and the temperatures were quite high. It was indeed time to dispose of the fish! So I took the parcel from my car went to the first lady and I said "Prominte, ale chcete riba ? (Excuse me, but would you like a fish?) She looked at me with disdain and sent me packing! I went to the next one – same result. And the next one! This fish was becoming a real problem. But at the end of one bench sat a small, grizzled old man. So I repeated "Chcete riba ?". He replied "Ktery riba ?" (what kind of fish?) so I told him it was a carp. He then asked if he could smell it and I quickly opened the parcel so that he could both see and smell the damned fish. He smelt it and then said "Kolik stoji ?" (How much?) So I told him nothing, at which a big smile came over his face; he got up and hurried home with his fish tucked under his arm as pleased as Punch. For that old man a carp would have been a luxury indeed, usually reserved for those who could afford it for Christmas Eve supper.

That was the occasion I played with the international football player, Pesek. He was brilliant and I became very friendly with him; however, I never kept in touch with him. Unfortunately I could only play the first half because I had a leg injury and I could not continue for the second half.

From the business point of view and looking back, I would say that perseverance and determination, which I have always possessed, again assisted me greatly and I was able to develop a number of new lines such as Noddy, Big Ears and Mr Plod in chocolate figurine form, Sooty &

Sweep in picture lollipop form and a number of other well known characters on TV. The Noddy idea came to me one day when leaning out of the window watching the children play in the grassed area before our block of flats and then, quite suddenly, they all vanished in a flash. Alarmed, I called out to Lynne, and asked her what was wrong? Smiling, she told me that nothing was wrong; it was only that the Noddy programme was due to begin on TV! Well, once again my business brain began to tick for it seemed to me that if children were so interested in Noddy, then I had better investigate and see if we can develop a line, or lines, based upon him and his pals Mr Plod and Big Ears.

To cut a long story short, I contacted the Head of the London School of Art, which I had attended myself in earlier years, and asked him if he had a sculptor pupil who could do a little job of work for me. He had such a person in mind and the young chap concerned came to my office; I explained very carefully to him what it was I wanted. After a number of sample shapes and with further evening meetings at my office, we eventually came up with a figure which was excellent. But it took such a lot of time that I decided just to restrict it to Noddy alone and that I would forget about Mr Plod and Big Ears for the time being. Well, Noddy was a big success, it even became a listed line with Woolworths, and some time later I had the pleasure to hand to Enid Blyton's agent, a chap called Ted Broadribb, a very nice cheque for royalties in a fine fish restaurant – Wheelers in Dover Street; I remember that lunch because I was introduced to Sole Veronique for the first time, a dish that I came to like very much and we drank a most perfect Chablis; I haven't tasted a Chablis like that ever since. I subsequently received a letter from Enid Blyton herself but I am afraid it either got misplaced during our move to Spain or perhaps more probably during the move back to England, and I very much regret to say I have lost it, along with other treasured papers and souvenirs.

We encouraged those importers who were covering the chain stores such as Woolworths, British Home Stores, etc., to offer our lines as widely as possible and a number of our items were so called 'listed lines' including Noddy as I have mentioned above, Liquid Centre Jellies, Vienna Wrapped Fruit BonBons and others, which meant that all Store Managers were aware that those lines were recommended by Head Office, that special prices had been negotiated and needed to be supported by all stores. For example, we supplied something like 1,000 tons of Vienna Fruit Bonbons a year to chain stores – it was big business!

A big help in this direction was a man called Frank Kress. I got to know Frank when he worked from my old friend Alex Kraus's office and often came to my office for a business chat together with Alex but I never knew what was his position or contractual relationship with him.

His story is worthy of mention. Frank was a Director of a substantial bank in Prague before, during and after the war and held an important part of the shareholding. I am unsure how he escaped the Nazi occupation as he was Jewish – but somehow he did. After the communist coup in Czechoslovakia following the war, which was certainly aided and abetted by Moscow – possibly even engineered by them – there was total nationalisation. The State took over everything – no private business was allowed to exist. When his bank was taken over Frank was told that he could still work there but only in a junior position and that he would be instructed as far as his duties were concerned by another man, obviously a good communist or maybe even a party member, who was formerly a lowly clerk. This is how the communists loved to humiliate former owners, directors and managers – by making them work as virtual 'underlings' and being ordered about by those who formerly worked beneath them. Of course his shareholding became worthless overnight and he received no compensation whatsoever.

Frank could not accept such a situation and quite rightly protested. But our 'friends' in the Communist Party would never brook any nonsense from those deprived of their business or their former station in life and in one way or another it was made clear to Frank that if he did not desist then he would be extremely sorry for having caused trouble. It was in fact a police chief who gave him the tip off that he was in dire danger, that fictitious excuses calling for his arrest were in preparation and that it would really be the best idea if he could leave the country. The same police chief enabled Frank and his family to get out of the country and organised all the necessary paperwork; in return Frank gave him his house containing many valuable items which kept the police chief happy.

So Frank came to this country with virtually nothing except the clothes he stood in and a small amount of money he succeeded to transfer to London. But it wasn't much and so Frank had to find a way of earning a living; he found that in the confectionery world which then brought him eventually into contact with Alex Kraus. I was told later that Frank began his association with confectionery via another company, Buxley Trading Co. Ltd., who were also clients of mine. Buxley was run by a Mr Englander and a Mr Frankel – both were Czechs originally but had left Czechoslovakia when the danger of a communist coup arose. They were a funny couple and I used to call them 'Mutt & Jeff' after the cartoon characters. It was from this very same firm that I was lucky enough to obtain my first class secretary, Joan Gloster. I believe that Mr Englander either became ill or maybe he even passed away but Buxley closed down and that is almost certainly the reason why Frank Kress gravitated to Alex Kraus.

Anyway, Frank had a very charming personality coupled with a sense of humour in the way he described matters to you or in the way he would ask for a small reduction in price. 'David,' he would say as only Continental Jewish people can say, 'please can you let an old friend live a little – be a nice fellow and reduce your price – only 5% do I need!' When I declined, which was very difficult when he put propositions to you in such an appealing way, he would then look at me very quizzically, and say, '2.5% perhaps?' and I have to confess that on occasions I weakened and promised to persuade Prague to agree such a reduction and usually they accepted my recommendations for the simple reason I always tried to make them reasonable. But Frank, using the same charm as with me, had excellent relationships with the buyers of the chain stores. In fact one of them, who shall be nameless, would pop into Frank's flat on his way home, walk in, go to the drinks cabinet and without asking just pour himself a large whisky! The relationship was that close. Well, such valuable relationships with such important buyers was very appealing to Alex Kraus as well and so somehow they formed a cooperation between them which worked right up to the time that poor old Frank passed away. He had Parkinson's Disease; that I know and when he came to my office I always had to order his coffee cup to be only half full because of his shaking hand.

Whether it was that which caused his death I do not know. But he was a character, that is for sure, and I missed him a lot following his departure from this world because I liked him very much indeed. I too had a very close relationship with Frank. One day he told me of the skullduggery that went on with certain store buyers who liked to be kept sweet but I always changed the subject very quickly – I didn't want to know about such things, for they were none of my business and best avoided.

Meanwhile I travelled around the country visiting our agents in all parts, including Scotland and Northern Ireland, to urge them to increase their sales and listen to any suggestions, complaints or queries that they may have had. In those days, travelling round the country was not the hardship it is today and there were many great places to stay. I got my secretary to reserve accommodation for me, mainly at Trust House Hotels which were all over the country and which were nice, clean, comfortable and if I remember correctly, they charged only £5 per night back then!

And that included full English breakfast! Wherever I went I always took my golf clubs, space permitting, my fishing rods and my football boots – even when I went by car to Czechoslovakia! I believe in hard work and, believe me, I worked long and hard hours. I was like a bulldog – once I had my teeth into something I would never let go until I had ended the matter with a satisfactory conclusion. But I always believed too that *all work and no play makes Jack a dull boy*. And so I took advantage of whatever opportunities that presented themselves wherever I went. I was a great believer in mixing business with pleasure and did not hesitate to use pleasure as a means to get what I wanted.

I remember one occasion when one of our important clients informed me that they would not be able to renew their contract with us for an item, Vienna Wrapped Fruit BonBons of which, as I related earlier, we used to supply some 1,000 tons per year. That was very important business to us. It appeared that his Polish suppliers were offering an identical line at a cheaper price. Hearing this very bad news, I went to see him but I decided not to kick up a fuss immediately but to adopt a nonchalant response. I changed the subject and began talking about other things – including golf. By good fortune I had got to hear that my client had recently taken up the game and he enthusiastically discussed it with me. I cannot claim to be an expert on golf but I was certainly becoming better in finding out what makes people tick. I was playing off 14 handicap at that time therefore I wasn't all that bad, so we discussed the best grip, the best balls, what kind of clubs he had, and then I spoke about golf courses and asked him if he had ever played Betchworth Park Golf Course, quite near to Dorking, Surrey in the lovely Box Hill country. I saw his eyes light up as I described the course and so I said quite casually – 'Why don't we have a game there sometime?' He said he would love to and would I mind if he brought along his co-director, Skip Wright? Of course I said – he would be very welcome. So I needed a partner to make up a foursome. I couldn't think of anyone else at that moment and so I invited Karel Jiracek, the Commercial Delegate, to join us. He didn't play very well but at a pinch, I thought, he'll do. Karel liked a day out!

On the appointed day we met at the course. I had planned everything down to the last detail – golf carts, three balls each, tees, course card and small pencil and additionally I had asked Mr Mantell, the Steward, if he would prepare a nice lunch for us and to put some good German wine in the refrigerator as I knew that my client loved German wine.

Well we began the game; the first hole was quite easy and just as we were going to tee off, a weasel or a stoat ran right across our front followed by a number of little ones. Where they were off to Heaven only knows! Maybe Mum was searching for lunch! The second tee was rather amazing because at that point we were quite high up and from the tee the whole of the fairway with its bunkers lay right down there before us like a carpet. But before you reached the fairway there was a large area of ferns and small bushes. Obviously it was better to hit one's ball well, and clear it, because if you landed in that area you were in big trouble. Well three of us hit our balls quite well and were on the fairway. But my client's co-director, Skip, had a bad shot and landed right in the middle of the ferns and bushes. As I wended my way down, I saw him searching and called out: 'Can't you find your ball, Skip?' and he replied, 'Yes, I have found my ball – but I have lost my clubs!!' Of course we all roared at that and finished a nice nine holes in the morning and at the ninth green I suggested we stop there and return to the clubhouse for lunch. Fortunately, it was a very nice day and the weather was kind to us. I didn't mention a single word about Fruit BonBons or contracts, prices or anything.

Well, Mr Mantell did us proud. We had a splendid lunch, I think we drank three bottles of wine – I must say that Karel Jiracek polished off almost a whole bottle by himself! And so, now in very good spirits, we resumed our game although I have to say that the standard of our golf had mysteriously fallen! I kept quite close to my client and so had the opportunity to chat with him as we walked on. At what I thought was the right moment, I raised the subject and said that not only I but our people in Prague, and certainly the factory concerned, were very unhappy that we were going to lose his contract and without saying so directly, I hinted that of course we would have no other choice but to offer the item to other buyers who may then be in competition with him. He asked me then if something could be done in terms of price and I said that regretfully it was not possible because he was already buying at the lowest level – I had no room for price reductions. He thought for a moment and then, without further prompting from me, suggested that maybe a way round the problem might be if he split his contract so that the Poles would enjoy 50% and we would retain 50% – without any price adjustment of course. I replied to him that I was sure that Prague would readily agree to such a compromise – and they were happy to do so. Of course, to lose 500 tons of business could not be regarded as a great victory for us but as we were originally in danger of losing the lot, I think the result achieved was not at all bad. I am absolutely sure that without that day at Betchworth Park Golf Course the outcome would have been quite different.

Also on my trips to Prague I played football for the Orion Factory which was near Prague. It began in this way: actually the HQ of Ceskoslovenske Cokoladovny was situated within the Orion Factory complex and one day we were sitting in a conference room discussing business when the door opened and a fit looking, smiling, man poked his head through. He said something in Czech but I caught the word 'football'. So I asked if he played and he said that he did and that in fact there was a game on later that afternoon – and would I like to play? I most certainly would like to play and, as I have explained, I had my football boots with me. Accompanying me on that trip was Bob Warrior who was my Sales Manager and he too said he would like to play. Well, the football pitch and small stadium was quite close to Modrany where the factory was situated and so within minutes we were there. In the dressing room I was introduced to the other players and to my amazement a number of them were ex-professional players; they were guest players invited by the factory to play for them. Their reward? A few boxes of confectionery! The reader may find this hard to believe but please try to imagine being in a country where almost everything was in short supply or so expensive that most people could not afford to buy boxes of chocolates for their wives and families. There was not a lot of opportunity for these ex-footballers to earn extra money but to come home occasionally with a few nice boxes of confectionery – well, that was something very special indeed! And so they were glad to play.

It was a good match. Bob Warrior was rather hopeless, I am afraid, but I hope it doesn't sound like boasting if I say I didn't play too badly although I did not play as well as I knew I could.. That is only because back home I played every Sunday morning with the boys down in Grange Park. The boys consisted of all ages. My own son took part, his friend Bill McGahey, whose father was at the Australian Embassy, boys from the avenue in which we lived and every Sunday we made up two teams depending on how many boys had turned up. To give them all a game sometimes we played maybe twelve or more a side!! Sometimes only nine a side! It all depended who turned up!

But it was great fun and kept me fit – in fact I played football until I was 56 years of age or so and, therefore, I kept myself in trim. My wife, however, will never forget the Sunday morning when, knowing about our football arrangements, four little boys knocked at our door to ask, 'Is Mr Mitchell coming out to play?'. Well we found that very amusing and I used to say that those boys only let me play on Sunday mornings because I supplied the footballs to play with! But, as I say, it was great fun and those Sunday mornings went on almost until I went to Spain in 1985. In those years we had a lot of boys who played with us and were good enough to have trials with Arsenal and Leicester City. Sometimes I felt like 'Mr Chips' as these boys grew up into young men, then girlfriends came along and in a number of instances, that was the end of football for them. But never mind, a new crop of youngsters would always come along to take their place. Also, in addition to playing with my son, Philip, and the boys every Sunday morning, I used to run them all over the place to matches when the team we all supported, Crystal Palace, was playing away from home. I took them in my car to Southampton, Luton, Aston Villa – to many such places. To see my car flowing with Crystal Palace scarves from the windows as we left the avenue in which we lived must have been quite a sight.

I would like to mention that in March of this year, 2007, Crystal Palace was playing away at Plymouth and two of the lads I used to play with, and who formed part of our away travels years ago, contacted me to say they were coming down to see the match and would it be possible to meet up somehow? To cut a long story short, my son-in-law obtained tickets for the match and so we were able to meet them afterwards at a restaurant where we enjoyed some beer and wine plus some not bad food. Of course, instead of lads these were now middle-aged men and I have to admit that in one case at least I would have found it difficult to recognise them if I passed them in the street. We had a marvellous time reminiscing about days gone by when one of the chaps, Paul Pettigrew, made a short speech thanking me on behalf of the lads for what I did for them when young, then presented me with a Crystal Palace scarf, and proposed a toast in my honour. I was very touched by this and was so glad we were able to meet after so many years. I sat throughout the dinner with the scarf around my neck and I must have looked like a Rabbi! I told them I was only there to collect petrol money which I had neglected to charge them nearly half a century before! Plus interest of course!

But in Czechoslovakia I played with some very good footballers, including, as I mentioned before in the fishing story, a nice chap called Pesek who had played for the Czechoslovak National Team – and he was excellent. He spoke a lot about Aston Villa but I wasn't clear whether he played for them – or against them. Somewhere I have a photograph of him and me together.

Back to business. I was very conscious now of the added responsibilities on my shoulders because not only was I in charge of sales but I was also responsible for purchases. Forward buying was a necessity and the decisions what to buy and how many was a matter for me. But it was my view that every good buyer should have an escape hatch if it was possible to arrange. I wanted someone with the possibility of disposing of merchandise surplus to requirements so that should I ever make a mistake I had the means to rectify it.

To this end, I befriended a young Jewish chap called Derek Nathan. He was a market man with a lot of other market men contacts. I quite liked Derek and believed he was a person I could do business with. And so I came to an agreement with him that he would take all our surplus to requirement goods and I would charge him as near to cost price as I could. True, we wouldn't make much out of such sales but on the other hand, we wouldn't lose anything either – however, the object of the exercise was to provide a safety net which would avoid possible losses on surplus goods which we had been unable to sell.

As our business relationship developed it was then that I thought of making up special packs of various confections suitable for market and possibly also supermarket outlets. Nobody had ever tried that before; well known British factories tended to steer clear of supermarkets back then because of price-cutting and the damage they thought that might do to their normal distribution channels. So I was the first to think of this idea and I wanted Derek to handle that for me – in other words, to act as a kind of guinea pig on my behalf. So I had three packs made up in one factory as a kind of trial and they sold quite well – I was much encouraged.

But then something happened to spoil everything. Derek owed a balance on his account of roughly £1,000 which I asked him to settle; he told me he couldn't! So there and then my relationship with him ended; I felt that he had let me down and I wanted nothing further to do with him. Little did he realise what he had sacrificed for the sake of a measly £1,000.

And now I would like to explain why and also how our supermarket programme came into being. In the latter part of that year I was contacted by Sidney Eagle, Managing Director of Eagle Bros. Ltd., a large wholesaler and distributor of confectionery and a great many other products He wanted to buy some of our Orange & Lemon Slices in drums of which I used to sell around 250 tons a year on the British market. Sidney dealt in a variety of goods, including confectionery, and so therefore I saw no reason not to do business with him. He bought there and then 200 cases of Orange & Lemon Slices and we discussed further possibilities. Sidney was accompanied on that occasion by his son, Geoffrey, who was a nice, pleasant young man and with whom I got on very well. As Sidney went on talking about his connections – especially with supermarkets – I found myself becoming more and more interested. He spoke of Jack Cohen, the king of supermarket trading at that time as if they were bosom pals – and indeed they were! He offered to introduce me to Jack Cohen and I said I would very much like to meet him; I did in fact meet him and had dinner with him twice as I shall relate later on. We agreed that a further chat would be a good idea and that meanwhile I would put on my thinking cap to see what we could come up with.

I didn't know it then but that first meeting with Sydney and Geoffrey Eagle was the birth of our business programme that became very substantial indeed – my supermarket programme.

To end this chapter, and this volume, I would like to describe our very first trip to Czechoslovakia by car in the year of 1960 because I think it is a story worth telling. I should have written about this before to place it in the right sequence – but better later than never! I had discussed with Karel Jiracek the idea of my making a combined business and holiday visit to Czechoslovakia. He thought it would be a good idea and suggested that after completing my business it would be good to go to Vysoky Tatry (the High Tatra mountains) and that maybe the people at Figaro factory in Bratislava might be helpful to me in arranging suitable accommodation. I therefore advised my principals in Prague of my intentions and also checked in with Cedok, the State Travel Bureau. That was not a good thing to do as I discovered – it caused confusion for it seemed everyone was booking accommodation for us! Then I put my car in for a thorough service; I was still driving my trusty Ford Prefect – a small car for such a long journey but that's all I had at that time.

I decided that the best and most simple route would be to fly our car across to Belgium from Southend and motor down via Brussels, Liege, cross into Germany and on via Cologne, Frankfurt, to Wurzburg in Bavaria where, in those days, the autobahn came to an end. The reader will appreciate that the roads and conditions then were quite different when compared to these days when you can motor from either the Belgian or Dutch coast right through to Prague via motorways and never stop.

Well the day came for our departure and my wife, Lynne, daughter Jackie (aged seven) and son Philip (aged six) set off on our great journey. But we only got as far as Gypsy Hill in South London when the excitement got to the children; firstly one began to be ill and that started the other one off! What a beginning! Never mind, we recovered from that or rather the children did, and before long we were entering the small Southend Airport. We looked at the plane then we looked at each other! Could this thing carry us, never mind our car, over the water? Well, there was nothing we could do about it now except cross our fingers and hope for the best!

So we boarded, our car was loaded, and shortly after we were airborne and making our way to Ostend. To our horror, when we looked down, we could see the sea through cracks in the floor! I swear that we were not more than 50-60 feet in the air – or at least it did not seem so judging by the sea below! Of course when you are young you tend to have these experiences and jest about them – and that's what we did. I think the plane journey was about an hour, maybe a little less, and then we were in Ostend. I gingerly headed out of the airport never having driven on the Continent before and soon we were on the road to Brussels.

When reading my maps I had gained the impression that we would take a ring road around Brussels but whether we missed a turning or not, I cannot now say. However, we found ourselves entering that large city and we just didn't quite know where to go from there. We knew we had to head towards Liege and so I thought the best idea would be to stop the car and ask for directions. My French is lousy and maybe I didn't make myself very clear but one man stopped, listened to my enquiry, scratched his head and was evidently puzzled. So he stopped the next person walking by and they started jabbering to each other; then a third person joined in the discussion quite ignoring me. So I left these people and slowly crept back to my car without a backward glance; I drove off leaving this bunch of people jabbering away and arguing with each other. I often wonder if they came to any conclusion as to how to get to Liege and what they must have thought when they discovered I had vanished!

It was a nightmare driving through Brussels but somehow we managed to find the road to Liege. However, as we went along I began to notice that something was not right with my car; it was stiff and acted as though it did not want to go another mile! So I limped off the main road and luckily found a garage near to a village or small town. The Belgian mechanic listened to what I had to say for I was trying to explain that before leaving England our car had been thoroughly serviced and so nothing should be wrong. Well he tinkered about and then motioned for me to come to the bonnet and engine compartment. He had the oil dipstick in his hand and placed it in the appropriate place, withdrew it, and showed it to me – it was bone dry! The engine had almost no oil in it! He motioned to me that if I had gone on for a few more miles my engine would certainly have seized up and that would have been the end of our business/holiday trip. So he filled the sump with oil, tested it, pronounced it OK and offering our grateful thanks we drove off. But not before my making a mental note to raise Merry Hell with that garage back in South London who carried out my service.

We found Liege alright and soon after we entered the German autobahn system. Again I must remind the reader that driving on the Continent in those days was a million light years away from the conditions of today. Lynne was our main map reader and it was a task she found very difficult for she had never done anything like that before – and frankly, so would I in a foreign country! So she was happier when we found ourselves on the autobahn. However, my poor little Prefect was not capable of high speeds but it was just as well because in any case, we wanted to absorb the sights and countryside as we passed through.

Eventually we stopped at one of the Rasthaus places for some refreshments. It was near to lunch time and so I ordered some ham sandwiches but unfortunately we didn't know that ham (or *Schinken* in German) was better known in that locality as smoked ham instead of cooked ham. We didn't enjoy those sandwiches very much at all. After that short break, off we went again and slowly the hours slipped by until we noticed the light was fading a bit. Never mind – we were nearly at Wurzburg where in those days the autobahn going eastwards ended.

Back in England I had been told that in Germany I would have no need to worry for there were plenty of Rasthausen along the autobahns and you could always get a room in one of those. What bad advice that was – for Rasthausen only serve food and drink etc., and none of them have rooms as I was to find out. I also had a problem now because, as the day had gone on, poor Lynne was quite ill with a most ferocious headache and general malaise very probably caused by the stress of map reading and looking for directions during our journey – but relief is at hand, or so I thought, for here we are at the Wurburg Rasthaus. The children were also tired and hungry and as I left the car they looked at me with appealing eyes hoping, I suppose, that I would return with good news. I so hoped that this Rasthaus would have a spare room for us. But when I entered the place it was almost as if nobody wished to talk to me. It was very busy and as I addressed each passing person they just brushed past me as if I were invisible or perhaps a slight nuisance in their way! I was gradually getting more and more desperate but eventually, thank goodness, someone deigned to speak with me – and that lady spoke English. Halleluja – this was a blessing! However, she immediately dashed my hopes by confirming that they had no rooms and that they only served food and drink. She advised me to go further on to a small town called Marktheidenfeld which was about 30 km distant; there, she said, you will be certain to find a room.

I really dreaded going back to the car to announce to Lynne and the kids that, sorry – we have to go on. None of us needed more motoring at that point. However, they took in what I had to say in good spirits but with anxious and wry smiles and so off we went in to the blackness of the German countryside. We really didn't have a clue as to where we were going but after a few kilometres we saw a signpost MARKTHEIDENFELD – 10 km. That cheered us up and I put my foot down and carried on. We came to a longish hill and at the bottom of this was a bridge to the right going over a river and signposted 'Marktheidenfeld'. We took that and somehow found ourselves in a small road just wide enough to take a car but nothing else. There I saw a pub/restaurant called Gulden Anchor. I stopped, went inside and once again I got the 'invisibility' treatment. The place was humming with people all eating and drinking and the waiters were very busy indeed. But eventually one stopped and I asked 'Haben sie frei zimmer?' The waiter simply said 'Nein' and off he went! What shall I do now? Well, I went outside and to my horror I saw a horse and cart which evidently wanted to bypass my car – but couldn't. Lynne was a bit frantic about this and the two little faces of our children were peeping through the window also wondering what would happen.

I am not certain now how we got out of this scrape because I couldn't go forward, and I don't think horses and carts can go backwards! Lynne thinks the man with the horse forced his way through over the pavement but I really cannot remember. But horse and cart or no I had now very urgently to do something about finding accommodation and something to eat and drink for my family and so I drove forward and there, within 60 yards of the Gulden Anchor we came to the town square where there was plenty of space in which to park our car. But were there plenty of hotels? At that moment I spotted an elderly man dressed in lederhosen and looking very German. So I hastily advanced towards him and thank my lucky stars – he too spoke English! I explained to him my desperate situation and pointed to my car in which poor Lynne, feeling by now absolutely rotten and the children, were sitting and looking very anxiously towards us. The old man nodded his head and said, 'Come with me,' and he led me some yards to a place I had not spotted before – Hotel Post.

We went inside, the man spoke to a lady there, she nodded her head and the kindly gentleman told me that indeed they had a spare room which was suitable for two adults and two small children. I thanked the old man profusely and hurried back to my car to fetch Lynne and the kids. Lynne was so ill by this time that as soon as we were shown to our room she went straight to bed. I asked her if she wouldn't come down to the restaurant to have something to eat and drink but she was beyond caring about food and drink; all she wanted to do was to close her eyes and sleep. I am afraid the stress and concentration during the whole day was just too much for her. I didn't want to leave Lynne alone, of course, but I had to get the children and myself something to eat and drink and so, reluctantly, we left the room and made our way downstairs to the restaurant. It was only half full and so we chose a table; very shortly a very pleasant young man came and asked in almost perfect English what we would like to eat and drink.

I asked him what was available and what would he recommend; he recommended the beef steaks and so I ordered that for all of us plus some beer and some soft drinks for the kids. This young man's name was Uli and I didn't know then that he was destined to become a good friend for many years to come until he sadly died a relatively young man from cancer. But I cannot tell or adequately describe the intense feeling of absolute relief that I felt sitting there waiting to be served with our supper. The only thing wrong was that Lynne was not there sitting at the table with us. The tranquility was only spoiled by a loud mouthed German who sat near to us and when enquiring where we were heading for then said loudly and in a scathing manner: 'Oh – Czechoslovakia – there you can get anything you want for a packet of cigarettes.' I knew this to be untrue but I was in no mood to argue with this stupid man who spoke far too loudly, as well as arrogantly, and in an objectionable manner about the country I was going to and which I had grown to like very much.

Never mind, soon our meals arrived – three glorious and very tasty looking steaks with some fried potatoes and vegetables. It looked wonderful – and indeed it was wonderful. The children ate every last morsel – even the vegetables, although I never thought they would. It shows how very hungry they must have been. However, we had only just begun our meal when all the lights went out; a common occurrence in recovering Germany at that time, I gathered. But Uli quickly came to the rescue with candles and there we sat eating our supper by candlelight; it was actually quite nice. And so, when we had finished eating, I took the kids up to our room. Lynne was fast asleep and the children started jumping up and down on their beds in their excitement until I stopped them. But not before they accidentally broke or rather dislodged the curtain rail. After settling them in, I asked Lynne again if I could bring her anything but she just wanted to sleep. So I went downstairs again to enjoy another glass of that delicious German beer and to speak further with Uli; by now the loud mouthed German had retired to his room and good riddance to him!

The next morning Lynne was feeling much better and refreshed after a good night's sleep. We told her about the delicious meal we had enjoyed the evening before and she was sorry that she missed it. The children were okay too and so we all went down for breakfast. After breakfast, as we were now in no special hurry, we thought we would take a look around Marktheidenfeld, look in the shops and see if there was anything worth buying. It is hard to believe now that at that time the exchange rate gave us over 12Dm per £ Sterling. In later years it fell to below 3Dm per £. But in 1960 it was a cheap country for British people to visit and although the war had ended some 15 years earlier, I didn't get the impression that the country, as a whole, had made a lot of real progress. Their economic miracle had not yet happened. So we bought a couple of things that caught our attention and went back to our hotel to enjoy one last beer, pay the bill and get on our way towards the Czech border. When Uli gave me my bill I looked at it and I had to ask if he had included everything? The room? The suppers? The beers? I think it came to about 100Dm which converted to about £8 something! Unbelievable! But such was the strength of Sterling at that time coupled of course with the low prices in Germany then.

We found our way back to the road taking us eastwards towards the Czech border. But first we had to go through Wurzburg itself. This was a busy and very attractive town but here I found for the first time that German drivers tended to be rather impatient with us. I was in a strange country and looking for the way ahead and naturally I would be going somewhat slowly at times when we were not sure of the direction. But I still got a couple of honks which I suppose were intended to speed me up but I ignored them. Once through Wurzburg the road ahead developed into just normal country roads such as we would have found in England before the spread of motorways. And I have to say how sorry I am that the majority of people today want or need to get where they are going as quickly as possible and so by going via autobahns and motorways, never have the opportunity to see and enjoy the country through which they are passing. I can only say that the journey from Wurzburg to the Czech border was a lovely, romantic trip through wonderful countryside and very attractive and unique small villages and it was a considerable pleasure to drive along that route. At one village at about twelve midday or so, we stopped at a small place we thought was a café – it was actually a butcher's shop! But they had two tables outside which must be there for a reason and so when the young lady came out to us I asked for 'Sausages and beer, bitte'. She must have guessed we were English and immediately began to make a fuss of us. She said, with a question in her voice, 'Ah – Wurst und bier?' and I replied 'Ja, bitte.' In due course she brought out a plate of steaming sausages, some delicious country bread, some beer for me and soft drinks for Lynne and the kids. And didn't we all tuck in – they were absolutely scrumptious and we ate the lot! And then the young lady reappeared carrying with her some pictures evidently taken from some magazines. They were pictures of our Royal Family and the two Princesses and as she spoke a little English she told us how she keeps a lot of pictures of them and that she loves them! I was quite taken aback but very pleased to hear this for I am a Royalist at heart, too!

So then we proceeded towards the Czech border and that, in the days of the Cold War, was an experience. We followed the signs to 'The Border' and 'Customs' etc. and arrived at the last stopping place in Germany. There were offices there and the road was closed with a barrier across. So you had to stop there, go into the office of the border guards or Customs with all your paperwork. There the Germans made a meticulous entry of us all and our car registration and then I was told we could go ahead. A man came out to lift the barrier and we slowly drove across into No Man's Land.

I suppose the distance between the German outpost and the Czech border was about 600-700 yards or so and you are warned to drive very slowly which I did.

Soon we spotted the Czech border control point; to our left and to our right were conning towers with border guards watching us through binoculars. Every border guard we saw seemed to be bristling with guns of all sorts – and binoculars. Not ever having done anything like this before it was quite nerve-wracking to drive across No Man's Land and enter Czechoslovakia. We had the feeling that many eyes were upon us. When we approached the Czech barriers we passed more and more border guards and again all were armed to the teeth. What a contrast to the other side, we thought.

Eventually we stopped at the Czech Customs and I had to go into the office once again with our passports, in which our visas were entered and all my paperwork. Back then there was a strict control over money and so I had to declare what I had in Sterling and in Deutschmarks or any other currency and give an undertaking that I was not carrying any

Czechoslovak money into the country which was strictly forbidden. All of this was entered on to a special form, of which they kept a copy, and a copy was tucked into your passport. Every time you changed money whilst in the country it had to be recorded on that form. The idea was to check if you had maybe stayed a month in the country at various hotels etc., but let us assume you had only changed £10. In that case you would be suspected of illegal sale of foreign currency on the 'black market' and you would need to explain how you managed with so little money and be subjected to a lot of questions. I am not sure what happened to those who were unable to satisfy the Customs or Control people on the question of currency. But it was evidently necessary to be very careful. It took well over half an hour to get through the Czech border controls and then we were on our way but not before every inch of our car including the engine and of course the boot – and even underneath – had been closely inspected! We also had to open one or two cases to show them that only our clothing was contained in them. It was a degree of control that I had never experienced before.

Once through Customs and Immigration Control our first impression was that everything we passed looked in a state of neglect. The villages could have been attractive but it looked as if nobody cared about painting their houses or cottages etc. I discovered later that since nobody was allowed to own their own home in communist Czechoslovakia and just paid rent, nobody bothered about the state of their home. In some cases these homes had formerly belonged to the people now inhabiting them – and now were forced to pay rent on what were their own properties!

But after a while we finally found ourselves at our first port of call – Karlovy Vary (maybe better known by it's German name Carlsbad – all towns close to the border have both Germanic and Czech names). It was not difficult to find our hotel which, although not grand, was quite acceptable. There I found a message waiting for me; it was from my artist friend Jiri (Georgie) Trnka, and it told me that I should expect a visit or a call from his good friend, Robert Robetin, who would like to welcome us to Czechoslovakia and to invite me to play a round of golf with him. Actually I was quite honoured for Robert Robetin was no ordinary person; he was a famous international ice-hockey player and known by virtually everybody in Czechoslovakia where that sport is as popular as football. Well Robert did in fact call upon us at the hotel and not wishing to offend, and being assured by Lynne that she and the children would be quite OK, I went off to play a round of golf with him at the Karlovy Vary

Golf Club. I found the course to be interesting and challenging and I enjoyed playing there very much.

When I returned to our hotel I found Lynne waiting there quite perplexed because she had asked in the restaurant for three lemonades. I had told her how to ask for it, i.e. 'Tri limonady prosim vas' and how to pronounce it but evidently the waitress misunderstood her and served them three lunches which they didn't want but felt obliged to eat. But whatever it was they didn't like it! I must say, unequivocally, that our stay in Karlovy Vary was very pleasant indeed and we were pleased that we had chosen this town as our first stop.

As English people were so very few and far between, they welcomed us wherever we went and I have to remark how very kind the people there were to us. It was a pleasure to be there. Yes – their smiles may have been a little wistful as if, perhaps, they envied us coming from a free country where we can travel anywhere we liked, anytime but we found their attitude towards us to be nothing but excellent.

However, at this point I have to carry us forward to the 21st century when together with Jackie, my eldest daughter and her husband, Ray, we visited Prague again for a couple of days in 2004. We flew from Bristol Airport to Ruzyne (Prague) Airport. In Prague we stayed at one of the nicest hotels I ever stayed at in my life, the Inter-Continental – and I have experienced quite a few in various countries. But this was arranged by my good friend, Jiri Stepan, who has good contacts everywhere. There in Staromestske Namesti (Old Town Square) I held a dinner for my remaining friends which was very pleasant but it was sad that the numbers were growing fewer each time I visited. After Prague, our first stop on our way was to be Plzen, the famous beer city, but somehow we missed a turning and found ourselves instead going directly to Karlovy Vary which ought to have been our second stop. Sadly, Jackie couldn't remember a lot about her previous visit there years before when she was little and so I described to her how it was then and we looked forward to a very pleasant visit.

However, it was anything but. We managed to park our car and then called in to a café which looked quite nice and we sat there for far too long waiting to be served. Meanwhile, we noticed that Germans, of which there were many, were being attended and pandered to in a rather self serving manner. After a while this became a bit annoying and so I spoke to one of the passing waiters in Czech and told him we had been waiting there for quite a while. He served us but in a rather surly manner which was absolutely nothing like the attitude towards English people such as we had experienced years before and at first I found that very difficult to understand because back then they had everything to be sad about and yet they were not, and now they have everything to be happy about – and yet they are not ! Except when talking to Germans!

Talking about it later, we were reminded that these border towns had become heavily reliant on German custom. It was so easy for Germans to pop across the border these days – for a weekend, or even on a day trip – and they did so in large numbers. So whilst my much earlier experiences showed a marked leaning towards people from the West but certainly not those from Germany whom they tended to hate, the pendulum had turned and now it was the other way around. 'Never mind,' I told the others, 'just wait until we get to Marianske Lazne – it will be different there, you will see,' But I have to say that it wasn't. The old attitude towards us English, so wonderful many years before, had vanished in Marianske Lazne, too!

Anyway, let me return to our trip in 1960. We had a great, but short, time in Karlovy Vary and now it was time to continue our itinerary. We didn't think we were in any hurry and so we didn't leave until after lunch. The problem was that just before leaving home I had received conflicting messages from Prague and we were not sure if we were booked in at a hotel in a town called Usti-nad-Labem or the Hotel Grand in Decin. Both towns were in the same general direction however and so off we went. We soon learned that when crossing railway crossings one had to do that very gingerly because they were really quite atrocious with great holes and prominent rails. If you went across them any faster than 10mph you soon knew about it.

Now it was getting a little darker and then I came to a full stop because before me was a fork in the road. To the left was Usti-nad-Labem and to the right was Decin! Which way should I go? Well we decided to go to Usti first which we did. There I stopped at the hotel, the name of which escapes me for the moment; I went to the Reception Desk and asked if they had a room reserved for me – they hadn't. So obviously we must be booked into Hotel Grand at Decin. In those days most places in Czechoslovakia were grim, dark, places and the fading light didn't help either. I took the most likely route but as we went on, the absence of any signposts made me slightly nervous.

We came to a railway crossing where traffic had stopped to allow a freight train, which seemed to me to be a half a mile long, to pass through. I took this opportunity to hop out of my car and ask the lorry driver just in front of us for directions. My Czech was in its early learning stages then but I managed to understand from him that I should follow him and he would show me the way to Decin. Actually, I was on the right road and it was straight ahead so really, although it was very kind of the lorry driver, I needn't have followed him at all.

So finally we arrived at Decin and there on my left I saw a grassed park like area and on the other side of that I could see 'Hotel Grand' illuminated. So I took the next turning left, then left again and there we were – right in front of the hotel. Both Lynne and I breathed a sigh of relief whilst we sat for a moment after that gruelling journey. We were all hungry and thirsty and so my first objective was to report to Reception, go to our room, and then immediately come down to the Restaurant below to satisfy our hunger and thirst.

But before we could move our car was surrounded by people – mainly young ones but a number of older ones too – and they were smiling at us, saying things in Czech which we didn't understand, of course. However we knew they were words of welcome by the expressions on their faces. They asked for chewing gum, they asked for cigarettes and to us it was quite bewildering. I mean, we weren't film stars or famous in any way. We were just simple visitors from England. I had never experienced a welcome like that then and I never have since but it just goes to show how visitors from the West were regarded in those days – not so much in Prague but certainly in outlying towns.

However, it didn't lessen our need for sustenance and so we extricated ourselves from these wonderful people and entered the hotel. Standing there at the entrance was a gentleman who asked me, in English, 'Are you Mr Mitchell?' I replied that I was and he introduced himself to me as Dr. Chraska who was an economist and mathematical expert. A very clever man indeed and much too intelligent to do the job he had back in the HQ at Prague which was making cost calculations for the various confectionery products.

I didn't know him before but I believe he was asked to be there in Decin for my visit in case price problems came up. Anyway, Dr Chraska was very attentive towards us and when I explained that we had not had anything to eat or drink for some hours he hastened to open the door of the restaurant. Immediately a great cloud of smoke hit us in the face; the room was filled to capacity by men drinking beer, smoking, laughing and shouting to each other. It was obviously no place for women and children. Seeing this Dr Chraska hastily closed the door, went to Reception, had a word with them and soon we were ushered to a private back room where we were served a very tasty meal of pork cutlets and vegetables washed down with some great beer Now we felt much better – but very tired. And so we excused ourselves and retired.

The next day our colleagues from Prague met with us and we went to the Diana Factory there where I was introduced to the Director of the Diana Factory, Jaromir Koci – another gentleman who was very kind to us and who I got to know very well over the coming years. I did my business in the morning whilst Lynne and the children were invited to sit in a pleasant little garden and later asked if they would like to pick and enjoy some fresh strawberries which they did. I had high hopes of this factory, which as time proved were not misplaced, as I shall relate later on; this was but a fleeting visit and I intended to include as many factories as I possibly could. However, as I had my family with me and being the hospitable kind of people that they were, in the afternoon we drove outside Decin to a lovely area in the countryside to a forested hill called Ruzova where one of the people who worked at Decin had a very nice wooden lodge buried in the deep forest which he used for hunting and keeping bees! This gentleman's name was Vaclav Kolacny and we nicknamed him 'Baron' Kolacny for he was the owner of this fine lodge. High in the sky above, eagles were wheeling and calling to each other in that unmistakable cry that all birds of prey use. Here you were certainly in the middle of the wilderness.

But actually Vaclav was a previous director and part owner of the Diana Factory before it was nationalised and he was lucky because although he did not have a high position in Diana, he was not put into a humiliating situation as most previous owners and directors were. He was fortunate that the Director, Mr Koci, was a very nice man – not the type to humiliate anybody. I didn't know it then but that was the first of many visits of mine to Ruzova.

There the children were in their element and when invited to help make a fire on which we were going to cook some special little, dumpy, sausages called Knacka, they joined in and worked like beavers, collecting wood and keeping the fire going. I shall always remember their little black faces looking up at me with a big grin whilst they were tending the fire. So we sat around the fire, drinking beer, cooking sausages and chatting – it was a very enjoyable break and it was then that I was introduced to hunting. I went with one of the foresters to hunt for wild boar and although we sat in a tree for hours, we didn't see anything and so we decided to wend our way back to the lodge to rejoin the others. What I was unaware of until the following day was that in the forest I had picked up an unwanted stranger in the crook of my arm – a forest leech which horrified me when I found it. I then did the wrong thing by pulling the insect out because, apparently, as I was told afterwards, if you leave the head buried in your flesh, some nasty complications can follow. But in my case, thank goodness, I had no such bother. I am told the best way to rid oneself of these insects is to touch them with a lighted cigarette and then they are supposed to release themselves from your body.

At the end of our visit to Decin, Mr Koci gave me a note on which there were three names; he explained that these were doctors at the sanatorium in Marianske Lazne, which would be the last place we would visit before our departure for home, and that they were all very interested in hunting and would perhaps be of help to me if I wished to try my luck at hunting there. I took the note, put it into my pocket, and forgot about it!

From the business point of view, my visit to Decin was very useful in connection with my ideas of formulating a range of boxed items for direct sale and distribution to the supermarket trade in the UK. As I have indicated before, nobody had ever done this previously in Britain as the leading British manufacturers tended to shun supermarkets in those days and regarded them simply as price cutters who would only spoil their main market but because our Czech factories were all nationalised, I had a whole industry behind me! And so if anyone could do this kind of business satisfactorily then it should be us, with all our possibilities from the various factories. From our discussions there I developed a number of ideas which eventually came to fruition. Mr Koci was very interested to hear about my plans for supermarket trading – especially when I told him that if we can succeed to produce the right type of lines, the volume would be considerable. I promised Mr Koci that I would return to Decin – and I did, many times. We developed excellent relations and a very nice business with the Diana factory. In fact, for marketing purposes, I eventually used the name "Diana" (Goddess of Hunting!) on all supermarket packs that we produced and sold.

After we had finished our business in Decin, we made our way to Hradec Kralove, stopped very briefly at a factory in Liberec and continued our journey, leaving Bohemia towards Olomouc which was and still is the most historic town in Moravia. As I described in the previous Chapter, situated there was the Zora Factory controlled by the Director, Mr Valka. He was a very nice and exceedingly hospitable gentleman and I came to know him very well in due course. I was only sorry that I was not able to generate a large amount of business for their particular type of products back in England. At Olomouc we stayed at Hotel Statni Dum (State House) which is a very old hotel. In its day it must have been a wonderful place for we must not forget that prior to the First World War, the whole of this area formed part of the old Austro-Hungarian empire and so royals, counts and barons were many in the old days.

We were given a small suite of rooms which was very suitable for Lynne, me and two children and above our large double bed was an insignia in the wall. I cannot recall now exactly but I do know the insignia was topped by a crown. In fact it looked like a bed in which a king, or some royal person may have once slept! We liked it at Statni Dum – especially the large lounge on the ground floor in the corner of which was a small stage and at weekends or on special days, a small orchestra played there. The orchestra consisted of a small, dumpy lady who played the violin in a very energetic manner which looked very humorous. She was accompanied by a pianist and maybe a drummer but he was mostly not required because they played slow, serious music – music was also controlled by the Communist authorities – so for this kind of music you did not require drums.

I had always been very surprised to learn that musicians could not play whatever they liked and western music was regarded by them as decadent, capitalist rubbish. Myself, I rather liked this somewhat old fashioned music because it was in harmony with the atmosphere of the old hotel. However, very pleasant though it was, soon it was time to leave Olomouc but not before Mr Valka asked me privately if I could help him by obtaining a special drug, extracted from the digitalis plant, in England for him. He explained to me that he suffered from a lack of pigmentation in the skin and his doctor had told him of this new drug which might help him. I even remember its name – Meladinine. Of course, it was unobtainable in Czechoslovakia and that was why he asked me to try to obtain it for him in the UK – and I did!

In the years I associated with the Czechs and because of the continued shortages of so many things in that country and as I have mentioned in passing before, I received many requests from people in the factories and also many others that I came into contact with. To begin with I did not realize that this would become quite a problem because such items ranged from drugs and medicines, tyres for cars, golf equipment, artists requisites, woollen sweaters, ball point pens, duffle coats and God knows what else! I do not think any of the people making these requests realised that they were not the only ones that were asking me to bring them things and that I, because of my frequent visits by car, received many such requests. It placed me in a difficult position because on the one hand I wanted to help anybody I could but, as I have also mentioned elsewhere, I had to buy such items from my own pocket. Of course some of them offered to recompense me – but with what? There was no point in paying me in Czech Crowns for I had enough of those; I received £10 per day travelling expenses, agreed with Jiracek of all people, and sometimes this was too much because £10 was a lot of money when converted to Czech crowns in those days. So when I had a surplus at the end of each trip, I either left money there in charge of good friends to be available for me on my next visit or spent it wildly on just anything I could see that was interesting in the shops because there were severe restrictions on the amount of Czech currency you could take out of the country – which was nil!. Over the years I spent a lot of my money in buying such items for various people – but they did appreciate it and it helped me to make a lot of friends. My visit to Olomouc was interesting and worthwhile but in the course of our visit, Mr Valka asked me if I was interested in hunting. Being interested in the outside and wild life in general, I replied that I had taken part in a hunt at Ruzova without success. It was then that Mr Valka arranged my small 'hunting trip' which I described in the previous chapter when I ate cold duck and drank home made Slivovice at 6.00am to celebrate 'Grandfather's' birthday!

On the subject of shortages in Czechoslovakia at that time, I would like to explain that this arose because of a number of reasons. First of all the demands of the Soviet Union were heavy and all the satellite countries were expected to supply all kinds of goods to them for which there may be some payment but at very low prices or on occasions, perhaps no payment at all – such transactions were recognised as being a contribution towards the glorious people of the even more glorious Soviet Union! This was a severe drain on the economy of Czechoslovakia. Partly as a result of this unequal trade situation with the Soviet Union, they were also very short of foreign currencies and this obviously inhibited their ability to purchase abroad. Consequently, items that we in Britain regarded as every day necessities were either in very short supply or were completely unobtainable.

Those people who were lucky enough to have relatives or friends abroad and who received foreign currency allowances from them, were able to go to the special shops called Tuzex where they could buy a great many things which were not available in normal shops. Others had to go without and that is what they learned to do! Another factor which had a great deal of influence on shortages was the cumbersome and very inefficient Communist system which was more aligned to ideology rather than commonsense. However, shortages may be necessary for the common people – but not for the top people and leading party members. No sir! Such people had their own special shop where only they and their families could go and there they could buy everything they could possibly want. In Prague, this special shop was situated in a district called Holesovice and I am sure that such special shops existed all over the country – but only for the top Communists! In the words of George Orwell in his book *Animal Farm*, 'Citizens are all equal, but some are more equal than others'!!

And so we left Olomouc and continued eastwards towards Jihimoravska, a small place also in Moravia and near to a town called Rohatec, where the Marysa Factory was situated. These people really rowed the boat out for us. We stayed at a very nice hotel and we saw in the restaurant a large table laid out with Union Jack flags on it. This was prepared for us and it really looked magnificent with cut crystal glasses and flower arrangements – it was all very elegant. But there was a change of plan, for when the people in the factory heard I was interested in wine, without asking me, they cancelled the prior arrangements and instead arranged a visit to a wine cellar where we could taste a variety of wines made in that district. So instead of the hotel dinner that was originally planned, off to the wine cellar we went. Moravian wines are very good; my favourite was a white wine called Tramin. I heard subsequently that the hotel management at Rohatec was very disappointed at being asked to arrange a big evening for this English family and then have it cancelled at the last minute. But what could we do? Lynne and I were in the hands of our hosts.

After Rohatec we then left to continue our journey and now we were heading towards Bratislava, capital city of Slovakia, on the banks of the River Danube. As we travelled through the Moravian countryside and eventually into Slovakia, it was very nice indeed how people, seeing our foreign car and number plate, waved to us as we drove through. It was not difficult to find our hotel by the river. And what a lovely hotel it was, too – I have seldom stayed at a hotel with such a nice atmosphere and it was so comfortable; it became one of my favourites. It was called Hotel Devin. We were very satisfied there.

The next day I had to go to the factory called Figaro and we discussed many points and looked at a range of their possibilities. But, to be honest, I could see little there that would be of interest on the British market. During the coffee break a young man came to me and spoke to me in excellent English. In a low voice, so that nobody else could hear, he told me that before the Communist coup, the Figaro factory belonged to his father. It was a little difficult for me to speak with him at length but I did ask him what he did now in the factory. He told me that generally speaking they used him to do all kinds of small, unimportant jobs, even sweeping floors which he, as an intelligent young man, obviously disliked; I uttered a word or two of sympathy – what else could one do? He said he was only present at these discussions because he spoke English and that his services might be needed for translation purposes. I then saw that others in the room were looking at us and so I thought it would be prudent to end this conversation although I truly had a lot of sympathy for him – he was a very nice and pleasant young man. In the years during which I represented the Czechoslovaks in the UK, I was to meet a number of people in this young man's situation and on every occasion I felt embarrassment and sadness but there was nothing I could do to help them.

Well, we ended the discussions at Figaro and now the work element of our trip had finished; then the Director and his colleagues told us that they had reserved a family room for us at a hotel in a small place in the Vysoky Tatry (High Tatra Mountains) called Stary Smokovec. And so the following morning we departed from Bratislava and made our way North Eastwards across Slovakia and in the direction of Kosice – but beforehand we were warned where we had to turn off on the road which would take us to the mountains. We were assured that we would be able to follow the route without difficulty, and even furnished us with an ornate road map of Slovakia in case we got lost somehow.

Our impression was that the quality of the roads in Slovakia were better than those in the Czech part of the country and so we found our way very well. When turning off on to the road leading to the mountains we stopped because there, before us was the lovely scene of the mountain range. It looked very beautiful and the mountains were topped with snow even though this was early summer and I took a picture or two before proceeding. Finally, after climbing and climbing for ever and ever we finally reached our destination – we were at Stary Smokovec and on top of the world so it seemed.

We found our hotel without too much difficulty. To be frank, it didn't look all that attractive; never mind, we thought, we shall see what it is like when we get inside. Well the inside was not a great deal better than the outside; our first impressions were not at all good. But we presented ourselves to Reception to obtain our keys and started to go upstairs to our room when a gentleman speaking impeccable English spoke to me and asked where in England did I come from? I told him and a short conversation ensued. But I asked him to excuse me for a few minutes for I wanted to get Lynne and the children upstairs to our room.

The room, as a matter of fact, was not all that bad and so we just decided to accept what the people at Figaro had reserved for us. I may be wrong but I think they were probably thinking of my pocket when selecting this hotel – they needn't have. I returned downstairs to the gentleman I had been speaking to and he told me that he was teaching English to the doctors in the quite large sanatorium situated nearby where people who mainly suffered from tuberculosis and other lung conditions came in order to be in perfect and pure mountain air conditions. I nodded as he told me and then he came straight to the point. He said that as very few English people visit the area, none of the doctors had ever had an opportunity to talk to an Englishman; would I be prepared to come to the sanatorium to meet the doctors, speak with them and answer a few questions that they may have? At first I found the idea very funny because this man before me spoke better English than I and without doubt I was no teacher of the English language! But he persisted and said that he would deem it a great personal service if I would come along. So, rather reluctantly, I agreed and he said he would be in touch to let me know which evening it would be. Meanwhile I returned to Lynne and the children upstairs.

But now it was necessary to feed our children who, as usual, were hungry and thirsty. So we went downstairs to the Restaurant and, quite frankly, we were astounded to see the whole room, which was quite large, filled with literally hundreds of children who were shouting, screaming, punching each other and generally misbehaving as children do when in large groups like that. Evidently these were schoolchildren on a school holiday. But with the noise they were making we could hardly hear ourselves talk. We love children but the very thought of Lynne and I having dinner there in the evening filled us with absolute horror.

Well, after quite a long wait a waitress came to us and we ordered a kind of tea for the kids but she served us in a rather impatient manner, probably because the poor girl had a great deal to cope with. Lynne and I looked at each other and I could see she was unhappy here – especially after the lovely hotels we had stayed at in Bratislava and before that, so we agreed to talk about it over dinner. We returned to Reception and whilst talking with them we gathered that as long as you notified them they had a listening service which enabled parents to go out in the evening if they so desired if they had children. Well we did so desire – and therefore, having noticed a large, much better looking hotel across the road, but lying back in a large grassed area, we decided that might be a good place to have dinner. And indeed it was.

When entering the Restaurant they gave us a nice welcome and we tried to reciprocate with smiles but our poor faces would hardly allow it. We were not happy. Anyway, we were shown to a table and we ordered dinner and a bottle of wine. Then, I am afraid we sat there with rather glum faces because no way could we stay in that horrid hotel across the road for very long. In fact, by that time we had already made the decision to reluctantly wend our way home and so end our holiday there. We ate our meal rather slowly and just before we had finished the waitress came back to see if we were OK; seeing our faces she said, 'Pane, proc jste tak smutny?' (Sir, why are you so sad?) In my very poor Czech I tried to explain that we were staying at the hotel across the road, that we did not like it there, that our holiday had been rather spoilt and that we were thinking of going home the following day. She nodded her head in an understanding manner and went away.

She returned after five minutes explaining that they had no free rooms there but she gave me a piece of paper on which was written 'Hotel Grand Praha – Tatranske Lomnice' and she told us that she had phoned there, that it is a beautiful hotel and that as long as I went there immediately, they had a nice room which they would hold for us. I don't think I had even finished dinner but simply got up and went after agreeing with Lynne that she would wait for me there or perhaps we agreed to meet back at our hotel. I ran to my car and drove like a bat out of Hell in the direction of Tatranske Lomnice.

As I drove through this mountainous but forested road, I saw many deer grazing by the roadside which were caught in my headlights. It was certainly a wild country – they even had bears and lynx in the area! I think Tatranske Lomnice was about 10 km from Stary Smokovec but there was absolutely no traffic whatsoever and I arrived there very quickly. And although in an isolated spot, what a hotel it was – all red, plush carpets with exactly what we were seeking – an exclusive kind of atmosphere and a classy hotel at that. Truly a beautiful hotel and the views from the bedroom windows were breathtaking. I knew Lynne would be happy here and so I confirmed immediately that we would check out of our present hotel and come there the next morning. And that is exactly what we did. The Reception people at the Stary Smokovec hotel seemed to understand when I explained that we were cutting short our stay with them – but I did remember to leave a message for the teacher gentleman who had asked for my assistance so that he would know where to contact me.

As I anticipated Lynne was very happy with the change and, like me, she and the children were much more content now that we had a nice hotel at which to stay. We explored a little of the outside and found a mountain path that we made a mental note of; it looked interesting – but perhaps we would tackle that the following day because it was late afternoon and we all wanted to have a bath to freshen ourselves up before dinner. The bathroom was absolutely perfect – just as you would expect in a hotel of that quality.

And so later we meandered down to dinner and, walking through the lounge, we saw a man, alone and perhaps in his middle 30s. We gave him a smile and walked on into the restaurant. We were shown to our table and almost immediately a waiter came and placed a Union Jack on our table. In those days that was the custom almost everywhere in Czechoslovakia; it was a charming custom that eventually petered out unfortunately with the increased quantity and variety of visitors. Shortly afterwards the man in the lounge came in to the restaurant; he sat down at a table, and once again a waiter placed a Union Jack on his table! So he was British too! We took longer than him to consume dinner and so after he had finished he went back into the very plush and comfortable lounge to sit and relax with a coffee and brandy. Very shortly after, we followed him and as I passed, I spoke with him and asked where in England did he come from. I nearly fell over, for it was totally unbelievable when he told me that he came from Coulsdon in Surrey! When I told him we came from Old Coulsdon just up the hill from him, he too was very surprised. What are the chances, I wondered, of meeting someone from the same hometown as you in a lonely, out of the way hotel, way up in the mountains well over a thousand miles from home?

We were now enjoying our holiday very much. We toured the area and explored various places recommended to us at Reception including Strbske Pleso – a mountain lake area; it was a strenuous but relaxing, holiday and the kids, especially, loved it When we returned to our hotel, a message awaited me from the English speaking gentleman we had met at Stary Smokovec asking me if the following evening would be convenient for him to collect me, take me to the sanatorium, and meet his doctor pupils. I agreed with this and carried out my promise. The doctors were a group of both men and women and they gave me a nice welcome. But it was a bit nerve-wracking, for I had never done anything like this before in my life and in any case, I certainly did not consider myself to be any kind of an expert on the English language. However, to my great surprise it went very well. I made some kind of little speech, included a few humorous quips which amused the doctors and I can only say that they clapped me at the end. Now was the time for questions but I found I was able to answer them all without too much difficulty. The question I found most difficult to answer was: 'Mr Mitchell, what is the difference between the words "should" and "would"?' I thought very quickly for a moment and then explained the difference by saying that it was an example of the indefinite and definite forms of speech which also exist in the Czech language. I suggested that 'should' is indefinite because it suggests there is a choice; whereas 'would' suggests a more positive form of speech. I have never checked to find out if I was correct – I hope I was!!

Soon the time came for our departure and we decided to go by the most direct route which would be via Olomouc, the town we stayed at on our way to Slovakia. As we had liked Hotel Statni Dum there, we returned to the same venue and, thankfully, they had a room for us. After checking in we went into that lounge which I described earlier but today was Sunday and it was absolutely packed. The little, dumpy, lady on the small stage was still playing away furiously; her music was still old fashioned, which as I have said I happen to like and it really did suit the atmosphere of that lounge. It was like a throwback to the earlier 1900s. The only table I could see free was situated by the waiters' entrance and exit; not ideal but we had no other choice. I caught the attention of a waitress and ordered tea for the children. Just soft drinks with some bread, butter, and jam. But I had a little difficulty in making her understand the word 'jam' as I pronounced the word in English style, i.e. with a long 'a'. She eventually understood but she pronounced it as 'jem', i.e. with a short 'a'.

The following morning we left Olomouc, went via Prague; I cannot now recall if we stayed overnight there but anyway we eventually made our way to Marianske Lazne where we had reserved rooms at Hotel Esplanade. We were very pleased with this hotel although it was obviously a relic of much earlier times, and looked it! In the days of King Edward VII, when he was still Prince of Wales, this was the spa where he met his then German lady friend; it must have been some hotel. Inside, we were again given a nice welcome and shown to our room which was old in every way – but adequate. Again we wanted to bathe and freshen up before dinner but, to our horror, we found the water to be of a dirty brown colour. Well, we were certainly not going to bathe our children in that! However, later we were told that the water is only discoloured because of the high level of certain spa mineral properties and that it is very healthy to bathe in it. I am not sure this was the whole truth and I had a kind of feeling that the ancient plumbing had something to do with it too. But in every other way the hotel was good and we were happy there – especially when we went down for dinner as the dining room was a lovely, palatial room with fantastic huge, crystal glass chandeliers which were truly beautiful. One could easily imagine how wonderful this restaurant must have been and what great occasions must have taken place in its heyday. We were shown to a table and shortly a very nice waiter, fully dressed as waiters in fine restaurants and hotels used to be, presented us with menus. The menu was extensive and the meal served to us was excellent in every way.

After spending two days there we were reluctant to leave. We had explored the area around the hotel, walked down the hill to the town, walked up the hill to the golf course which was specially constructed for our Prince of Wales and in fact officially opened by him in the early 1900s. I played a game there and met the so called 'pro' whose name was Jiri Stanek. He was to escape from the country later on in 1968 as did many people because after the invasion by the Warsaw Pact nations, led by the Soviet Union of course; the borders were wide open and anyone could leave. I liked Jiri a lot and I cannot forget our discussion about beer; you could not get Pilsner beer everywhere – there was a shortage of that although it was only brewed in Plzen about an hour away (which is why it is called Plzenske Pivo – i.e. the beer of Plzen). Most people know the city as Pilsen. But Jiri took us to a restaurant on the main road, just opposite the golf course, and there in a back room we ordered and we received Plzenske Pivo. We had to drink it secretly in that back room otherwise everybody else would want it too but because the beer from Plzen was in very short supply, it was reserved for special customers only of which Jiri was certainly one! Inferior beers from other breweries were of course in plentiful supply.

I would like to describe more fully my first game of golf there in Marianske Lazne. My old friend, Jiri Trnka, back in Prague was the person who had arranged for me to play a round or so with Jiri Stanek, the pro. Lynne and the children sat in the area outside the club house where there were a number of tables and chairs and there you could sit, drink beer or soft drinks or do anything you wanted because the golf course was used also as a park by the general public! This hardly made for good golf because you could hit a ball down the fairway only if you could avoid the people crossing over and they did so almost all the time; they even held picnics on the greens! Sometimes you arrived near to a green but before you could play you had to ask the people having picnics, politely, if they would mind moving off the green! I should explain that the communist authorities would have liked to close the golf course and make it completely into a public park with a portion of it used for agriculture.

But the members of the club, which included a number of doctors from the spa sanatorium and people like my friend Jiri Trnka and his friends, fought furiously against this intention. One can but admire the courage of those people because in those days it was not healthy to argue with the communists. But for them there would be no golf course at Marianske Lazne. However, it was agreed that the course would remain as such – but the public had to be allowed on the course and walk wherever and whenever they wanted. So, as I have remarked, these conditions hardly made for good golf.

During our visit in 2004 I visited the golf course and what a total difference – the old clubhouse was gone and in its place was a magnificent new building. It was a course and a clubhouse of which any country would be proud – probably championship class. Curiously, I walked into the clubhouse to see if a plaque or any kind of recognition existed of those past members whose courage in fighting for the continuation of the club and course was so crucial back in the bad times. Without them there would be no fine club today. I was sad to see that nothing existed – no recognition whatsoever of those brave people.

When I returned to England and home I sent an email to the Director of the course complimenting him on the truly splendid facilities now at the club but telling him of my sadness of what seemed to me to be an omission and suggested that a small plaque containing at least some of the prominent names back then of club members who fought for the club. I am afraid that I received neither an acknowledgement nor reply to my entreaties.

But let me return to that first game I played in 1960 with Jiri Stanek. It seemed that word had got around that an Englishman was playing the course that day because I was sitting with Lynne and the children at a table and noticed that quite a crowd had gathered around the first tee. Suddenly the crowd parted and through the gap there was Jiri beckoning me to come and start our game. What? In front of all those people? Lynne of course nearly died laughing at my predicament and as I walked towards the tee, I said to Jiri words to the effect that I was no Henry Cotton, just an ordinary player, and I asked him what these people expected? He replied to me saying that they wanted to see how an Englishman plays golf, for wasn't it in England that the game began? I corrected him by saying that it was started in Scotland, not England.

However, although I found this collection of people surrounding us to be unnerving I was so glad when I hit the ball fairly and squarely right down the middle of the fairway – and the small crowd clapped me! Believe me, that was pure luck because I was distracted and I was sure I was going to muff it! When we left the tee, the crowd followed us! But gradually as we advanced further round the course they thinned out until only two or three people were still following.

However, I have to remark that on a green there I made the finest putt in the whole of my life – really the best ever! It was a large and curving green and very difficult to judge; I was quite a long way from the hole but I made my putt very carefully. At first I was put off a little bit by a Russian man with a movie camera who was filming us play. I heard the faint noise of the camera, took careful aim and my ball went round and down from about 40 feet – and straight into the hole! If I may say so, it was a fine putt – the best I ever did and I was never able to equal it. Even Jiri Stanek gave me a clap! The Russian cameraman was of course delighted that he had captured this on film. One last comment on this golf course which involves a contest they had called King of Drivers. I took part in this and won it! So, as I have heard nothing to say otherwise, I must still be King of Drivers there!

On one of the days we were at the golf course, it began to rain very heavily. So not only us but many other people too took refuge inside the clubhouse. This crowd included a whole section of Russians who had evidently done something good at home and were being rewarded by such a holiday visit to Czechoslovakia. They were such nice people and it was evident that they absolutely loved children. They made a great fuss of our two kids and gave them some trinkets from Russia – unfortunately we had nothing with us to give them. And then, the Russians burst into song and I have to say it was quite wonderful. They were terrific singers – no doubt about that – and it turned our rainy afternoon into a very nice and most enjoyable sojourn.

On our return to the hotel which was only half a mile perhaps from the course, I changed my clothing and, in my pocket, I found the note that Mr Koci had given me earlier in Decin. So I went downstairs to Reception and there a very pleasant girl who asked how she could help me. I gave her the note and explained the situation. She nodded and asked me to return in one hour. I did so on our way to dinner but she told me that she had been quite successful in contacting the three doctors but the first one said he was going to Prague, the second said he was too busy and the third one just simply declined. Quietly she indicated that I should understand how some people are nervous when being in contact with anybody from the West – especially if they are in positions of importance. As she explained – in regard to taking the risks it very much depends on the person. Some do not care and are willing to do so. Others are more nervous and are not. I had no intention to, but I must have looked rather crestfallen at this rebuff.

The charming girl smiled and said that I shouldn't be sad and that she would try something else. So we went in to dinner and once again it was a very pleasant meal. The next day we had been out and were returning to the hotel following a chap on a small motorcycle. He turned in to the driveway of Hotel Esplanade and I followed him. After parking, I entered the hotel and found this chap talking to the Receptionist – a different one than the young lady earlier who must have gone off duty. But I could not help overhearing my name being mentioned and so I walked over and presented myself, at which the young chap shook my hand, introduced himself as Slavek Svinger, and told me he was a member of the Forest Organisation. He then continued by saying that if I would like to go hunting, he would be pleased to accompany me. He was, of course, the same Slavek whom I have written about earlier in connection with fishing

Obviously this had occurred only due to the kind efforts of the young girl in Reception earlier. But Slavek, who also became a life long friend, could only speak slow and stuttering English then and with almost every sentence he had to refer to a small Anglo-Czech translation booklet to find the right words! Anyway I told him that it was very kind of him and we made an agreement that he would come to the hotel later on in the afternoon and we would drive to the forest in my car.

He duly arrived at the hotel spot on time – a very unusual event in Czechoslovakia then! So we drove a few miles out of Marianske Lazne and there, standing by a small junction at the entrance to the forest was another forester – apparently I was to go with him. His name was Antonin (Tonda in the familiar form) Moucha and he was a very nice chap. Anyway, they asked me if I was familiar with guns and I told them that I was a British ex-soldier which seemed to satisfy them. So off the two of us went; Tonda ahead and me following behind. In all, I think we had walked at least three kilometres and the light was beginning to fade. We had stopped at various points where the forester knew deer were normally grazing in the early evening; we saw only one roe buck but this one had a fine trophy and those specimens were not hunted – they were needed to keep up good genes in the herd, for it is the quality of the trophy which tells a hunter that he may, or may not, shoot.

Well, my companion turned to me and gestured that as we have had no luck we should return to the spot where Slavek and my car were. As we trudged through the fields, I saw to my left a deer; evidently Tonda had not seen it so I tapped him on the shoulder. He looked at the deer through his binoculars and then motioned me to shoot. To be quite honest, I didn't know if I wanted to and so I hesitated briefly. I was really more interested in watching these animals and not so much in shooting them. But my companion motioned again that I should shoot – and so I did.

Now the procedure after a kill is that you must respect the animal and so one has to wait for a few minutes. Meanwhile, Slavek had heard the shot and found where we were. We all walked towards the deer and it lay there motionless. But Slavek told me that it had a very poor trophy, that it was sick and that it was better that such specimens are removed from the herd. He said that sooner or later it would have been seen either by the foresters or perhaps by one of the hunting clubs, and dealt with. I felt a little bit better after knowing that. My feelings now about hunting, for I had a number of adventures after my introduction at Marianske Lazne, are absolutely different from then. I quite realise that like it or not, culling is part of the necessary preservation of the herd and the forest but if I were invited to participate in hunting now, I would politely decline; I prefer to leave the task of herd control to others. Back at the hotel I felt obliged to offer Slavek a drink at the bar and, in fact, we had several – to celebrate my initiation to hunting Slavek said, after looking the words up in the book, of course!

We stayed another day or so in which time we met Slavek's charming wife when he brought her to the hotel the next day. Her name was Jarmila (or Jarka in the familiar case – yes the same Jarka who cooked my fish) and we entertained both her and Slavek to lunch. We, and especially me, because I came there many times over the next eight years, got to know Jarka quite well and many is the meal she cooked at all hours of God's night and day for me. She was, and still is, a lovely person and extremely pleasurable company. She got on with Lynne very well. In the years to follow, I invited Slavek and Jarka to come to England for a visit. They did and stayed with us during which I think they had a nice time. Sadly the marriage between Slavek and Jarka broke down and they were divorced some years later. But Jarka still lives in Marianske Lazne and when we visited we saw her and I still write to her now and then. I try very hard not to forget my old friends.

But now it was time to wend our way home again. The way to the border was not complicated but our examination at the control point was just as bad as when we had arrived in Czechoslovakia! The control on money was very strict and they examined my currency form given to me when we entered the country very closely to see what I had exchanged and then tried to catch me out by asking what foreign currency I had left. I counted the Sterling, Deutschmarks and Belgian Francs I had and fortunately it all seemed to match up. I was not into currency deals – far too dangerous, especially for me in my position.

Anyway, after all the formalities we then had to cross No Man's Land and go through the German Customs and border control. But driving away from the Czech border point was again rather eerie; we felt as if our every movement was being watched, as it no doubt was, and that maybe even guns were trained upon us. So we were relieved to get through into Germany – especially to experience decent roads again, for the roads in Czechoslovakia back then were atrocious.

Our journey through Germany was uneventful. We decided to take a slightly different route going back which brought us to Aachen, quite near to the border. As we had some Deutschmarks left, we thought it might be an idea to stay at Aachen for one night before proceeding to Belgium. We found a very nice, modern hotel without difficulty and it was a satisfying break. What was pleasurable was that we could ask for, and get, anything we liked – quite different from the situation in foreign currency starved Czechoslovakia. And the next morning we arose early and made our way to the border and through into Belgium. On the much better roads we made good headway and although we once again had difficulties in Brussels, we managed to find our way eventually and now we were on the excellent road between Brussels and Ostend. But we were quite early to catch the plane back and so when I spied what looked like a first class restaurant on the opposite side of the road we stopped and enjoyed a truly excellent lunch. I took the opportunity whilst there to phone the airport just to confirm that there were no delays – there weren't and so when we had finished lunch we resumed our journey to Ostend but not before the staff at the restaurant all wished us a good trip. I must say that in those days it seemed to us that we English were liked very much by all the Continentals – even the Germans. I wonder what happened?

At Ostend Airport our plane was ready. Once again it looked a rickety affair. We hoped it was efficient enough to get us across the Channel but our fears, or rather our anxieties, were eliminated once we had touched down at Southend.

From Southend to our home in Old Coulsdon, Surrey was about two hours or even less in those happy motoring days, when we hardly knew what a traffic jam was. And Oh Boy! Much as we had thoroughly enjoyed our interesting and adventurous journey, it was so good to be home once again and in our own surroundings. Lynne and the children were all very happy to have finally arrived home.

AFTERWORD

At this point I am afraid we have to leave my narrative for the moment. Mine has been a long life filled with many adventures and experiences and to try to put all of this into one book would result in a much too long and unwieldy affair.

So do look out for Volume 2. Don't miss it for in it I will tell more human, even inhuman, stories of my adventures behind the Iron Curtain, how I became mixed up with spies, how MI6 asked for my help, how I further developed Czechoslovak confectionery sales and distribution in the UK – especially with the supermarkets – and why I decided to resign my position as UK Director for confectionery products. I describe how my career went from there, how I started my own successful business from nothing, why we subsequently decided to quit the rat race and retire to our villa in the Costa Blanca. I describe our lives there, how much we enjoyed our stay in Spain, and finally why we decided to return home to England. We did so after nine wonderful years during which, in my opinion, I believe we experienced the very last of what I would describe as good old Spain. It only remains for me to say ADIOS AMIGOS!

BUT I TRULY HOPE WE SHALL MEET AGAIN
VERY SHORTLY!